Electrical principles
for technicians
volume 2

G. Wa
Lectu
Leeds

illustr
R. P.
Lectu
Carlet

Edward Arnold
A division of Hodder & Stoughton
LONDON   MELBOURNE   AUCKLAND

© 1982 G. Waterworth and R. P. Phillips

First published in Great Britain 1982
Reprinted 1985, 1987, 1989, 1990

British Library Cataloguing in Publication Data

Waterworth, G.
  Electrical principles for technicians.
  Vol. 2
  1. Electric engineering
  I. Title   II. Phillips, R. P.
  621.3   TK145

  ISBN 0-7131-3443-7

Typeset by Reproduction Drawings Ltd, Sutton, Surrey. Printed and
bound in Great Britain for Edward Arnold, a division of Hodder
and Stoughton Limited, Mill Road, Dunton Green, Sevenoaks, Kent
TN13 2YA by Clays Ltd, St Ives plc

Contents

Preface

This second volume of *Electrical principles for technicians* extends the basic theory developed in volume 1 and describes the application of the various theorems and techniques discussed. It covers the objectives of the Technician Education Council standard units Electrical and electronic principles III (U81/742 and U76/360) and Electrical principles III (U75/010). Together, the two volumes aim to foster the understanding of electrical principles required by technician students as a basis for a range of specialisms in electrical, electronic, and communications engineering.

To help the student obtain a real working grasp of the subject matter, I have tried to integrate worked examples with the text and have made extensive use of photographs to relate the principles under discussion to their practical applications.

I would like to thank the following organisations for permission to reproduce photographs: Gresham Transformers Ltd (fig. 5.11), GEC Power Transformers Ltd (fig. 5.12), GEC Large Machines Ltd (figs 6.3(a) and (b), 6.4(a) and (b), 7.5, and 7.6), GEC Small Machines Ltd (figs 7.7 and 9.4), Brush Electrical Machines Ltd (figs 9.1, 9.5, and 9.6), Marconi Instruments Ltd (figs 10.4 and 10.15), and Mullard Ltd (fig. 11.1).

I would also like to thank Sheila Henderson for translating my manuscript into typescript.

G. Waterworth

1   Circuit theorems

1.1 Introduction
The various circuit theorems used in electrical engineering have been
developed to aid the engineer in analysing electrical circuits. They are a means
of simplifying the calculations involved in determining a current or a voltage
in any part of an electrical network.

You will already have met and applied Kirchhoff's laws and the super-
position theorem. Three more useful theorems will now be discussed.

1.2 Maximum-power-transfer theorem
This theorem states that the power transferred from a signal source into a
load will be maximum when the load resistance is equal to the resistance of
the source.

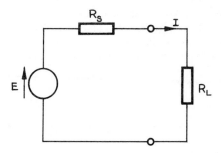

Fig. 1.1 Signal source with resistive load

Consider the circuit of fig. 1.1 in which a voltage source E is connected
across a load of resistance R_L. The resistance of the voltage source is R_S. The
power transferred to the load is given by

$$P = I^2 R_L \text{ watts}$$

where $\quad I = \dfrac{E}{R_S + R_L}$

$$\therefore \quad P = \left(\frac{E}{R_S + R_L}\right)^2 R_L$$

The maximum-power-transfer theorem states that this power transfer is maximum when $R_L = R_S$,

$$\therefore \quad P_{max.} = \frac{E^2 R_S}{(2R_S)^2} = \frac{E^2}{4R_S}$$

Example 1   A 20 V d.c. supply feeds a load resistance R_L via a 10 Ω source resistance. Plot a graph of power P transferred to the load resistor against load resistance R_L for values of R_L between 0 and 20 Ω and hence show that maximum power transfer occurs when $R_L = R_S = 10 \Omega$. What is the maximum power transferred?

The graph of power P transferred to the load against load resistance R_L is shown in fig. 1.2, from which it can be seen that maximum power transfer occurs when $R_L = R_S = 10 \Omega$.

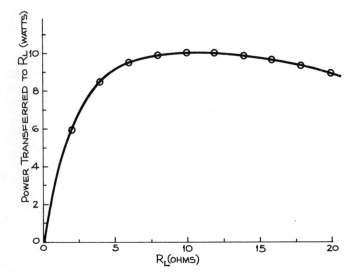

Fig. 1.2 Graph of power transferred to load against load resistance

The maximum power transferred is given by

$$P_{max.} = \frac{E^2}{4R_S} = \frac{(20\,V)^2}{4 \times 10\,\Omega} = \frac{400}{40}\,W = 10\,W$$

i.e. the maximum power transferred to the load is 10 W and occurs when $R_L = R_S = 10 \Omega$.

Example 2   A signal source has resistance of 300 Ω and is to be recorded on an ultra-violet recorder which has an input resistance of 1000 Ω. Calculate the percentage of possible maximum power delivered to the recorder.

Power P delivered to load $= I^2 R_L$

where $I = \dfrac{V_S}{R_S + R_L} = \dfrac{V_S}{300\,\Omega + 1000\,\Omega} = \dfrac{V_S}{1300\,\Omega}$

$\therefore \quad P = \dfrac{V_S^2}{(1300\,\Omega)^2} \times 1000\,\Omega = V_S^2 \times 5.92 \times 10^{-4}$

Now, for maximum power to be delivered to the recorder, $R_L = R_S = 300\,\Omega$.

$\therefore \quad P_{max.} = \dfrac{V_S^2}{(600\,\Omega)^2} \times 300\,\Omega = V_S^2 \times 8.33 \times 10^{-4}$

$\therefore \quad$ percentage of maximum power delivered to recorder $= \dfrac{P_{max.} - P}{P_{max.}} \times 100\%$

$$= \dfrac{8.33 - 5.92}{8.33} \times 100\% = 29\%$$

i.e. the percentage of possible maximum power delivered to the recorder is 29%.

The maximum-power-transfer theorem applies equally well to both d.c. and a.c. sources, provided that the load and source are purely resistive.

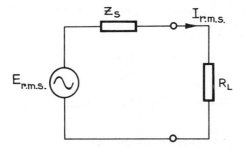

Fig. 1.3

We will now consider the case where the load R_L is purely resistive but the source is an a.c. supply with source impedance Z_S as shown in fig. 1.3. In this case, maximum power is transferred to the load when R_L is equal to the *magnitude* of the source impedance,

i.e. $R_L = \sqrt{(R_S^2 + X_S^2)} = Z_S$

where R_S and X_S are the resistance and reactance of the source impedance.

In this case the maximum power transferred, $P_{max.}$, is given by

$$P_{max.} = \frac{(E_{r.m.s.})^2}{4Z_S}$$

For a.c. circuits other than those considered, the situation is more complex and a more advanced text should be consulted.

Example 3 An a.c. voltage source has an internal resistance of 400 Ω and a reactance of 300 Ω. Calculate the value of the load resistance for maximum power transfer, and calculate the maximum power transferred if the voltage source has a peak value of 339 V.

Magnitude of source impedance Z_S is given by

$$Z_S = \sqrt{(R_S{}^2 + X_S{}^2)}$$

where $R_S = 400\,\Omega$ and $X_S = 300\,\Omega$

$\therefore$ $Z_S = \sqrt{(400\,\Omega)^2 + (300\,\Omega)^2} = 500\,\Omega$

For maximum power transfer, $R_L = Z_S = 500\,\Omega$.

Maximum power transferred is given by

$$P_{max.} = \frac{(E_{r.m.s.})^2}{4Z_S}$$

where $E_{r.m.s.} = (339\,V)/\sqrt{2} = 240\,V$ and $Z_S = 500\,\Omega$

$\therefore$ $P_{max.} = \dfrac{(240\,V)^2}{4 \times 500\,\Omega} = 28.8\,W$

i.e. the value of the load resistance for maximum power transfer is 500 Ω, and the maximum power transferred is 28.8 W.

Impedance matching is used extensively in communications and audio engineering where it is desired to transfer the maximum power from a signal source into a load. It is particularly important where the signal source is of low power. A transformer may be used to 'match' a load resistance to a signal source to ensure maximum power transfer. Transformer matching is considered in chapter 5. Impedance matching of attenuators is considered in section 2.13.

1.3 Voltage sources and current sources
When considering a network of voltage sources and resistances as shown in fig. 1.4(a), we could regard the network as consisting of a *single* constant-voltage source E and a source resistance R_S as shown in fig. 1.4(b). In fact we could not tell the difference between the network and the equivalent

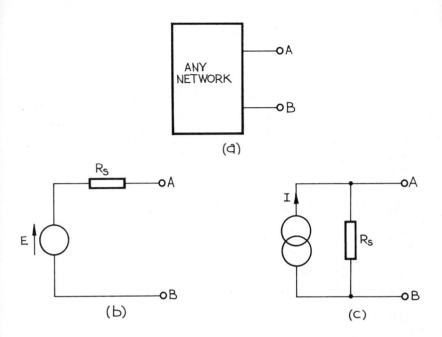

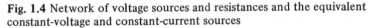

Fig. 1.4 Network of voltage sources and resistances and the equivalent constant-voltage and constant-current sources

voltage circuit if they were hidden from view and only the terminals A and B were accessible. This is the basis of Thévenin's theorem.

An alternative viewpoint would be to consider the network as a *single* constant-current source with a parallel source resistance as shown in fig. 1.4(c). This is the basis of Norton's theorem.

The two networks in figs 1.4(b) and (c) are completely interchangeable. Although a constant-current source is less common, it is equally valid and often very useful as a network representation.

1.4 Thévenin's theorem

Thévenin's theorem states that any network can be replaced by a *single* source of e.m.f. E and a series internal resistance R_S, as shown in fig. 1.5. The source of e.m.f. E is the open-circuit terminal voltage of the network measured between terminals A and B. The internal resistance R_S is the resistance of the network measured between A and B with all internal voltage sources replaced by short circuits (or by their internal resistances) and all internal current sources replaced by open circuits (or by their internal resistances).

Example 1   Replace the circuit of fig. 1.6(a) by the Thévenin equivalent circuit.

5

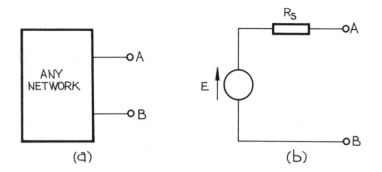

Fig. 1.5 Thévenin equivalent circuit

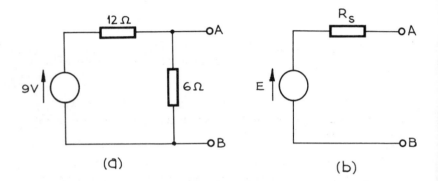

Fig. 1.6

We replace the circuit by a voltage generator E and an internal resistance R_S as shown in fig. 1.6(b). The e.m.f. E of the voltage generator is found by calculating the open-circuit terminal voltage across AB in fig. 1.6(a):

$$E = \left(\frac{6\,\Omega}{12\,\Omega + 6\,\Omega}\right) 9\,V = 3\,V$$

The internal resistance R_S is found by replacing the voltage generator by a short circuit and measuring the resistance across AB. This leaves us with $12\,\Omega$ in parallel with $6\,\Omega$,

$$\therefore \quad R_S = \frac{12\,\Omega \times 6\,\Omega}{12\,\Omega + 6\,\Omega} = \frac{72\,\Omega}{18} = 4\,\Omega$$

i.e. the Thévenin equivalent circuit is as shown in fig. 1.6(b), with a source voltage E of 3 V and an internal resistance R_S of $4\,\Omega$.

Example 2 Replace the circuit of fig 1.7(a) by the Thévenin equivalent circuit.

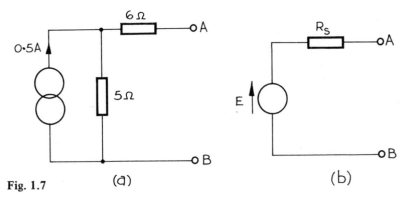

Fig. 1.7   (a)   (b)

The Thévenin equivalent circuit is shown in fig 1.7(b).

The source voltage E is the open-circuit voltage measured across AB in fig 1.7(a),

$$\therefore \quad E = 0.5\,\text{A} \times 5\,\Omega = 2.5\,\text{V}$$

The internal resistance R_S is found by open-circuiting the current source and measuring the resistance across AB:

$$R_S = 5\,\Omega + 6\,\Omega = 11\,\Omega$$

i.e. the Thévenin equivalent circuit is as shown in fig 1.7(b), with a source voltage E of 2.5 V and an internal resistance R_S of 11 Ω.

Now let us see how Thévenin's theorem can be used to simplify the solving of network problems.

Example 3 Use Thévenin's theorem to calculate the current in the 1.2 Ω load resistance of fig. 1.8.

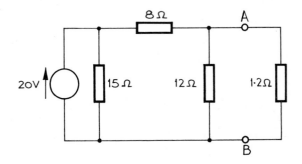

Fig. 1.8

We could obviously do this problem without the aid of Thévenin's theorem, but notice how easy the theorem makes this problem.

Firstly, remove the $1.2\,\Omega$ load resistor as shown in fig. 1.9(a) and replace the network that is left by its Thévenin equivalent circuit. From fig 1.9(a), the open-circuit voltage across AB is

$$V_{AB} = \left(\frac{12\,\Omega}{12\,\Omega + 8\,\Omega}\right) 20\,V = 12\,V$$

$$\therefore \quad E = 12\,V$$

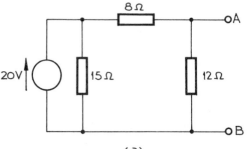

(a)

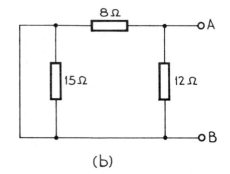

Fig. 1.9

(b)

In fig. 1.9(b) we have replaced the voltage generator by a short circuit. The resistance measured across AB is thus

$$R_{AB} = \frac{8\,\Omega \times 12\,\Omega}{8\,\Omega + 12\,\Omega} = \frac{96\,\Omega}{20} = 4.8\,\Omega$$

$$\therefore \quad R_S = 4.8\,\Omega$$

Notice that in fig. 1.9(b) the $15\,\Omega$ resistor is shorted out by the short circuit.

We may now draw the Thévenin equivalent circuit as shown in fig. 1.10 and replace the $1.2\,\Omega$ load resistor. The current in the $1.2\,\Omega$ resistor is then simply found from

8

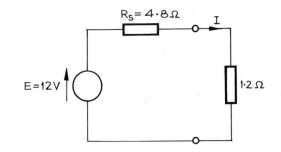

Fig. 1.10

$$I = \frac{12\,\text{V}}{4.8\,\Omega + 1.2\,\Omega} = \frac{12\,\text{V}}{6\,\Omega} = 2\,\text{A}$$

i.e. the current in the 1.2 Ω resistor is 2 A.

Notice that once you have mastered the method it is much less cumbersome than the alternative procedure using, say, Kirchhoff's laws.

Example 4 Use Thévenin's theorem to find the current in the 3.74 Ω resistor in fig. 1.11.

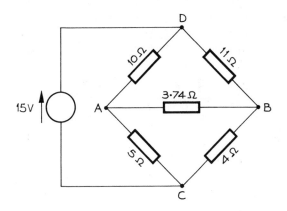

Fig. 1.11

Firstly remove the 3.74 Ω resistor as shown in fig. 1.12(a) and replace what is left by the Thévenin equivalent circuit. From fig. 1.12(a), the voltage between A and C is given by

$$V_{\text{AC}} = \left(\frac{5\,\Omega}{10\,\Omega + 5\,\Omega}\right) 15\,\text{V} = 5\,\text{V}$$

Similarly the voltage between B and C is given by

$$V_{\text{BC}} = \left(\frac{4\,\Omega}{11\,\Omega + 4\,\Omega}\right) 15\,\text{V} = 4\,\text{V}$$

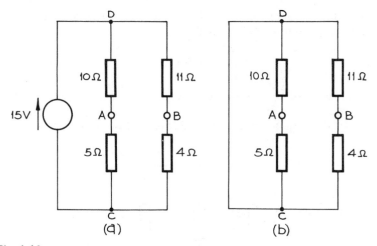

Fig. 1.12

Therefore the voltage between A and B is given by

$$V_{AB} = V_{AC} - V_{BC} = 5\,V - 4\,V = 1\,V$$

This is the open-circuit voltage between terminals A and B. Thus, in the Thévenin equivalent circuit, $E = 1\,V$.

In fig. 1.12(b) we have replaced the voltage generator by a short circuit. The resistance between A and B in fig. 1.12(b) is given by

$$R_{AB} = \frac{10\,\Omega \times 5\,\Omega}{10\,\Omega + 5\,\Omega} + \frac{4\,\Omega \times 11\,\Omega}{4\,\Omega + 11\,\Omega}$$

$$= \frac{50\,\Omega}{15} + \frac{44\,\Omega}{15}$$

$$= 3.33\,\Omega + 2.93\,\Omega = 6.26\,\Omega$$

$$\therefore \quad R_S = 6.26\,\Omega$$

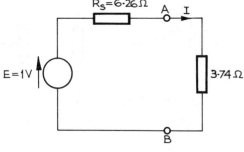

Fig. 1.13

Now use these values in the Thévenin equivalent circuit as shown in fig. 1.13 and replace the 3.74 Ω resistance:

$$I = \frac{1\,\text{V}}{6.26\,\Omega + 3.74\,\Omega} = \frac{1\,\text{V}}{10\,\Omega} = 0.1\,\text{A}$$

i.e. the current in the 3.4 Ω resistor is 0.1 A.

Example 5   Calculate the current in the 5 Ω resistor in the network of fig. 1.14.

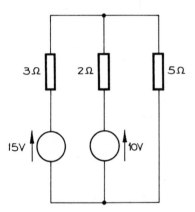

Fig. 1.14

This could readily be calculated by using Kirchhoff's laws or the super-position theorem. It may be calculated using Thévenin's theorem by first removing the 5 Ω resistor as shown in fig. 1.15(a) and replacing what is left by the Thévenin equivalent circuit.

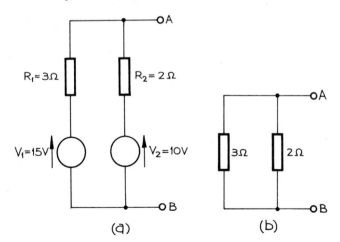

(a)   (b)

Fig. 1.15

11

Notice that it is not quite so simple to calculate V_{AB} in fig. 1.15(a). However, a useful rule to remember in circuits such as these is

$$V_{AB} = \left(\frac{V_1}{R_1} + \frac{V_2}{R_2} \right) r$$

where r = parallel combination of R_1 and R_2 = $\dfrac{R_1 R_2}{R_1 + R_2}$

(This useful rule may be extended to cover any number of voltage sources and internal resistances. A simple proof is shown in section 1.5, example 4, using Norton's theorem.)

Applying the rule to fig. 1.15(a) gives

$$V_{AB} = \left(\frac{15\,V}{3\,\Omega} + \frac{10\,V}{2\,\Omega} \right) \left(\frac{2\,\Omega \times 3\,\Omega}{2\,\Omega + 3\,\Omega} \right)$$

$$= (5\,V + 5\,V) \frac{6\,\Omega}{5\,\Omega} = 10\,V \times \frac{6}{5}$$

$$= 12\,V$$

Therefore, in the Thévenin equivalent circuit, $E = 12\,V$.

In fig. 1.15(b) we have replaced the voltage generators by short circuits,

$$\therefore \quad R_{AB} = \frac{3\,\Omega \times 2\,\Omega}{3\,\Omega + 2\,\Omega} = 1.2\,\Omega$$

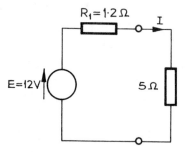

Fig. 1.16

We may now draw the Thévenin equivalent circuit as shown in fig. 1.16 and replace the 5 Ω resistor,

$$\therefore \quad I = \frac{12\,V}{1.2\,\Omega + 5\,\Omega} = \frac{12\,V}{6.2\,\Omega} = 1.94\,A$$

i.e. the current in the 5 Ω resistor is 1.94 A.

1.5 Norton's theorem

Norton's theorem states that any network can be replaced by a *single* current source I and a parallel internal resistance R_S, as shown in fig. 1.17. The current source is the current that would flow into a *short circuit* connected across AB. The internal resistance is the resistance of the network measured between A and B with voltage sources replaced by short circuits (or by their internal resistances) and current sources replaced by open circuits (or by their internal resistances). Notice that the source resistance R_S is the same in both the Norton and Thévenin equivalent circuits. In the Norton circuit the resistance appears across the source instead of in series with it.

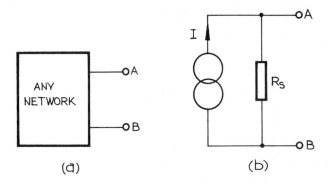

(a)   (b)

Fig. 1.17 Norton equivalent circuit

Example 1   Replace the circuit of fig. 1.18(a) by the Norton equivalent circuit.

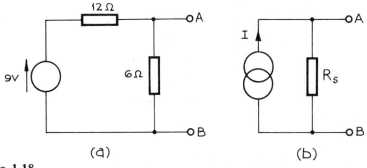

(a)   (b)

Fig. 1.18

The Norton equivalent circuit is shown in fig. 1.18(b). The current source I is the current that would flow into a short circuit connected across AB in fig. 1.18(a),

13

$$\therefore \quad I = \frac{9\,\text{V}}{12\,\Omega} = 0.75\,\text{A}$$

The source resistance R_S is found by replacing the voltage generator by a short circuit and determining the resistance between A and B.

$$\therefore \quad R_S = \frac{12\,\Omega \times 6\,\Omega}{12\,\Omega + 6\,\Omega} = \frac{72\,\Omega}{18} = 4\,\Omega$$

i.e. the Norton equivalent circuit has a current source I of 0.75 A and an internal resistance R_S of 4 Ω.

Example 2 Replace the circuit of fig. 1.19(a) by its Norton equivalent circuit.

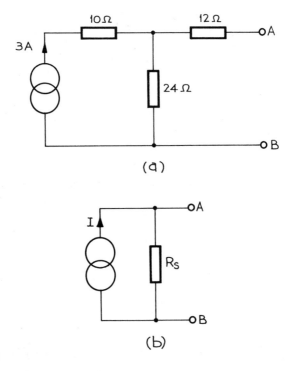

(a)

(b)

Fig. 1.19

The short-circuit current I flowing into a short circuit across the network terminals AB is found using the current-divider rule:

$$I = \left(\frac{24\,\Omega}{24\,\Omega + 12\,\Omega}\right) 3\,\text{A} = \frac{24}{36} \times 3\,\text{A} = 2\,\text{A}$$

The source resistance R_S is found by replacing the network current generator by an open circuit and calculating the resistance across AB:

$$R_S = 24\,\Omega + 12\,\Omega = 36\,\Omega$$

i.e. the Norton equivalent circuit has a current source I of 2 A and an internal resistance R_S of 36 Ω.

Now let us consider some network problems where Norton's theorem may be used to assist the solution.

Example 3   Calculate the current in the 10 Ω resistor in the network of fig. 1.20.

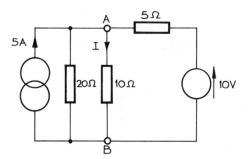

Fig. 1.20

First remove the 10 Ω resistor and replace the 10 V voltage generator and its 5 Ω source resistance by the Norton equivalent circuit as shown in fig. 1.21(a). Since we now have two current generators in parallel, we may simply add their effects and take the parallel combination of internal resistances to give the Norton equivalent circuit of fig. 1.21(b).

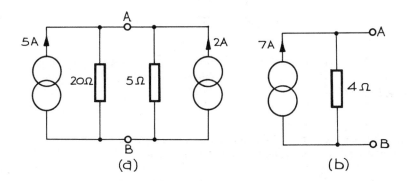

Fig. 1.21

15

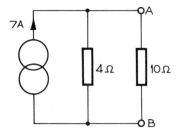

Fig. 1.22

Now replace the 10 Ω resistor as shown in fig. 1.22. The current I in the 10 Ω resistor is found by using the current-divider rule:

$$I = \left(\frac{4\,\Omega}{10\,\Omega + 4\,\Omega}\right) 7\,\text{A} = \frac{4}{14} \times 7\,\text{A} = 2\,\text{A}$$

i.e. the current in the 10 Ω resistor is 2 A.

Example 4   Use Norton's theorem to calculate the open-circuit voltage across AB in the network of fig. 1.23.

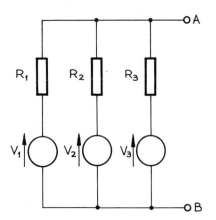

Fig. 1.23

First replace each voltage generator by its Norton equivalent circuit to give the network of fig. 1.24(a). Now, by simply adding the currents and taking the parallel combination of the resistors, we have the circuit of fig. 1.24(b) where

$$I = \frac{V_1}{R_1} + \frac{V_2}{R_2} + \frac{V_3}{R_3}$$

and $\dfrac{1}{r} = \dfrac{1}{R_1} + \dfrac{1}{R_2} + \dfrac{1}{R_3}$

16

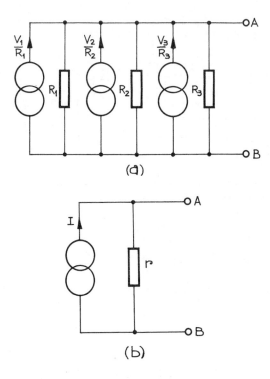

Fig. 1.24

The open-circuit terminal voltage V_{AB} is given by

$$V_{AB} = Ir$$

$$\therefore \quad V_{AB} = \left(\frac{V_1}{R_1} + \frac{V_2}{R_2} + \frac{V_3}{R_3} \right) r$$

where r = parallel combination of resistors R_1, R_2, and R_3

This result is often useful in simplifying networks and is the equation used in example 5 on Thévenin's theorem in section 1.4.

1.6 Combinations of Norton's and Thévenin's theorems
It is often necessary to use Thévenin's and Norton's theorems together to simplify networks, and they can be used together quite freely. When simplifying networks, it should be remembered that

a) voltage generators in series may be added,
b) current generators in parallel may be added.

The approach to the solution of problems is best demonstrated by several examples.

17

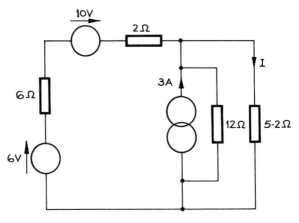

Fig. 1.25

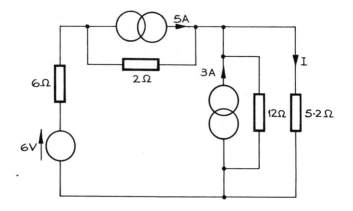

(a)

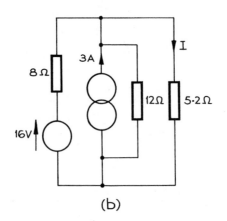

Fig. 1.26   (b)

18

Example 1 Calculate the current in the 5.2 Ω resistor in the network of fig. 1.25.

First replace the 5 A current generator by its Thévenin equivalent circuit as shown in fig. 1.26(a). The voltage generators may then be added to give the network of fig. 1.26(b).

Now replace the 16 V voltage generator by its Norton equivalent as shown in fig. 1.27(a). By simply adding current generators, this reduces to the network of fig. 1.27(b).

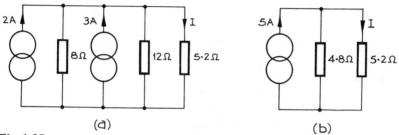

(a)   (b)

Fig. 1.27

Now, by the current-divider rule,

$$I = \left(\frac{4.8\ \Omega}{4.8\ \Omega + 5.2\ \Omega} \right) 5\ A = \frac{4.8}{10} \times 5\ A = 2.4\ A$$

i.e. the current in the 5.2 Ω resistor is 2.4 A.

Example 2 By successive application of Thevenin's and Norton's theorems, determine the Thévenin equivalent circuit of the network in fig. 1.28.

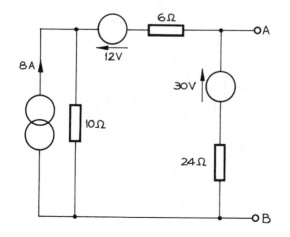

Fig. 1.28

First replace the current generator by the equivalent voltage generator as shown in fig. 1.29(a). This may be simplified to the arrangement of fig. 1.29(b). Notice that, since the 80 V and 12 V generators are in opposition, you subtract one from the other.

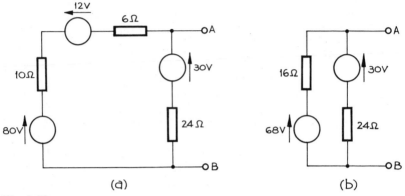

(a)   (b)

Fig. 1.29

Now replace these by their equivalent current generators as shown in fig. 1.30(a). This may be simplified to the arrangement of fig. 1.30(b), where the 9.6 Ω resistor is made up of the 16 Ω and 24 Ω resistors in parallel.

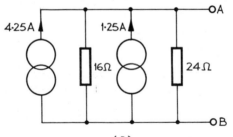

(a)

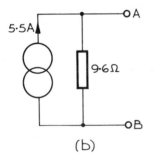

(b)

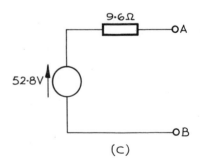

(c)

Fig. 1.30

The current generator may now be replaced by the equivalent voltage generator as shown in fig. 1.30(c); i.e. the Thévenin equivalent circuit consists of a 52.8 V generator in series with a 9.6 Ω resistor.

Exercises on chapter 1

1   The equivalent circuit of a generator is represented by a constant-current generator of 20 A in parallel with a resistance of 5 Ω. Convert this to the equivalent constant-voltage generator and calculate the constant voltage and internal resistance of the generator.   [100 V; 5Ω]

2   The equivalent circuit of a generator is represented by a constant-voltage generator of 20 V in series with a resistance of 15 Ω. Convert this to the equivalent constant-current generator and internal resistance.   [1.67 A; 15 Ω]

3   A 10 V d.c. generator with an internal resistance of 4 Ω has a parallel network connected across it consisting of a 6 Ω resistance in parallel with a 3.6 Ω resistance. Use Thévenin's theorem to calculate the voltage across the 3.6 Ω resistance.   [3.6 V]

4   A current source of 1 A with an internal resistance of 10 Ω is connected across 15 Ω and 10 Ω resistors in parallel. Calculate the current in the 15 Ω resistor.   [0.25 A]

5   A 10 A current source with an internal resistance of 8 Ω is connected across a resistive network. The network consists of 10 Ω in parallel with 5 Ω, the combination being connected in series with a 2 Ω resistor. Calculate the current in the 5 Ω resistor.   [4 A]

6   A 20 V battery with internal resistance of 5 Ω has terminals AB. A 10 V battery with internal resistance of 2 Ω has terminals CD. A 15 Ω resistor is connected across AB and an 8 Ω resistor across CD. A 10 Ω resistor connects A and C, and B connects to D such that the batteries oppose one another. Use Thévenin's theorem to calculate the current in the 10 Ω resistor. [0.46 A]

7   State Thévenin's theorem as it is applied to the solution of simple resistive circuits.

A network consists of a 110 V generator with an internal resistance of 0.25 Ω, connected in parallel opposition with a 100 V generator with an internal resistance of 0.20 Ω. The two are connected across a 10 Ω resistor. Use Thévenin's theorem to calculate the current in the 10 Ω resistor. [10.34A]

8   A resistive bridge ABCD is made up of resistors 10 Ω, 15 Ω, 20 Ω, and 25 Ω respectively from A to D. A 6 V d.c. supply is connected across AC and a 5 Ω resistor across BD. Use Thévenin's theorem to calculate the current in the 5 Ω resistor.   [42 mA]

9   A resistive bridge network ABCD is made up of resistors between A and D as follows: 20 Ω, 30 Ω, 30 Ω, 20 Ω. A 50 V d.c. supply is connected across AC. Derive the Thévenin and Norton equivalent circuits across the terminals BD.   [10 V, 24 Ω; 0.42 A, 24 Ω]

10   A constant-voltage generator has an internal resistance of 1 kΩ and an e.m.f. of 100 V and is connected to a resistive load. Draw the equivalent constant-current circuit and calculate the value of constant current and the internal resistance.   [0.1 A, 1 kΩ]

11   20 V generator with internal resistance 8 Ω and a 12 V generator of internal resistance 6 Ω have their negative terminals connected together. Their positive terminals are connected via a 3.6 Ω resistor. A 12 Ω resistor is connected across the terminals of the 20 V generator, and a 3 Ω resistor across the terminals of the 12 V generator. Calculate the current in the 3.6 Ω resistor.   [1.60 A]

12   A 10 V generator of internal resistance 6 Ω is connected in series aiding with a 1 A current generator of internal resistance 4 Ω. The combination is connected in parallel aiding with an 0.6 A current generator of internal resistance 10 Ω across a 15 Ω load resistor. Calculate the current in the load. [0.5 A]

13   A 15 V generator with internal resistance 12 Ω has terminals AB. This is connected in series aiding with a 6 V generator of internal resistance 3 Ω. The combination is connected in parallel opposition with a 4 A generator of internal resistance 5 Ω. By successive application of Thévenin's and Norton's theorems, determine the Norton equivalent circuit of the terminals AB. [2.6 A, 3.75 Ω]

14   Explain the meaning of the term 'maximum power transfer'. The primary of an audio-frequency transformer has 4000 turns and the secondary has 200 turns. If the resistance connected across the secondary is 10 Ω, calculate the value of internal resistance of the supply to give maximum power transfer.   [4 kΩ]

15   What are meant by the terms 'output resistance' and 'input resistance' of an amplifier?

   An amplifier having an output resistance of 36 kΩ is to be used to supply a load of 1 kΩ. Show by means of a diagram how matching can be effected to ensure maximum power transfer from the amplifier to the load and give any necessary numerical information.   [turns ratio 6:1]

2   Single-phase a.c. circuits

2.1 Introduction

You will already have considered the analysis of single-phase a.c. circuits containing resistive and reactive components and found that the phasor diagram is a simple yet accurate method of relating the voltage, current, and phase angle in a.c. circuits.

It should be remembered when using phasor representation that

a) the magnitude of the phasor represents the r.m.s. value of the sinusoidal current or voltage (the peak value may be used instead, provided the user is consistent);

b) the angle which the phasor makes with the horizontal axis represents the phase angle of the sinusoidal quantity relative to the reference quantity.

We shall consider a number of a.c. circuits in which phasor representation is used extensively, but let us first consider the electrical components themselves.

It is important to realise that electrical components are not perfect elements. A coil of wire possesses both inductance and resistance as well as some small capacitance. A capacitor possesses both capacitance and some leakage resistance as well as some small inductance. In order to simplify the analysis of these *real* components, we represent them by *equivalent circuits* made up of pure inductance, pure capacitance, and pure resistance.

In the analysis that follows, the terms 'inductance', 'capacitance', and 'resistance' will be used to denote pure inductance, pure capacitance, and pure resistance.

We shall first consider the various combinations of components in *series* a.c. circuits. Remember that we are concerned with finding the relationship between the voltage and current in the circuit (magnitude and phase).

2.2 Circuits possessing resistance and inductance in series

Figure 2.1(a) shows a series circuit consisting of an inductance L and a resistance R. We use a phasor diagram to represent the current and voltages. The phasor diagram is shown in fig. 2.1(b). Notice that the current is used as the reference phasor, since the same current flows in both components.

Representing the voltages across the components and the current through them by their r.m.s. values, V_R is in phase with I and V_L leads I by $90°$. The resultant (or phasor addition) of the two voltages is the supply voltage V.

By the theorem of Pythagoras,

$$V^2 = V_R{}^2 + V_L{}^2$$

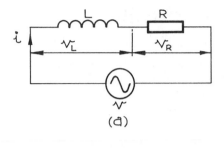

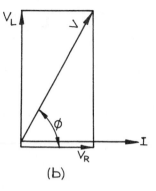

Fig. 2.1 Series R–L circuit and phasor diagram

$$\therefore \quad V = \sqrt{V_R^2 + V_L^2}$$

The phase angle ϕ between the supply voltage V and the current I is given by

$$\tan \phi = V_L/V_R$$

The phasor diagram may be redrawn as shown in fig. 2.2(a) in terms of the current I, the resistance R, the inductive reactance X_L, and the impedance Z. This may be simplified to the impedance triangle of fig. 2.2(b).

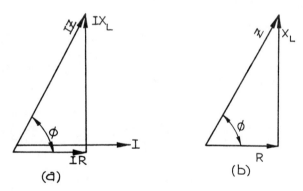

Fig. 2.2 Phasor diagram and impedance triangle

From the impedance triangle, we have

$$Z = \sqrt{R^2 + X_L^2}$$

But $\quad X_L = \omega L = 2\pi f L$

where $\quad f$ = frequency of supply

$$\therefore \quad Z = \sqrt{R_2 + \omega^2 L^2}$$

Also $\quad \tan\phi = X_L/R = \omega L/R$

Example A coil of inductance 2 H and resistance 100 Ω is fed from a 50 Hz supply of 200 V r.m.s. Calculate (a) the inductive reactance of the coil, (b) the impedance of the coil, (c) the magnitude of the current in the coil, (d) the phase angle between the voltage and current.

a) $\quad X_L = 2\pi f L$

where $\quad f = 50\,\text{Hz} \quad$ and $\quad L = 2\,\text{H}$

$\therefore \quad X_L = 2\pi \times 50\,\text{Hz} \times 2\,\text{H}$

$\qquad = 628\,\Omega$

b) $\quad Z = \sqrt{R^2 + X_L{}^2}$

where $\quad R = 100\,\Omega \quad$ and $\quad X_L = 628\,\Omega$

$\therefore \quad Z = \sqrt{(100\,\Omega)^2 + (628\,\Omega)^2}$

$\qquad = 636\,\Omega$

c) $\quad I = V/Z$

where $\quad V = 200\,\text{V} \quad$ and $\quad Z = 636\,\Omega$

$\therefore \quad I = \dfrac{200\,\text{V}}{636\,\Omega} = 0.314\,\text{A}$

d) $\quad \tan\phi = X_L/R$

where $\quad X_L = 628\,\Omega \quad$ and $\quad R = 100\,\Omega$

$\therefore \quad \tan\phi = \dfrac{628\,\Omega}{100\,\Omega} = 6.28$

$\therefore \qquad \phi = 80.9°$

i.e. the inductive reactance of the coil is 628 Ω, the impedance is 636 Ω, the current is 0.314 A, and the phase angle between the voltage and current is 80.9°.

The most common use of the series $R-L$ circuit is in the representation of a coil. Although the inductance and resistance of the coil cannot physically be separated, the analysis requires this separation into the two ideal components of inductance and resistance for ease of calculation. The $R-L$ circuit is referred to as the *equivalent circuit* of the coil.

2.3 Circuits possessing resistance and capacitance in series
Figure 2.3(a) shows a series circuit consisting of a capacitance C and a resistance R. The corresponding phasor diagram is shown in fig. 2.3(b). The

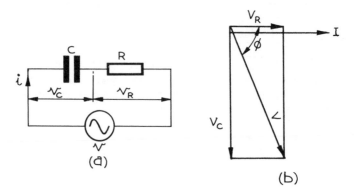

Fig. 2.3 Series $R–C$ circuit and phasor diagram

current I is used as the reference phasor, V_R is the phase with I, and V_C lags I by $90°$.

The resultant of the two voltages is the supply voltage V, where

$$V^2 = V_R^2 + V_C^2$$

$$\therefore \quad V = \sqrt{V_R^2 + V_C^2}$$

The phase angle ϕ may be found from

$$\tan \phi = V_C/V_R$$

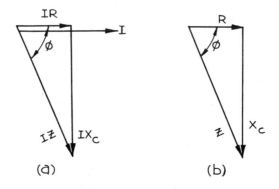

Fig. 2.4 Phasor diagram and impedance triangle

The phasor diagram may be redrawn as shown in fig. 2.4(a) in terms of the current I, the resistance R, the capacitive reactance X_C, and the impedance Z. The corresponding impedance triangle is shown in fig. 2.4(b), where

26

$$Z = \sqrt{R^2 + X_C{}^2}$$

But $\quad X_C = \dfrac{1}{\omega C} = \dfrac{1}{2\pi f C}$

where $\quad f$ = frequency of supply

$\therefore \quad Z = \sqrt{R^2 + \dfrac{1}{\omega^2 C^2}}$

Also $\quad \tan \phi = \dfrac{X_C}{R} = \dfrac{1}{\omega C R}$

Example A series R-C circuit consists of a $100\ \Omega$ resistor and an unknown capacitor. When a 20 V supply of frequency 2.5 kHz is connected across the combination, a current of 0.123 A flows. Calculate (a) the circuit impedance, (b) the circuit reactance, (c) the value of the capacitor, (d) the voltage across each component.

a) $Z = V/I$

where $\quad V = 20\,\text{V}$ and $\quad I = 0.123\,\text{A}$

$\therefore \quad Z = \dfrac{20\,\text{V}}{0.123\,\text{A}} = 163\,\Omega$

b) $X_C = \sqrt{Z^2 - R^2}$

where $\quad Z = 163\,\Omega$ and $\quad R = 100\,\Omega$

$\therefore \quad X_C = \sqrt{(163\,\Omega)^2 - (100\,\Omega)^2}$

$\qquad = 129\,\Omega$

c) $X_C = \dfrac{1}{2\pi f C}$

$\therefore \quad C = \dfrac{1}{2\pi f X_C}$

where $\quad f = 2.5\,\text{kHz} = 2500\,\text{Hz}$ and $\quad X_C = 129\,\Omega$

$\therefore \quad C = \dfrac{1}{2\pi \times 2500\,\text{Hz} \times 129\,\Omega} = 0.5\,\mu\text{F}$

d) $V_R = IR = 0.123\,\text{A} \times 100\,\Omega = 12.3\,\text{V}$

$\quad V_C = IX_C = 0.123\,\text{A} \times 129\,\Omega = 15.87\,\text{V}$

i.e. the circuit impedance is $163\,\Omega$, the reactance is $129\,\Omega$, the value of the capacitor is $0.5\,\mu\text{F}$, and the voltages across the resistor and capacitor are 12.3 V and 15.87 V respectively.

The series R–C circuit is one equivalent circuit for representing a practical capacitor. The series resistance represents the dielectric-loss resistance of the capacitor. Since dielectric loss increases with frequency, the series R–C circuit is generally used as the high-frequency equivalent-circuit representation of the capacitor. The low-frequency equivalent circuit is discussed in section 2.8 under parallel circuits.

2.4 Power, volt amperes, reactive volt amperes, and power factor

We often need to calculate the power dissipated in a.c. circuits. Figure 2.5(a) shows the phasor diagram for an inductive and resistive circuit where I and V are the current through and the voltage across the combination. The power phasor diagram is shown in fig. 2.5(b).

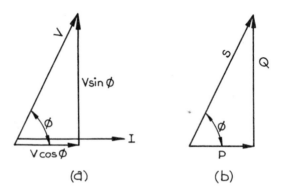

Fig. 2.5 Voltage and power phasor diagrams

Power is dissipated only in the *resistive* component of the circuit. This is referred to as the 'true power' dissipated in the circuit and is represented by the phasor P in fig. 2.5(b). True power is measured in watts (W).

The true power may be calculated by taking the product of the current I and the in-phase component of the voltage, $V \cos \phi$, as shown in fig. 2.5(a):

$$P = VI \cos \phi$$

where V and I are r.m.s. values.

True power may also be calculated by using the equation

$$P = I^2 R$$

These two equations are interchangeable, since one may be derived from the other.

The 'apparent power' S is defined as the voltage V multiplied by the current I:

$$S = VI$$

This is represented by phasor S in fig. 2.5(b). Apparent power is measured in volt amperes (V A).

The ratio of the true power to the apparent power is called the *power factor* of the circuit:

$$\text{power factor} = \frac{\text{true power}}{\text{apparent power}} = \frac{P}{S}$$

$$= \frac{VI \cos \phi}{VI}$$

i.e.   power factor $= \cos \phi$

The 'reactive volt amperes' Q is defined as the current I multiplied by the quadrature voltage $V \sin \phi$:

$$Q = VI \sin \phi$$

This is represented by the phasor Q in fig. 2.5(b). Reactive volt amperes are measured in volt amperes reactive (V Ar).

It can be seen from fig. 2.5(b) that

$$S^2 = P^2 + Q^2$$

Example 1   A single-phase induction motor is connected to a 240 V a.c. supply. A wattmeter connected in the circuit reads 960 W, and an ammeter connected in series with the motor reads 5 A. Calculate (a) the true power, (b) the apparent power, (c) the reactive volt amperes, (d) the power factor.

a)   A wattmeter reads true power,

∴   true power $P = 960$ W

b)   Apparent power $S = VI$

where $V = 240$ V   and $I = 5$ A

∴ $S = 240$ V × 5 A = 1200 V A

c)   Reactive volt amperes $Q = \sqrt{S^2 - P^2}$

where $S = 1200$ V A   and $P = 960$ W

∴ $Q = \sqrt{(1200 \text{ V A})^2 - (960 \text{ W})^2} = 720$ V Ar

d)   Power factor $= P/S$

where $P = 960$ W   and $S = 1200$ V A

∴   Power factor $= \dfrac{960 \text{ W}}{1200 \text{ V A}} = 0.8$

i.e. the true power is 960 W, the apparent power is 1200 V A, the reactive volt amperes is 720 V Ar, and the power factor is 0.8.

Example 2 Calculate the power dissipated in a coil which has a resistance of 30 Ω and an inductive reactance of 40 Ω, if the coil is connected across a 240 V a.c. supply.

Power $P = VI \cos \phi$

But $I = V/Z$ and $\cos \phi = R/Z$

$$\therefore \quad P = \frac{V^2}{Z} \times \frac{R}{Z} = \frac{V^2 R}{Z^2}$$

where $V = 240\,\text{V}$

and $Z = \sqrt{R^2 + X^2} = \sqrt{(30\,\Omega)^2 + (40\,\Omega)^2} = 50\,\Omega$

$$\therefore \quad P = \frac{(240\,\text{V})^2 \times 30\,\Omega}{(50\,\Omega)^2} = 691.2\,\text{W}$$

i.e. the power dissipated is 691.2 W.

It is worth noting that capacitors are relatively perfect components and in practice dissipate very little power. In a perfect capacitor, the voltage and current are $90°$ out of phase and therefore the power dissipated is zero.

2.5 Resonant circuits
In series or parallel circuits containing both capacitive and inductive com-ponents, it is found that both components store energy but on different parts of the applied-voltage waveform. The inductor stores energy in the form of a magnetic field, while the capacitor stores energy in the form of an electric field.

On one part of the applied-voltage cycle, the inductor is storing energy while at the same time the capacitor is discharging. At another part of the waveform the capacitor is charging while the magnetic field in the inductor is collapsing. The result is that energy is passed backwards and forwards between the two components. There is, of course, always resistance in the circuit, which dissipates some of this energy – this may be referred to as 'damping'.

This passing backwards and forwards of stored energy means that at any instant there can be more energy stored in the components than is being supplied from the applied sinusoidal voltage. It is rather like the build-up of oscillations of a child's swing – keep giving a small push and eventually the oscillations will become very large.

The frequency at which the energy passes backwards and forwards between the two components is referred to as the natural-oscillation frequency, f_0.

Consider the case where the circuit is fed from an a.c. supply voltage and the resistive damping is small. When the supply-voltage frequency is the *same* as the natural-oscillation frequency of the circuit, the energy oscillations will be greatest. (Remember that when pushing a swing you must push it at just the right moment to get the largest oscillations; i.e. at its natural-oscillation frequency.) This condition is called *resonance* and will be considered for both series and parallel *L-C-R* circuits.

We will first consider a series resonant circuit in which a capacitor is connected in series with a coil (containing both inductance and resistance).

2.6 Series combinations of resistance, inductance, and capacitance

A series *L-C-R* circuit is shown in fig. 2.6(a). The corresponding phasor diagram is shown in fig. 2.6(b).

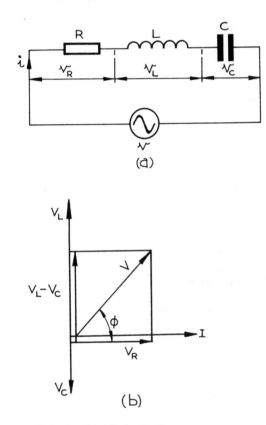

Fig. 2.6 Series *L-C-R* circuit and phasor diagram

The current is used as the reference phasor, since the same current is common to all three components. V_R is in phase with I, V_L leads I by $90°$, and V_C lags I by $90°$. Since V_L and V_C are in direct opposition, we may easily calculate the resultant of these two alone, shown on the phasor diagram as $V_L - V_C$.

To find the applied voltage V, we take the resultant of $V_L - V_C$ and V_R.

From the phasor diagram,

$$V^2 = V_R^2 + (V_L - V_C)^2$$
$$\therefore \quad V = \sqrt{V_R^2 + (V_L - V_C)^2}$$

The phase angle of the complete circuit is given by

$$\tan \phi = \frac{V_L - V_C}{V_R}$$

We can represent the phasor diagram in terms of the current I and the component resistance R and reactances X_L and X_C as shown in fig. 2.7(a), where

$$V = IZ$$
$$V_R = IR$$
$$\text{and} \quad V_L - V_C = I(X_L - X_C)$$

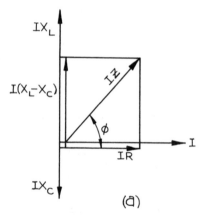

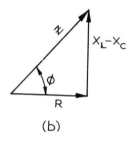

Fig. 2.7 Phasor diagram and impedance triangle for a series L-C-R circuit

The corresponding impedance triangle is shown in fig. 2.7(b).
From fig. 2.7(b) it may be seen that

$$Z^2 = R^2 + (X_L - X_C)^2$$
$$\therefore \quad Z = \sqrt{R^2 + (X_L - X_C)^2}$$
$$\text{and} \quad \tan \phi = \frac{X_L - X_C}{R}$$

The particular shape of the phasor diagram depends on the supply frequency being considered. There are three conditions worth considering in more detail:

a) $X_C > X_L$

b) $X_C = X_L$

c) $X_C < X_L$

The phasor diagrams for these three conditions are shown in fig. 2.8.

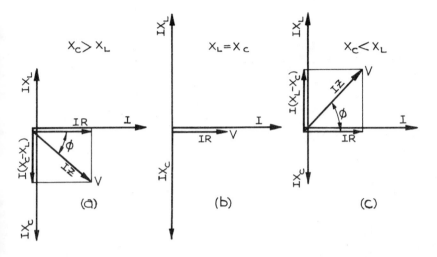

Fig. 2.8 Phasor representation of a series L-C-R circuit at various frequencies

For $X_C > X_L$ the circuit is mainly capacitive and has a leading phase angle (i.e. the current leads the voltage) as shown in fig. 2.8(a).

For $X_C < X_L$ the circuit is mainly inductive and has a lagging phase angle (i.e. the current lags the voltage) as shown in fig. 2.8(c).

At $X_C = X_L$ the circuit is at the condition of resonance. The inductive and capacitive effects cancel each other out and the circuit is purely resistive. The phase angle is therefore zero as shown in fig. 2.8(b).

Notice that V_L and V_C may be much greater than the applied voltage V.

Consider the condition of resonance shown in fig. 2.8(b).

Since $V_L = V_C$

then $IX_L = IX_C$

$\therefore$ $X_L = X_C$

$\therefore$ $\omega L = \dfrac{1}{\omega C}$

$\therefore$ $\omega^2 = \dfrac{1}{LC}$

$$\therefore \quad \omega = \frac{1}{\sqrt{(LC)}}$$

$$\therefore \quad f = \frac{1}{2\pi\sqrt{(LC)}}$$

This is the resonant frequency and is given the symbol f_0.

i.e. $\quad f_0 = \dfrac{1}{2\pi\sqrt{(LC)}} \quad$ for a series L–C–R circuit

$$\therefore \quad \omega_0 = 2\pi f_0 = \frac{1}{\sqrt{(LC)}}$$

Now the equation for the impedance of an L-C-R circuit is

$$Z = \sqrt{R^2 + (X_L - X_C)^2}$$

At the resonant frequency,

$$X_L = X_C$$

$$\therefore \quad Z = R$$

i.e. at resonance the circuit is purely resistive and has a zero phase angle.

Example 1 A circuit consists of a coil of inductance 10 mH and resistance 100 Ω connected in series with a 20 nF capacitor. It is supplied from a 10 V variable-frequency supply. Calculate (a) the resonant frequency, (b) the impedance at resonance, (c) the current at resonance, (d) the inductive and capacitive reactances at resonance.

a) $\quad f_0 = \dfrac{1}{2\pi\sqrt{(LC)}}$

where $\quad L = 10\,\text{mH} = 10 \times 10^{-3}\,\text{H}$

and $\qquad C = 20\,\text{nF} = 20 \times 10^{-9}\,\text{F}$

$$\therefore \quad f_0 = \frac{1}{2\pi\sqrt{(10 \times 10^{-3}\,\text{H} \times 20 \times 10^{-9}\,\text{F})}}$$

$$= 11\,260\,\text{Hz} = 11.26\,\text{kHz}$$

b) At resonance, $Z = R$

where $\quad R = 100\,\Omega$

$\therefore \quad$ impedance at resonance $= 100\,\Omega$

c) At resonance, $I = V/R$

where $\quad V = 10\,\text{V} \quad$ and $\quad R = 100\,\Omega$

$$\therefore \quad I = \frac{10\,V}{100\,\Omega} = 0.1\,A$$

d) At resonance, $X_L = \omega_0 L = 2\pi f_0 L$

where $f_0 = 11\,260\,\text{Hz}$ and $L = 10\,\text{mH} = 10 \times 10^{-3}\,\text{H}$

$\therefore \quad X_L = 2\pi \times 11\,260\,\text{Hz} \times 10 \times 10^{-3}\,\text{H} = 707\,\Omega$

Also at resonance, $X_L = X_C$

$\therefore \quad X_C = 707\,\Omega$

i.e. the resonant frequency is 11.26 kHz, the impedance at resonance is 100 Ω, the current is 0.1 A, and the inductive and capacitive reactances are 707 Ω.

Q factor

To see how impedance varies with frequency in a series L–C–R circuit, let us plot a graph of impedance Z against supply frequency f. This is shown in fig. 2.9(a).

For $f < f_0$ the circuit is mainly capacitive with a leading phase angle.

For $f = f_0$ the circuit is purely resistive with the impedance at its *minimum* value of $Z = R$.

For $f > f_0$ the circuit is mainly inductive with a lagging phase angle.

The variation of current I with frequency f is shown in fig. 2.9(b). Notice that the current reaches a *maximum* value at the resonant frequency, as would be expected.

The variation of voltage V_C across the capacitor with frequency f is shown in fig. 2.9(c). At very low frequencies this voltage is equal to the supply voltage V.

Notice that V_C increases as the frequency approaches f_0. At the resonant frequency, V_C may be many times the supply voltage V.

The ratio V_C/V at resonance is defined as the Q factor, or quality factor, of the series circuit:

$$Q = \frac{V_C}{V} \quad \text{at resonance}$$

Since the capacitor voltage may be many times the supply voltage V, the Q factor of a series resonant circuit may be defined as the 'voltage magnification factor'.

Notice that, since $V_L = V_C$ at resonance, we may also define the Q factor as

$$Q = \frac{V_L}{V} \quad \text{at resonance}$$

However, since we cannot physically separate the inductance and resistance of the coil, we cannot measure V_L.

35

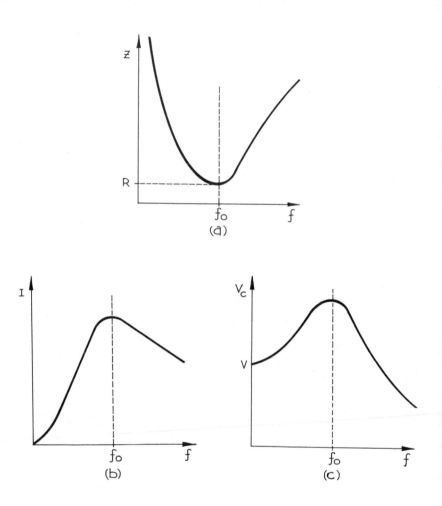

Fig. 2.9 Variation of impedance, current, and capacitor voltage with supply frequency in a series L–C–R circuit

Now, at resonance,

$$V_C = IX_C = \frac{I}{\omega_0 C}$$

and $\quad V = IR$

$$\therefore \quad Q = \frac{V_C}{V} = \frac{IX_C}{IR} = \frac{X_C}{R} = \frac{1}{\omega_0 CR}$$

Also, since $X_L = X_C$ at resonance,

$$Q = \frac{X_L}{R} = \frac{\omega_0 L}{R}$$

and, since $\omega_0 = 1/\sqrt{(LC)}$,

$$Q = \frac{L}{R\sqrt{(LC)}} = \frac{1}{R}\sqrt{\frac{L}{C}}$$

Since the resistance of the circuit is often simply the resistance of the coil, the Q factor of a series L-C-R circuit is a measure of how good the coil is at resonating with a capacitor at a particular frequency.

Example 2 Calculate the resonant frequency and Q factor of a series circuit consisting of a coil of inductance 100 mH and resistance 18 Ω and a 0.25 μF capacitor.

a) $f_0 = \dfrac{1}{2\pi\sqrt{(LC)}}$

where $L = 100\,\text{mH} = 0.1\,\text{H}$ and $C = 0.25\,\mu\text{F} = 0.25 \times 10^{-6}\,\text{F}$

$\therefore\quad f_0 = \dfrac{1}{2\pi\sqrt{(0.1\,\text{H} \times 0.25 \times 10^{-6}\,\text{F})}}$

$= 1007\,\text{Hz} = 1.007\,\text{kHz}$

b) $Q = \dfrac{1}{R}\sqrt{\dfrac{L}{C}}$

where $R = 18\,\Omega$ $L = 0.1\,\text{H}$ and $C = 0.25 \times 10^{-6}\,\text{F}$

$\therefore\quad Q = \dfrac{1}{18\,\Omega}\sqrt{\dfrac{0.1\,\text{H}}{0.25 \times 10^{-6}\,\text{F}}} = 35$

i.e. the resonant frequency is 1 kHz and the Q factor is 35.

Example 3 A coil has an inductance of 10 mH and a Q factor of 25 at 12 kHz. Calculate (a) the resistance of the coil, (b) the capacitance to be connected in series with the coil to cause resonance at 12 kHz.

a) $Q = \omega_0 L/R$

$\therefore\quad R = \omega_0 L/Q$

where $\omega_0 = 2\pi f_0 = 2\pi \times 12\,000\,\text{Hz}$

$L = 10\,\text{mH} = 0.01\,\text{H}$ and $Q = 25$

$\therefore\quad R = \dfrac{2\pi \times 12\,000\,\text{Hz} \times 0.01\,\text{H}}{25} = 30\,\Omega$

b) $\omega_0 = 1/\sqrt{(LC)}$

$\therefore\quad C = 1/(L\omega_0^2)$

where $\quad \omega_0 = 2\pi \times 12\,000\,\text{Hz}\quad$ and $\quad L = 0.01\,\text{H}$

$$\therefore\quad C = \frac{1}{0.01\,\text{H} \times (2\pi \times 12\,000\,\text{Hz})^2}$$

$$= 0.018 \times 10^{-6}\,\text{F} = 18\,\text{nF}$$

i.e. the resistance of the coil is $30\,\Omega$ and the required capacitance is $18\,\text{nF}$.

In high-frequency electronic circuits, series resonance may be used to advantage. Since the series circuit has a minimum impedance at only one frequency (the resonant frequency), it may be used as a frequency-selective circuit. The higher the Q factor of the coil, the more frequency-selective is the circuit.

In series power circuits, a high Q factor could be a definite disadvantage, since, due to the voltage magnification, the voltage across the capacitor and across the inductance could be several times the supply voltage. In power circuits this could cause dangerously high voltages, with subsequent break-down of the insulation.

In practice, power series resonant circuits with high Q factor are uncommon.

Now let us consider the various combinations of components in *parallel* a.c. circuits.

2.7 Circuits possessing resistance and inductance in parallel

Figure 2.10(a) shows a resistance R and an inductance L connected in parallel and supplied from an a.c. voltage source V. The currents I_R and I_L are not in phase and therefore the phasor diagram of fig. 2.10(b) is used to analyse the circuit. In the phasor diagram, I_R is in phase with V and I_L lags V by 90°.

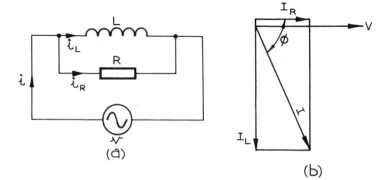

Fig. 2.10 Parallel R–L circuit and phasor diagram

Notice that in the parallel circuit the voltage across each component is the same, and therefore voltage is used as the reference phasor.

From the phasor diagram, the total current I is given by

$$I = \sqrt{I_R^2 + I_L^2}$$

but $\quad I_R = V/R \quad$ and $\quad I_L = V/X_L$

$$\therefore \quad I = \sqrt{\left(\frac{V}{R}\right)^2 + \left(\frac{V}{X_L}\right)^2} = V\sqrt{\frac{1}{R^2} + \frac{1}{X_L^2}}$$

The impedance Z of the total circuit is given by

$$Z = \frac{V}{I} = \frac{1}{\sqrt{(1/R^2 + 1/X_L^2)}} = \frac{1}{\sqrt{(1/R^2 + 1/\omega^2 L^2)}}$$

The phase angle ϕ is given by

$$\tan \phi = \frac{I_L}{I_R} = \frac{V/X_L}{V/R} = \frac{R}{X_L} = \frac{R}{\omega L}$$

The parallel R–L circuit is not a very commonly used arrangement, since the preferred representation of a coil is a series R–L circuit.

2.8 Circuit possessing resistance and capacitance in parallel

Figure 2.11 (a) shows a resistance R and a capacitance C connected in parallel and supplied from an a.c. voltage source. The corresponding phasor diagram is shown in fig. 2.11 (b). In the phasor diagram, I_R is in phase with V and I_C leads V by $90°$.

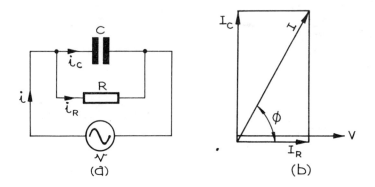

Fig. 2.11 Parallel R–C circuit and phasor diagram

From the phasor diagram,

$$I = \sqrt{I_R^2 + I_C^2}$$

but $\quad I_R = V/R \quad$ and $\quad I_C = V/X_C$

$$\therefore \quad I = \sqrt{\left(\frac{V}{R}\right)^2 + \left(\frac{V}{X_C}\right)^2} = V\sqrt{\frac{1}{R^2} + \frac{1}{X_C^2}}$$

and $\quad Z = \dfrac{V}{I} = \dfrac{1}{\sqrt{(1/R^2 + 1/X_C^2)}} = \dfrac{1}{\sqrt{(1/R^2 + \omega^2 C^2)}}$

The phase angle is given by

$$\tan \phi = \frac{I_C}{I_R} = \frac{V/X_C}{V/R} = \frac{R}{X_C} = \omega C R$$

Example A 2.2 μF capacitor has a parallel leakage resistance of 1 kΩ. Calculate (a) the phase angle of the circuit at 1 kHz, (b) the power loss in the capacitor if it is fed from a 20 V supply.

a) $\quad \tan \phi = \omega C R$

where $\quad \omega = 2\pi f = 2\pi \times 1000$ Hz $\qquad C = 2.2 \mu$F $= 2.2 \times 10^{-6}$ F

and $\quad R = 1$ kΩ = 1000 Ω

$\therefore \quad \tan \phi = 2\pi \times 1000$ Hz $\times 2.2 \times 10^{-6}$ F $\times 1000$ Ω

$\qquad = 13.8$

$\therefore \qquad \phi = \arctan 13.8 = 86°$

b) Power loss $P = V^2/R$

where $\quad V = 20 V \quad$ and $\quad R = 1$ kΩ = 1000 Ω

$\therefore \quad P = \dfrac{(20 V)^2}{1000 \Omega} = 0.4$ W

i.e. the phase angle of the circuit is 86° and the power loss is 0.4 W.

The parallel R–C circuit is an arrangement commonly used to represent a practical capacitor. In this case the parallel resistance represents the leakage resistance of the capacitor, which will usually be a very large resistance. This equivalent circuit is used to represent a practical capacitor at low frequencies.

2.9 Parallel circuits containing inductance and capacitance
Consider the parallel combination of a pure inductance and a pure capacitance supplied from an alternating voltage source, as shown in fig. 2.12. As discussed in section 2.5, the energy passes backwards and forwards between the inductor and the capacitor at a frequency determined by the values of L and C.

The currents I_L and I_C are exactly 180° out of phase. Current flows either from the inductor to the capacitor or vice versa. Since there is no resistance

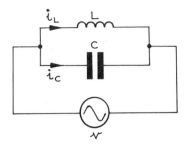

Fig. 2.12 Parallel L–C circuit

in the circuit, no continuous flow of energy is taken from the supply and the power consumed by the circuit is zero.

This is not a practically realisable circuit, since a coil possesses both inductance and resistance. A more practical arrangement will now be considered.

2.10 Parallel combinations of resistance, inductance, and capacitance

In practice, parallel combinations of L–C–R circuits are usually represented as shown in fig. 2.12 – this is because the coil possesses both inductance and resistance, while in comparison the capacitor is a relatively perfect component.

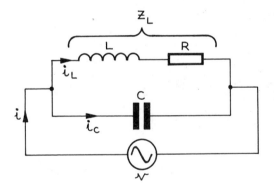

Fig. 2.13 Parallel L–C–R circuit

In the case of parallel circuits, we use the voltage V as the reference phasor, since this is common to both branches.

First consider the phasor diagram for the coil branch. This is shown in fig. 2.14(a) – the usual representation for a series R–L circuit with phase angle ϕ_L.

If we now rotate the diagram clockwise to make V the reference phasor, and add the capacitor current I_C, we have the complete-circuit phasor diagram shown in fig. 2.14(b). The total current I may then be found by taking the phasor addition of I_L and I_C. This is shown in fig. 2.14(c) for the condition of resonance with the total current I in phase with the voltage V.

41

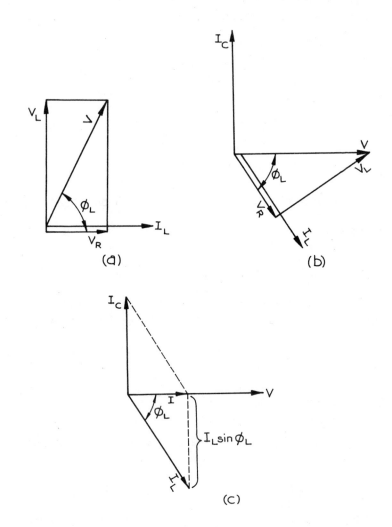

Fig. 2.14 Development of the phasor diagram for a parallel $L-C-R$ circuit at resonance

In the parallel $L-C-R$ circuit, resonance occurs when I_C is equal to the vertical component of I_L. At resonance,

$$I_C = I_L \sin \phi_L$$

as shown in fig. 2.14(c).

The circuit at resonance is purely resistive, since V and I are in phase. The total phase angle is therefore zero.

42

Now, we have stated that at resonance

$$I_C = I_L \sin \phi_L$$

where $I_C = V/X_C$ and $I_L = V/Z_L$

Z_L being the impedance of the coil

and $\sin \phi_L = X_L/Z_L$

$$\therefore \qquad \frac{V}{X_C} = \frac{V}{Z_L} \cdot \frac{X_L}{Z_L}$$

$$\therefore \qquad X_C X_L = Z_L{}^2 = R^2 + X_L{}^2$$

$$\therefore \qquad \frac{1}{\omega_0 C} \cdot \omega_0 L = R^2 + \omega_0{}^2 L^2$$

$$\therefore \qquad \frac{L}{C} = R^2 + \omega_0{}^2 L^2$$

$$\therefore \qquad \omega_0{}^2 L^2 = \frac{L}{C} - R^2$$

$$\therefore \qquad \omega_0{}^2 = \frac{1}{LC} - \frac{R^2}{L^2}$$

$$\therefore \qquad \omega_0 = \sqrt{\frac{1}{LC} - \frac{R^2}{L^2}}$$

and $$f_0 = \frac{\omega_0}{2\pi} = \frac{1}{2\pi} \sqrt{\frac{1}{LC} - \frac{R^2}{L^2}}$$

This is the equation for the resonant frequency in terms of L, C, and R.
Notice that when R is small such that

$$\frac{R^2}{L^2} \ll \frac{1}{LC}$$

then the equation approximates to

$$\omega_0 = \frac{1}{\sqrt{(LC)}}$$

which is the same as for series resonance.

Example 1 A coil of inductance 2 H and resistance 363 Ω is connected in parallel with a 2.5 μF capacitor and supplied from a 400 V 50 Hz a.c. voltage source. Calculate the current in each branch and, by use of a scaled phasor diagram, calculate the total current and the phase angle.

For the coil,

$$X_L = 2\pi fL$$

where $f = 50\,\text{Hz}$ and $L = 2\,\text{H}$

$\therefore \quad X_L = 2\pi \times 50\,\text{Hz} \times 2\,\text{H}$

$\quad\quad\quad = 628\,\Omega$

$$Z_L = \sqrt{R^2 + X_L{}^2}$$

where $R = 363\,\Omega$ and $X_L = 628\,\Omega$

$\therefore \quad Z_L = \sqrt{(363\,\Omega)^2 + (628\,\Omega)^2}$

$\quad\quad\quad = 725\,\Omega$

$$\tan\phi_L = \frac{X_L}{R} = \frac{628\,\Omega}{363\,\Omega} = 1.73$$

$\therefore \quad\quad \phi_L = \arctan 1.73 = 60°$

$$I_L = \frac{V}{Z_L} = \frac{400\,\text{V}}{725\,\Omega} = 0.55\,\text{A}$$

For the capacitor,

$$X_C = 1/2\pi fC$$

where $f = 50\,\text{Hz}$ and $C = 2.5\,\mu\text{F} = 2.5 \times 10^{-6}\,\text{F}$

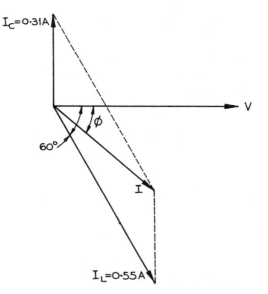

Fig. 2.15

$$\therefore \quad X_C = \frac{1}{2\pi \times 50\,\text{Hz} \times 2.5 \times 10^{-6}\,\text{F}}$$

$$= 1274\,\Omega$$

$$\therefore \quad I_C = \frac{V}{X_C} = \frac{400\,\text{V}}{1274\,\Omega} = 0.314\,\text{A}$$

The phasor diagram is drawn to scale in fig. 2.15. From this diagram,

$$I = 0.32\,\text{A} \quad \text{and} \quad \phi = 30.5°$$

i.e. the current in the coil is 0.55 A, the current in the capacitor is 0.31 A, and the total current and the phase angle are 0.32 A and 30.5°.

A scaled phasor diagram is one method for determining the sum of the branch currents in parallel *L-C-R* circuits. An alternative method is by resolution of the branch currents into *in-phase* and *quadrature* components. These are the phasor components of the current which are respectively in-phase with and at right angles to the reference quantity. An example will demonstrate this method.

Example 2 In the network of fig. 2.16, the generator maintains a sinusoidal voltage of 50 V r.m.s at 400 Hz. At this frequency the reactance of the capacitor is 6 Ω and that of the inductor is 8 Ω. Calculate the magnitude and phase of the current in each branch and the magnitude and phase of the generator current.

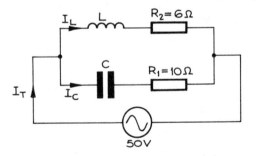

Fig. 2.16

An approximate phasor diagram is shown in fig. 2.17, where

$$I_C = \frac{V}{\sqrt{(X_C^2 + R_1^2)}}$$

$$= \frac{50\,\text{V}}{\sqrt{[(6\,\Omega)^2 + (10\,\Omega)^2]}} = \frac{50\,\text{V}}{11.66\,\Omega} = 4.29\,\text{A}$$

and $\quad \phi_C = \arctan(X_C/R_1) = \arctan(6/10) = 30.96°$

45

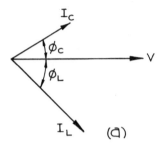

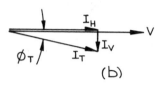

Fig. 2.17

$$I_L = \frac{V}{\sqrt{(X_L^2 + R_2^2)}}$$

$$= \frac{50\,V}{\sqrt{[(8\,\Omega)^2 + (6\,\Omega)^2]}} = \frac{50\,V}{10\,\Omega} = 5\,A$$

and $\phi_L = \arctan(-X_L/R_2) = \arctan(-8/10) = -38.66°$

Now take horizontal and vertical components of both currents.

The horizontal (in-phase) component I_H of the total current is given by

$$I_H = I_C \cos\phi_C + I_L \cos\phi_L$$

$$= 4.29\,A \times \cos 30.96° + 5\,A \times \cos(-38.66°)$$

$$= 7.58\,A$$

The vertical (quadrature) component I_V of the total current is given by

$$I_V = I_C \sin\phi_C - I_L \sin\phi_L$$

$$= 4.29\,A \times \sin 30.96° + 5\,A \times \sin(-38.66°)$$

$$= -0.92\,A$$

∴ $$I_T = \sqrt{(I_H^2 + I_V^2)}$$

$$= \sqrt{[(7.58\,A)^2 + (-0.92\,A)^2]}$$

$$= 7.64\,A$$

and $$\phi_T = \arctan\left(\frac{I_V}{I_H}\right) = \arctan\left(\frac{-0.92\,A}{7.58\,A}\right)$$

$$= -6.92°$$

i.e. the current through the capacitor is 4.29 A at a phase angle of 30.96°, the current through the inductor is 5 A at a phase angle of −38.66°, and the generator current is 7.64 A at a phase angle of −6.92°.

Dynamic resistance

Consider the phasor diagram of fig. 2.14(c), which shows a parallel L–C–R circuit at resonance.

The current taken from the supply is given by

$$I = I_L \cos \phi_L$$

Now $\quad I_L \cos \phi_L = \dfrac{V}{Z_L} \cdot \dfrac{R}{Z_L} = \dfrac{VR}{Z_L{}^2}$

but we have seen that, at resonance,

$$Z_L{}^2 = X_C X_L = \frac{1}{\omega_0 C} \cdot \omega_0 L = \frac{L}{C}$$

$\therefore \quad I_L \cos \phi_L = \dfrac{VRC}{L}$

At resonance, the impedance is

$$Z = \frac{V}{I} = \frac{V}{I_L \cos \phi_L} = \frac{VL}{VRC} = \frac{L}{CR}$$

The impedance at resonance is purely resistive and is therefore referred to as the *dynamic resistance*, R_D, where

$$R_D = \frac{L}{CR}$$

Example 3 A coil of inductance 200 mH and resistance 25 Ω is connected in parallel with an 0.1 μF capacitor and fed from a 20 V variable-frequency supply. Calculate (a) the resonant frequency, (b) the dynamic resistance, (c) the current taken from the supply at resonance.

a) $\quad f_0 = \dfrac{1}{2\pi} \sqrt{\dfrac{1}{LC} - \dfrac{R^2}{L^2}}$

where $\quad L = 200 \, \text{mH} = 0.2 \, \text{H}$

$\qquad\quad C = 0.1 \, \mu\text{F} = 0.1 \times 10^{-6} \, \text{F} \quad$ and $\quad R = 25 \, \Omega$

$\therefore \quad f_0 = \dfrac{1}{2\pi} \sqrt{\dfrac{1}{0.2 \, \text{H} \times 0.1 \times 10^{-6} \, \text{F}} - \dfrac{(25 \, \Omega)^2}{(0.2 \, \text{H})^2}}$

$\qquad = \dfrac{1}{2\pi} \sqrt{50 \times 10^6 - 15.6 \times 10^3}$

$\qquad = \dfrac{7070}{2\pi} = 1126 \, \text{Hz} = 1.126 \, \text{kHz}$

Notice that, in this example, the resistance produces negligible effect on f_0.

b) $R_D = \dfrac{L}{CR}$

where $L = 0.2\,\text{H}$ $C = 0.1 \times 10^{-6}\,\text{F}$ and $R = 25\,\Omega$

$\therefore\quad R_D = \dfrac{0.2\,\text{H}}{0.1 \times 10^{-6}\,\text{F} \times 25\,\Omega}$

$= 80\,000\,\Omega = 80\,\text{k}\Omega$

c) At resonance,

$I = V/R_D$

where $V = 20\,\text{V}$ and $R_D = 80\,\text{k}\Omega$

$\therefore\quad I = \dfrac{20\,\text{V}}{80\,\text{k}\Omega} = 0.25\,\text{mA}$

i.e. the resonant frequency is 1.126 kHz, the dynamic resistance is 80 kΩ, and the current at resonance is 0.25 mA.

Let us consider how the impedance varies with frequency.

The graph of impedance Z against frequency is shown in fig. 2.18(a). The impedance is a maximum at the resonant frequency f_0 and is then equal to the dynamic resistance R_D. At this frequency the phase shift is zero.

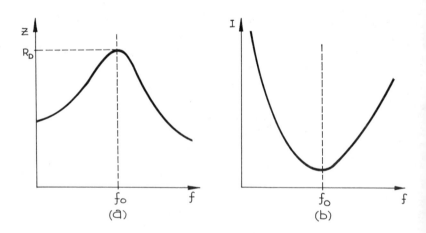

Fig. 2.18 Variation of impedance and total current with supply frequency in a parallel L–C–R circuit

48

The graph of the current variation with frequency is shown in fig. 2.18(b). This represents the current drawn from a fixed-voltage supply. At the resonant frequency f_0, the current is a minimum and is given by

$$I = \frac{V}{R_D}$$

For a parallel resonant circuit, the Q factor of the circuit is defined as the ratio of the capacitor current I_C to the total supply current I:

$$Q = \frac{I_C}{I} \quad \text{at resonance}$$

At resonance,

$$I_C = \frac{V}{X_C} = V\omega_0 C$$

$$\text{and} \quad I = \frac{V}{R_D} = \frac{VCR}{L}$$

$$\therefore \quad Q = \frac{V\omega_0 CL}{VCR} = \frac{\omega_0 L}{R}$$

This is the same equation as was obtained for the series resonant circuit.

Since the capacitor current I_C may be many times the supply current I, we may define the Q factor of a parallel resonant circuit as the current-magnification factor of the circuit.

Example 4   A coil of resistance 5 Ω and inductance 0.5 H is connected in parallel with a capacitor across a 240 V 50 Hz a.c. supply. Determine (a) the value of the capacitor if the current taken from the supply is to be a minimum, (b) the total current, (c) the Q factor of the circuit.

a)   For the current to be a minimum, the circuit must be at resonance at 50 Hz.

$$\text{Now} \quad \omega_0 = \sqrt{\frac{1}{LC} - \frac{R^2}{L^2}}$$

If we approximate this, we have

$$2\pi f_0 = \frac{1}{\sqrt{(LC)}}$$

$$\therefore \quad C = \frac{1}{L(2\pi f_0)^2}$$

where $L = 0.5$ H   and $f_0 = 50$ Hz

$$\therefore \quad C = \frac{1}{0.5 \, \text{H} \, (2\pi \times 50 \, \text{Hz})^2}$$

$$= 20.2 \, \mu\text{F}$$

Notice that, since $1/LC = 99 \times 10^3$ and $R^2/L^2 = 100$, then $R^2/L^2 \ll 1/LC$ and the approximation is acceptable.

b) $\quad R_\text{D} = \dfrac{L}{CR}$

where $\quad L = 0.5 \, \text{H} \qquad C = 20.2 \times 10^{-6} \, \text{F} \qquad$ and $\qquad R = 5 \, \Omega$

$$\therefore \quad R_\text{D} = \frac{0.5 \, \text{H}}{20.2 \times 10^{-6} \, \text{F} \times 5 \, \Omega} = 4.95 \, \text{k}\Omega$$

At resonance,

$$I = \frac{V}{R_\text{D}} = \frac{240 \, \text{V}}{4.95 \, \text{k}\Omega} = 48.5 \, \text{mA}$$

c) $\quad Q = \dfrac{\omega_0 L}{R} = \dfrac{2\pi f_0 L}{R}$

where $\quad f_0 = 50 \, \text{Hz} \qquad L = 0.5 \, \text{H} \quad$ and $\quad R = 5 \, \Omega$

$$\therefore \quad Q = \frac{2\pi \times 50 \, \text{Hz} \times 0.5 \, \text{H}}{5 \, \Omega} = 31.4$$

i.e. the capacitor is $20.2 \, \mu\text{F}$, the minimum total current is $48.5 \, \text{mA}$, and the Q factor is 31.4.

Example 5   A coil of resistance $100 \, \Omega$ and a Q factor of 8 is connected in parallel with a capacitor to produce resonance. When the circuit is connected to an a.c. supply at the resonant frequency, the current taken by the circuit is 15 mA. Calculate (a) the current through the capacitor, (b) the p.d. across the circuit.

We appear to have a minimum of information available in this question.

a)   Now $\quad Q = I_C/I \quad$ at resonance

$\therefore \qquad I_C = QI$

where $\quad Q = 8 \quad$ and $\quad I = 15 \, \text{mA}$

$\therefore \quad I_C = 8 \times 15 \, \text{mA} = 120 \, \text{mA} = 0.12 \, \text{A}$

b)   Now $\quad I = V/R_\text{D}$

$$\therefore \qquad V = IR_\text{D} = \frac{IL}{CR}$$

Also, we may say approximately that

$$\omega_0 = 1/\sqrt{(LC)}$$

$$\therefore \quad C = \frac{1}{L\omega_0{}^2}$$

Substituting in the equation for V, we have

$$V = \frac{IL^2\omega_0{}^2}{R}$$

Now $\quad Q = \omega_0 L/R$

$\therefore \quad \omega_0 L = QR$

$$\therefore \quad V = \frac{I}{R}(QR)^2 = IQ^2R$$

where $\quad I = 0.015\,\text{A} \quad\quad Q = 8 \quad$ and $\quad R = 100\,\Omega$

$\therefore \quad V = 0.015\,\text{A} \times 8^2 \times 100\,\Omega$

$\quad\quad = 96\,\text{V}$

i.e. the current through the capacitor is 0.12 A and the p.d. across the circuit is 96 V.

Notice how with a minimum of information we can use the known relationships to derive the other quantities.

2.11 Power-factor correction

We have considered in section 2.4 the difference between real power and apparent power. The real power is the power dissipated in the resistive component of the circuit, whereas the apparent power is the product of the voltage and the supply current.

In circuits containing both resistance and reactance, real and apparent power are different, due to some of the energy fed to the circuit being fed back into the supply on another part of the voltage cycle.

A typical example of such a circuit is an induction motor, which may be represented at any given speed by a series combination of resistance and inductive reactance. When the motor is running, it takes in more energy from the supply than is required to drive the motor. Some of the energy is converted into mechanical energy and produces torque at the motor shaft. The additional energy is stored as a magnetic field on one part of the cycle and is fed back into the supply on another part of the cycle. This means that the motor is taking more current from the supply than it requires.

The disadvantage of this situation is that the supply cable and control switchgear need to be rated at a higher current than is really necessary. Scale this up by all the induction motors running in a large machine factory and the additional cost of cable and switchgear is very large.

Some means is required which ensures that the motor takes only the current required to produce the necessary drive torque. This is very neatly arranged by connecting a capacitor in parallel with the motor. The reason for this may be understood by considering the phasor diagram of fig. 2.14(c). This shows the phasor addition of an inductive current I_L and a capacitive current I_C. In fact it represents the phasor diagram for just such a circuit as we are considering. Notice that the resultant current I is less than either I_C or I_L, and the circuit is purely resistive. In fact the only current which is taken by the combination is that which is required to produce the torque.

The result of connecting the capacitor across the inductive circuit is to reduce the phase angle from ϕ_L to zero. Since the power factor of a circuit is given by

power factor $= \cos \phi$

reducing the phase angle brings the power factor closer to unity.

The improvement of power factor by adding a capacitor in parallel with an inductive load is called *power-factor correction*.

The Central Electricity Generating Board requires all large-scale electricity consumers to maintain power factors within a fixed tolerance of unity, otherwise they will be charged an extra tariff. The reason for this is that the CEGB wishes to keep the size of cables and switchgear to a minimum for the particular load required, to reduce its costs.

In practice, large banks of capacitors are used in parallel with induction motors. A synchronous motor (see section 9.6) may be used instead for power-factor correction and be driven such that it provides a leading phase angle.

Example   A 240 V 50 Hz single-phase induction motor takes a current of 50 A. Its power factor at this load is 0.8 lagging. Determine the value of capacitor required to correct the power factor to unity.

The circuit arrangement is shown in fig. 2.19(a) and the corresponding phasor diagram in fig. 2.19(b).

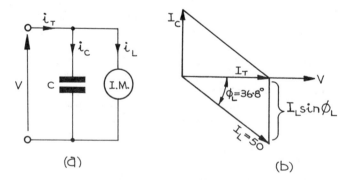

Fig. 2.19 Power-factor correction of an induction motor.

To correct the power factor to unity requires that the capacitor current I_C be equal to $I_L \sin \phi_L$.

$$\therefore \quad I_C = I_L \sin \phi_L$$

where $I_L = 50\,\text{A}$ and $\cos \phi_L = 0.8$ $\therefore$ $\sin \phi_L = 0.6$

$$\therefore \quad I_C = 50\,\text{A} \times 0.6$$

$$= 30\,\text{A}$$

The required capacitive reactance is given by

$$X_C = \frac{V}{I_C} = \frac{240\,\text{V}}{30\,\text{A}} = 8\,\Omega$$

$$\therefore \quad \frac{1}{\omega C} = 8\,\Omega$$

$$\therefore \quad C = \frac{1}{8\,\Omega \times \omega}$$

where $\omega = 2\pi f = 2\pi \times 50\,\text{Hz} = 314.2\,\text{Hz}$

$$\therefore \quad C = \frac{1}{8 \times 314.2}\,\text{F}$$

$$= 398 \times 10^{-6}\,\text{F} = 398\,\mu\text{F}$$

i.e. the required capacitance is $398\,\mu\text{F}$.

2.12 Bandwidth of resonant circuits

In any a.c. circuit containing reactive elements, the 'response' of the circuit is frequency-dependent. Consider, for example, the L–C–R circuit of fig. 2.20(a) and the graph of variation of voltage across the capacitor (V_C) with frequency (fig. 2.20(b)). It is evident that the value of V_C is very frequency-dependent.

Because we are often concerned with defining quantitively the sharpness of this response curve, we define a frequency f_L below the resonant frequency and a frequency f_H above it at which the voltage V_C is equal to $1/\sqrt{2}$ of its value at resonance. (i.e. 0.707 of its value at resonance). This figure is chosen since the power dissipated at these frequencies will be $(0.707)^2$ ($= 0.5$) times the power dissipated at resonance. The frequency values f_H and f_L are therefore known as the *half-power frequencies*.

The difference between these two frequencies ($f_H - f_L$) is called the *bandwidth*. Bandwidth may thus be defined as the frequency range over which the response is greater than its half-power frequency values.

It may be shown that, for a series resonant circuit,

$$f_H - f_L = \frac{f_0}{Q}$$

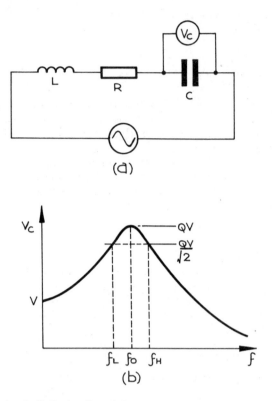

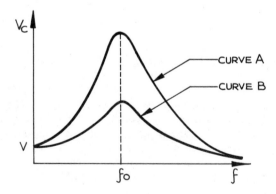

Fig. 2.20 Series L–C–R circuit and frequency-response curve of capacitor voltage

Fig. 2.21 Capacitor-voltage frequency-response curves with high and low Q factor

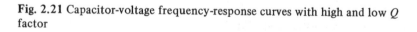

Now $Q = \dfrac{\omega_0 L}{R} = \dfrac{2\pi f_0 L}{R}$

$\therefore \quad f_H - f_L = \dfrac{f_0}{2\pi f_0 L/R} = \dfrac{R}{2\pi L}$

Figure 2.21 shows curves of V_C against frequency for two resonant circuits, both resonant at frequency f_0. Curve A has a higher Q and a smaller bandwidth than curve B. Curve A could be achieved by using a coil with a high ratio of inductance to resistance.

It may be shown that in the case of the parallel resonant circuit the same definition applies for bandwidth; i.e. $f_H - f_L = f_0/Q$. In this case the half-power frequencies are the points on the graph of impedance (Z) against frequency where

$$Z = \frac{R_D}{\sqrt{2}}$$

where R_D is the dynamic resistance L/CR (see fig. 2.22(a) and (b)).

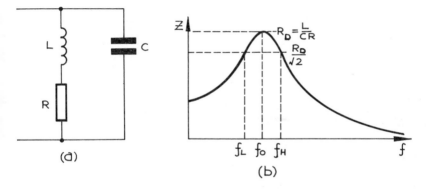

Fig. 2.22 Parallel L–C–R circuit and frequency-response curve of impedance

Example A coil with an inductance of $100\,\mu H$ is resonated with a $400\,pF$ capacitor connected in parallel and gives a Q factor of 50. Calculate (a) the resistance of the coil, (b) the dynamic resistance of the circuit, (c) the bandwidth of the circuit.

a) $\quad \omega_0 = \dfrac{1}{\sqrt{(LC)}}$

where $\quad L = 100\,\mu H = 100 \times 10^{-6}\,H$

and $\quad C = 400\,pF = 400 \times 10^{-12}\,F$

$$\therefore \quad \omega_0 = \frac{1}{\sqrt{(100 \times 10^{-6}\,\text{H} \times 400 \times 10^{-12}\,\text{F})}}$$

$$= \frac{10^9}{200} = 5 \times 10^6 \text{ rad/s}$$

$$Q = \frac{\omega_0 L}{R}$$

$$\therefore \quad R = \frac{\omega_0 L}{Q}$$

where $Q = 50$

$$\therefore \quad R = \frac{5 \times 10^6 \text{ rad/s} \times 100 \times 10^{-6}\,\text{H}}{50} = 10\,\Omega$$

b) $R_D = \dfrac{L}{CR}$

$$= \frac{100 \times 10^{-6}\,\text{H}}{400 \times 10^{-12}\,\text{F} \times 10\,\Omega}$$

$$= 25 \times 10^3\,\Omega = 25\,\text{k}\Omega$$

c) $f_H - f_L = \dfrac{f_0}{Q}$

where $f_0 = \dfrac{\omega_0}{2\pi} = \dfrac{5 \times 10^6}{2\pi}\,\text{Hz}$

$$\therefore \quad f_H - f_L = \frac{5 \times 10^6}{2\pi \times 50}\,\text{Hz} = 15.92\,\text{Hz}$$

i.e. the resistance of the coil is $10\,\Omega$, the dynamic resistance of the circuit is $25\,\text{k}\Omega$, and the circuit bandwidth is $15.92\,\text{kHz}$.

Due to the sharpness of their response curves, resonant circuits may be used to select and amplify signals.

The parallel resonant circuit, using a variable capacitor connected in parallel with a coil, is used in a radio receiver as a frequency-selective circuit to 'tune' to a particular frequency. It is also used in a 'tuned amplifier', where it is connected as the load of the amplifier circuit. If the bandwidth is narrow enough and the Q factor is high, then the tuned amplifier will amplify only a narrow band of frequencies near the resonant frequency and effectively reject other frequencies.

Tuned coupled circuits

A transformer-coupled circuit in which either the primary or the secondary of the circuit is tuned, by means of a capacitor, is referred to as a 'tuned coupled circuit'.

Tuned coupled circuits are used extensively in communication circuits where frequency-selective coupling is required. Typical examples are intermediate-frequency (i.f.) and radio-frequency (r.f.) tuned amplifiers, where the transformer constitutes the coupling between amplifier stages.

The most commonly used single-tuned coupled circuit has the secondary tuned by a capacitor as shown in fig. 2.23(a). This circuit is often used to provide tuned coupling between two high-impedance stages of a frequency-selective voltage amplifier.

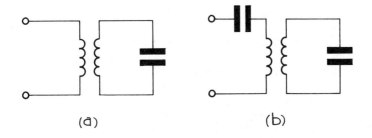

(a)   (b)

Fig. 2.23 Tuned coupled circuits: (a) single-tuned, (b) double-tuned

In the case of double-tuned transformer circuits, a commonly used arrangement is that shown in fig. 2.23(b), in which the primary is series-tuned. The usual application is with primary and secondary tuned to the same resonant frequency. The response curves for this network are shown in fig. 2.24 for various coupling factors (i.e. degrees of coupling between the two coils).

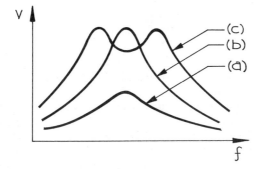

Fig. 2.24 Response curves of a tuned coupled circuit for various coupling factors: (a) under coupling, (b) optimum coupling, (c) over coupling

Curve (b) shows the case for optimum coupling and shows a single maximum. Curves (a) and (c) show the case for under coupling and over coupling respectively. Notice that with over coupling the response exhibits two maximum values and a correspondingly larger bandwidth. This effect of widening the bandwidth is often useful in r.f. and i.f. amplification stages of communication equipment.

2.13 Attenuators and filters

These are networks which modify the voltage gain (attenuators) or the frequency response (filters) of a system. They are usually inserted between the signal source and the system input, or between the system output and the load.

Attenuators

An attenuator is a network which provides a voltage reduction (attenuation). When a load is connected to a signal source via an attenuator, it is usually desirable that maximum power is delivered to the load. From the maximum-power-transfer theorem, this requires that the network output impedance be matched to the load.

Also, for maximum power to be delivered from the signal source to the attenuator, the attenuator input impedance must be matched to the signal source impedance.

Example 1 The arrangement of fig. 2.25 shows a T-shaped attenuator inserted between a signal source and a load (both 600 Ω). Calculate

a) the resistance 'seen' by the signal source (across AB) when the load is connected across CD,
b) the resistance 'seen' by the load (across CD) when the signal source is connected across AB,
c) the ratio of the voltage v_L across the load to the supply voltage v_S.

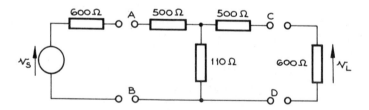

Fig. 2.25 A T-shaped attenuator

a) With the load connected across CD, the network is as shown in fig. 2.26(a). The resistance R_{AB} seen looking into AB is

58

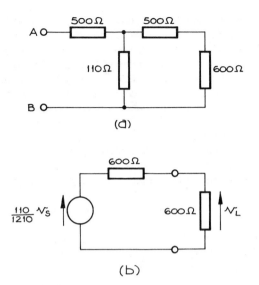

Fig. 2.26

$$R_{AB} = 500\,\Omega + \frac{1100\,\Omega \times 110\,\Omega}{1100\,\Omega + 110\,\Omega}$$

$$= 500\,\Omega + 100\,\Omega$$

$$= 600\,\Omega$$

b) Similarly, with the source connected across AB, the resistance R_{CD} seen looking into CD is

$$R_{CD} = 500\,\Omega + \frac{1100\,\Omega \times 110\,\Omega}{1100\,\Omega + 110\,\Omega}$$

$$= 600\,\Omega$$

c) The voltage attenuation may be found by first finding the Thévenin equivalent circuit of the source and attenuator and then calculating the voltage ratio as shown in fig. 2.26(b).

Hence $v_L = \dfrac{600\,\Omega}{1200\,\Omega} \times \dfrac{110}{1210}\, v_S$

$\therefore \quad \dfrac{v_L}{v_S} = 0.045$

i.e. the attenuator is matched both to the source resistance and to the load, presenting a 600 Ω resistance in each case. This network therefore provides maximum power transfer at the chosen voltage reduction of 0.045.

In communication circuits, matched attenuation networks such as that shown in example 1 are commonly used. These are referred to as symmetrical T attenuators where both arms have the same value. The impedance presented to the source and load in this case is referred to as the *characteristic impedance*.

Symmetrical attenuators may be either T-shaped or π-shaped. Other types of attenuator are used, such as for example half-T or half-π sections.

In practice, attenuators are often used with an attenuation which is variable by means of switches. They provide voltage reduction in terms of decibels (dB) (see chapter 10), and a typical variable switched attenuator would provide attenuation variable in multiples of say 10 dB and 1 dB.

Example 2　A half-π attenuator is shown in fig. 2.27 with a 75 Ω load connected across the output. Calculate values of R_1 and R_2 such that the attenuation is 10 dB (i.e. $V_2/V_1 = 0.316$) and the resistance seen looking into AB is also 75 Ω.

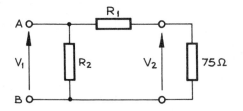

Fig. 2.27 A half-π attenuator

Since　　$V_2/V_1 = 0.316$

then　　$\dfrac{75\,\Omega}{R_1 + 75\,\Omega} = 0.316$

$\therefore$　　　　$R_1 = 162\,\Omega$

Also　$\dfrac{R_2(R_1 + 75\,\Omega)}{R_2 + R_1 + 75\,\Omega} = 75\,\Omega$

$\therefore$　　　　$R_2 = 110\,\Omega$

i.e. the values of the resistors in the half-π attenuator are 16 Ω and 110 Ω.

Filters
A filter is a network which has a particular shape of frequency response. Filters are used to 'pass' one band of frequencies and 'filter' or 'reject' others. The most common types of filter are low-pass, high-pass, band-pass, and band-stop.

A low-pass filter has zero attenuation (i.e. no gain reduction) up to the cut-off frequency and a large attenuation above this (see fig. 2.28(a)).

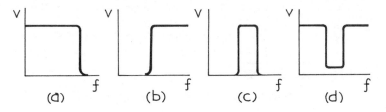

Fig. 2.28 Filter frequency-response characteristics: (a) low-pass, (b) high-pass, (c) band-pass, (d) band-stop

A high-pass filter has large attenuation at frequencies up to the cut-off frequency and zero attenuation above this (see fig. 2.28(b)).

A band-pass filter has zero attenuation over a specified frequency band and large attenuation at all other frequencies (see fig. 2.28(c)).

A band-stop filter has large attenuation over a specified frequency band only (see fig. 2.28(d)).

Perfect filters with abrupt cut-off frequencies as shown in the ideal cases of fig. 2.28 are impossible to achieve in practice. There are many designs of filter, some of which attempt to meet these characteristics.

A simple low-pass filter is shown in fig. 2.29(a). The ratio of the magnitudes of the voltages, v_o/v_i, is given by

$$\frac{v_o}{v_i} = \frac{1}{\sqrt{(1 + \omega^2 C^2 R^2)}}$$

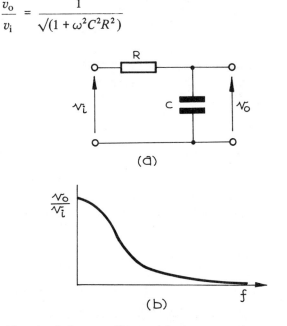

Fig. 2.29 A simple low-pass filter and frequency response

which has the frequency response shown in fig. 2.29(b). Both the voltage gain and the phase shift of the network are frequency-dependent.

A simple high-pass filter is shown in fig. 2.30(a). It has a voltage ratio

$$\frac{v_0}{v_i} = \frac{\omega CR}{\sqrt{(1 + \omega^2 C^2 R^2)}}$$

with a frequency response as shown in fig. 2.30(b).

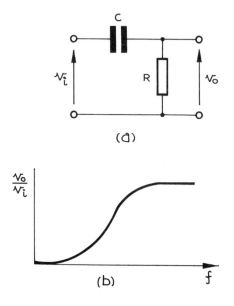

(a)

(b)

Fig. 2.30 A simple high-pass filter and frequency response

In practice, filter networks are more complex than this in order to provide a sharp cut-off characteristic.

'Passive filters' use various combinations of inductors and capacitors and are generally made up by using standard designs and a table of component values to give well-defined characteristics. 'Active filters' use various combinations of resistors and capacitors connected around operational amplifiers to achieve the same result.

Exercises on chapter 2
1   a) A coil has an inductance of 0.08 H and a resistance of 20 Ω. Calculate its impedance at (i) 50 Hz, (ii) 5 kHz.

b) a 0.1 μF capacitor is connected in parallel with a 20 kΩ resistor across a 240 V 50 Hz supply. Calculate (i) the capacitor reactance, (ii) the total current.   [32 Ω, 2.5 kΩ; 31.8 kΩ, 6.39 mA]

2   A 2 μF capacitor is connected across a variable-frequency supply. The frequency may be varied between 500 Hz and 5 kHz. Calculate the reactance at these two frequencies and sketch a graph, approximately to scale, of reactance against frequency within this range.   [159 Ω; 15.9 Ω]

3   A coil of inductance 0.5 mH and negligible resistance is connected in series with a coil of inductance 1.5 mH and resistance 100 Ω across a supply of frequency 5 kHz. Calculate the circuit impedance.   [118 Ω]

4   An inductor is connected to a d.c. supply of 10 V and passes a current of 100 mA. The inductor is now connected to a 10 V 50 Hz supply and the new current is 50 mA. Calculate the resistance and inductance of the coil. [100 Ω, 0.55 H]

5   Two coils of inductance 0.02 H and 0.05 H and resistance 8 Ω and 10 Ω respectively are connected in parallel across a 240 V 50 Hz supply. Determine (a) the current in each coil, (b) the total current, (c) the overall power factor. [23.6 A, 12.9 A; 36 A; 0.7071]

6   A coil is connected to a 200 V 50 Hz a.c. supply and consumes 1414 W at a current of 10 A. A second coil is connected in parallel and the total current is then 20 A at a power factor of 0.866 lagging. Calculate (a) the current taken by the second coil, (b) the reactance and resistance of the coil.   [13.73 A; 9.67 Ω, 10.87 Ω]

7   Define the term 'power factor'.

A 240 V a.c. supply feeds the following loads:

a) an a.c. motor load of 1.96 kW at a power factor of 0.75 lagging,
b) incandescent lamps taking a load of 1.92 kW,
c) fluorescent lamps taking a load of 1.2 kVA at a power factor of 0.8 leading.

Calculate the total current, the kW and the kVA, and the overall power factor.   [20.6 A; 4.84 kW; 4.94 kVA; 0.98 lagging]

8   The following loads are supplied by a power station: 1 MW at 0.8 power factor lagging, 1.5 MW at 0.9 power factor lagging, 700 kW at 0.9 power factor leading, and 250 kW at unit power factor.

a) Calculate the overall kVA and power factor of the power station.
b) If all the loads are carried by the same feeder cable, calculate the total load at unity power factor, which the cable would carry with the same losses.   [3633 kVA, 0.95; 3633 kW]

9   A capacitor of 10 nF is connected in series with a coil of inductance 10 mH and resistance 500 Ω to a supply of 20 V at 12 kHz. Calculate (a) the impedance, (b) the current, and (c) the phase angle. Sketch the phasor diagram, showing all voltages and current.   [761 Ω; 26.3 mA; 49° leading]

10   A coil has an inductance of 0.191 H and a resistance of 25 Ω. It is connected in series with a 125 μF capacitor to a 200 V 50 Hz a.c. supply. Calculate (a) the impedance of the network, (b) the total current taken by

the network, (c) the voltages across the coil and across the capacitor.

Sketch a phasor diagram of the voltages, showing their phase relationships to the current.   [42.6 Ω; 4.69 A; 304.9 V, 119.6 V]

11   Calculate the resonant frequency and Q factor of a series circuit containing a coil of 20 mH and 2 Ω and a 2 μF capacitor.   [796 Hz, 50]

12   Define the term 'Q factor' as applied to a series resonant circuit.

A coil has an effective resistance of 10 Ω and an inductance of 1 mH. It is connected in series with a 500 pF capacitor to a 1 V supply of variable frequency. Calculate (a) the circuit resonant frequency, (b) the current at resonance, (c) the Q factor.   [225 kHz; 0.1 A; 141]

13   Explain the term 'resonance' as applied to a coil connected in parallel with a capacitor.

A coil has an inductance of 0.5 H and a resistance of 18.7Ω. It is connected in parallel with a 20 μF capacitor across a 250 V variable-frequency supply. The frequency is varied such that the network power factor is unity. Calculate (a) the frequency of the supply, (b) the dynamic impedance, (c) the current taken from the supply, (d) the current passing through the coil.   [50.0 Hz; 1337 Ω; 187 mA; 1.58 A]

14   a) A coil of inductance L henrys and resistance R ohms is connected in parallel with a capacitor having capacitance C farads. (i) Draw a phasor diagram to show the resonant condition of this circuit. (ii) Derive the expression for the resonant frequency.

b) If the coil has inductance 0.5H and resistance 100 Ω, calculate the value of the capacitor to produce resonance at a frequency of 38.5 Hz. [20.3 μF]

15   A coil has a resistance of 50 Ω and produces resonance when connected across a capacitor of unknown value. The Q factor of the circuit is 5 and the total current at resonance is 10 mA. Calculate (a) the current taken by the capacitor, (b) the supply voltage.   [50 mA; 13 V]

16   A 100 μF capacitor is connected across an inductive circuit for power-factor correction. Calculate the kVA rating of the capacitor if the supply is 240 V 50 Hz.   [1.81 kVA]

17   A coil has an inductance of 31.8 mH and a resistance of 10 Ω. It is connected in parallel with a capacitor across a 240 V 50 Hz supply. If the total current is to be a minimum, calculate the value of the capacitor. Sketch a phasor diagram to show the currents and their phase relationship to the supply voltage.   [159 μF]

18   A 240 V 50 Hz single-phase motor takes a current of 40 A. At this load its power factor is 0.8 lagging. Calculate the value of capacitor required to correct the power factor to unity, and its kVA rating.   [318 μF; 5.76 kVA]

19   For a series L–C–R circuit supplied at constant voltage, we may say that bandwidth = f_0/Q. Hence show that an alternative definition is

$$\Delta\omega = \omega_H - \omega_L = R/L$$

The Q factor and resonant frequency of such a circuit are 100 and 51 kHz respectively. Determine the bandwidth between the half-power points. [510 Hz]

20 Define the term 'bandwidth'.

A coil has an inductance of $200\,\mu H$ and when connected in parallel with a capacitor of $200\,\mu F$ gives a Q factor of 70. Calculate (a) the resonant frequency, (b) the resistance of the coil, (c) the dynamic impedance of the circuit, (d) the bandwidth of the circuit. (Hint: the approximate equation for parallel resonance is valid in this case.)   [796 Hz; 14.3 mΩ; 70 Ω; 11.4 Hz]

21 Explain the terms 'bandwidth', 'Q factor', and 'resonance'.

A series tuned circuit has a Q factor of 120 and a resonant frequency of 9 kHz. A 200 mV variable-frequency supply is set to this frequency and when connected across the network supplies a current of 5 mA. Determine the values of R, L, and C and the bandwidth.   [40 Ω; 85 mH; 3.68 nF; 75 Hz]

22 Explain the purpose of an attenuator.

A T-shaped attenuator has outer arms each of 160 Ω and a centre limb of 240 Ω. When terminated by a load resistor R ohms, the resistance seen looking into the input of the attenuator is also R ohms. For a supply voltage of 30 V, calculate (a) the value of R, (b) the voltage across the load, (c) the voltage attenuation, (d) the power loss in the network.   [320 Ω; 13.85 V; 3.2 dB (0.69); 2.21 W]

23 What is the advantage of using an attenuator instead of a potential-divider for reducing the output of a signal generator?

A T-shaped attenuator has arms each of 200 Ω and a centre limb of 800 Ω. It is fed from a signal generator with an internal resistance of 600 Ω. Calculate (a) the resistance presented to the load, (b) the proportion of the supply voltage that appears across a load of 600 Ω.   [600 Ω; 25%]

24 Explain the purpose of a filter. Sketch the gain/frequency characteristic of a simple low-pass filter consisting of a resistor and a capacitor.

A low-pass filter is made up of a 4.7 kΩ resistor and a 0.01 μF capacitor. Calculate the filter bandwidth.   [21.2 kHz]

3   Three-phase supply

3.1 Introduction
Electricity is transmitted via the National Grid using a three-phase supply system. One reason for this is that many of the major consumers use electricity to drive electric motors and require the efficiency and good starting characteristics provided by three-phase a.c. motors (induction motors). Another reason is the economy effected in the quantity of copper or aluminium required for a three-phase transmission as compared to a single-phase system.

3.2 Single-phase and three-phase generators
You will have already considered the generation of a single-phase e.m.f. using an alternator. A simple but inefficient single-phase alternator is shown in fig. 3.1 (a). It consists of a coil rotating in a magnetic field, with the ends of the coil connected to 'slip rings' so that the induced e.m.f. may be connected via 'brushes' to an external circuit.

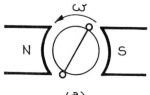

(a)

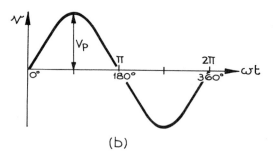

(b)

Fig. 3.1 A simple single-phase alternator and voltage waveform

The voltage waveform produced is shown in fig. 3.1(b). The voltage is at its maximum V_p when the coil sides are cutting through the magnetic flux at right angles, and is zero when the coil sides are moving parallel to the magnetic flux. The voltage waveform is sinusoidal, going both positive and negative about the zero axis.

The same principle can be applied to the generation of a three-phase electricity supply. A simple three-phase alternator is shown in fig. 3.2(a). In

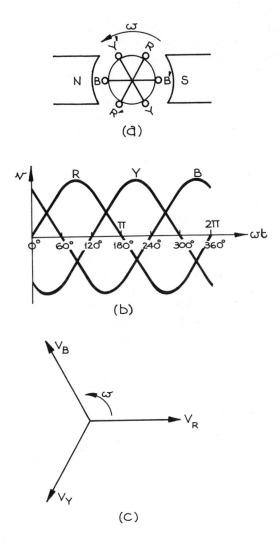

Fig. 3.2 A simple three-phase alternator, voltage waveforms, and phasor diagram

this case three coils are mounted on the same axis such that they are equally spaced around the circumference. The coils are usually referred to as R (red), Y (yellow), and B (blue) and produce voltages which are referred to as the red, yellow, and blue *phases*. The three coils would require six slip rings if they were to be connected to an external circuit.

If we consider the red coil, this has one end marked R to signify the 'start' of the coil, and the other end marked R' to signify the 'finish' of the coil. The other two coils are similarly marked.

Notice that the R, Y, and B starts are arranged to be separated by 120° ($2\pi/3$ radians) and that, with the direction of rotation as shown, the usual convention for the order of the coils (i.e. the order in which they would pass any particular point in the magnetic field) is R, Y, and B in that order. The corresponding voltage waveforms are shown in fig. 3.2(b) for one complete rotation of the coils.

It may be seen that the three voltage waveforms are separated by 120° and that they each have the same amplitude. The phasor representation of these waveforms is shown in fig. 3.2(c). In this figure, the red phasor is used as the reference and is therefore drawn horizontally from left to right.

The three voltages are referred to as the 'phase' voltages. Their instantaneous values may be represented by the expressions

$$v_R = V_p \sin \omega t$$

$$v_Y = V_p \sin (\omega t - 2\pi/3)$$

$$v_B = V_p \sin (\omega t - 4\pi/3)$$

Notice that their maximum (or peak) values are the same, and that the voltages are separated from each other by $2\pi/3$ radians.

This is referred to as a *symmetrical* three-phase system and is the type considered in the remainder of the chapter.

In any three-phase system there are two possible sequences in which the voltages may pass through their maximum possible values. One sequence is red–yellow–blue, which is known as the *positive sequence*. An alternative sequence is red–blue–yellow, which is known as the *negative sequence*. We shall consider only the positive sequence, which is the one represented in the phasor diagram of fig. 3.2(c). In negative sequence, the blue and yellow phases would be interchanged.

3.3 Star-connected three-phase systems

One method of connecting the three coils to resistive loads is shown in fig. 3.3. The three phases are used independently of each other, as three separate single-phase systems. This method does not provide the advantages of three-phase systems described in the introduction.

An alternative method which does provide these advantages is the star-connected system shown in fig. 3.4(a). In this method of connection, the three coil finishes R', Y', and B' are connected together, and the three starts R, Y, and B are taken to three separate slip rings. The common point is refer-

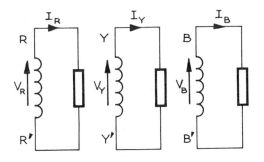

Fig. 3.3 One method of connecting the three-phase windings to resistive loads

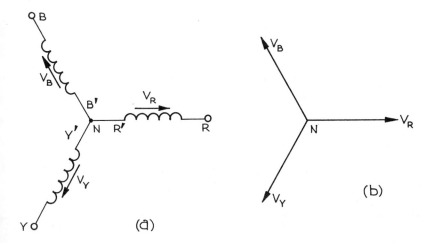

Fig. 3.4 A star-connected three-phase supply and its voltage phasor diagram

red to as a *neutral* and may be brought out to a fourth slip ring if required. This neutral provides a common point for the currents in the three phases. This will be discussed in more detail in section 3.4. The phasor diagram of the star-connected system is shown in fig. 3.4(b).

Since we have connected all the coil finishes to a common point, then, as well as the phase voltages between the starts of the coils and the neutral, there will also be a voltage between any two lines, say R and Y. The voltage between lines is referred to as the *line voltage* and in a symmetrical system all the line voltages will be the same, as shown in fig. 3.5(a). The voltage between each line and the neutral is called the *phase voltage*.

The relationship between the line voltage and the phase voltage may be seen by considering the phasor diagram of fig. 3.5(b). This phasor diagram shows both the phase and the line voltages, where the line voltages are

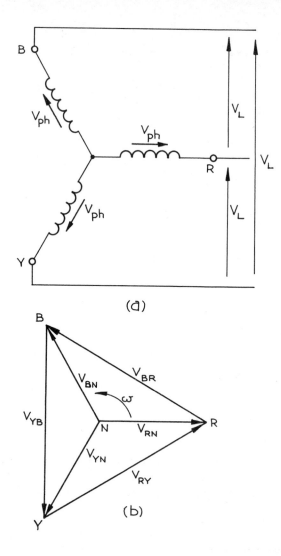

Fig. 3.5 Line and phase voltages in a three-phase star-connected supply

obtained by phasor addition of the phase voltages. This needs some explanation.

Consider the line-voltage phasor V_{RY}. This may be considered as the phasor addition of the two voltages V_{RN} and V_{YN}. Redrawing just that part of the phasor diagram with which we are concerned and extending YN backwards gives the diagram of fig. 3.6. The line DN has been added, and is equal to RY.

Now   DN = 2CN

70

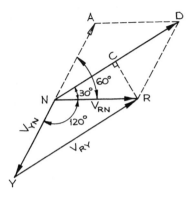

Fig. 3.6 Part of phasor diagram of fig. 3.5(b) to show relationships between line and phase voltages

$$\therefore \qquad DN = 2RN \cos 30°$$

but $\quad \cos 30° = \sqrt{3}/2$

$$\therefore \qquad DN = 2RN\sqrt{3}/2$$

$$= \sqrt{3}.RN$$

But, since $V_{RY} \equiv RY = DN$,

$$V_{RY} = \sqrt{3}.V_{RN}$$

therefore we may say that, in a symmetrical star-connected three-phase system,

line voltage $= \sqrt{3} \times$ phase voltage

or $\qquad V_L = \sqrt{3}.V_{ph}$

3.4 Star-connected resistive loads

Let us consider how we might connect the three-phase supply to a resistive load.

Figure 3.7(a) shows a three-phase alternator supplying a three-phase star-connected load. The neutral point is taken to the star connection of the load, thus providing a fourth wire in which the neutral current (if any) may flow.

If all three phase resistances are equal then the current in each line will be the same ($I_R = I_Y = I_B$) and the system is said to be *balanced*. Also, if the load is purely resistive, these currents will be in phase with the phase voltages.

Although in fig. 3.7(a) the three line currents are all shown as flowing from the alternator to the load, the directions of the currents *at any instant* will not be the same. The directions of the currents at any instant will depend

71

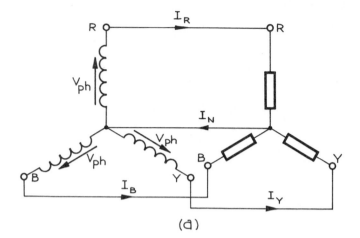

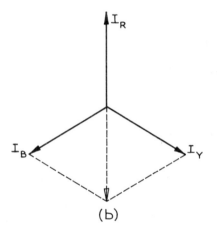

Fig. 3.7 A three-phase star-connected load and its current phasor diagram.

on the instantaneous polarities of the phase voltages. As the voltages go positive and negative as shown in the sinusoidal representation of the three-phase voltages in fig. 3.2(b), then the currents will go forward and reverse.

If we represent these currents by their r.m.s. values, as shown in the phasor diagram of fig. 3.7(b), then it may be seen that, in a balanced three-phase system, the resultant of phasors I_Y and I_B is exactly equal and opposite to I_R. This means that the resultant current at any instant is zero in a *balanced* system and therefore I_N is zero. We may therefore remove the neutral wire without affecting the system in any way.

In the star-connected system of fig. 3.7(a), the currents $I_R, I_Y,$ and I_B flowing in the connecting lines are referred to as the line currents, I_L. The currents which flow in the phase windings are referred to as the phase currents, I_{ph}. In the star-connected system it is apparent that

$$I_L = I_{ph}$$

Example A balanced three-phase star-connected load has a resistance of 10 Ω per phase. Calculate (a) the phase voltage and (b) the phase and line currents when the network is connected to a 415 V three-phase supply.

a) $V_{ph} = V_L/\sqrt{3}$

where $V_L = 415$ V

$\therefore$ $V_{ph} = \dfrac{415\,\text{V}}{\sqrt{3}} = 240\,\text{V}$

b) $I_{ph} = V_{ph}/R$

where $V_{ph} = 240$ V and $R = 10\,\Omega$

$\therefore$ $I_{ph} = \dfrac{240\,\text{V}}{10\,\Omega} = 24$ A

Since $I_L = I_{ph}$ in a star-connected load then $I_L = 24$ A

i.e. the phase voltage is 240 V and the phase and line currents are 24 A.

3.5 Star-connected reactive loads

The three-phase load may not always be resistive; for example, in the case of a three-phase motor the load is inductive and resistive. Capacitive loads also sometimes occur. In any event, if the reactive–resistive load is balanced, the treatment of problems is almost as simple as for the case with purely resistive loads.

Consider the phasor diagram of fig. 3.8, which shows the voltages and currents in a balanced three-phase inductive–resistive load. Each phase current lags the phase voltage by the phase angle ϕ.

The phase current is related to the phase voltage by the equation

$$V_{ph} = I_{ph} Z_{ph}$$

where $Z_{ph} = \sqrt{R_{ph}^2 + X_{ph}^2}$

The power consumed by a balanced three-phase load is equal to three times the power consumed by each phase.

The power per phase is found from the equation

$$\text{power per phase} = V_{ph} I_{ph} \cos \phi$$

where $\phi = $ phase angle

$\therefore$ total power $= 3 V_{ph} I_{ph} \cos \phi$

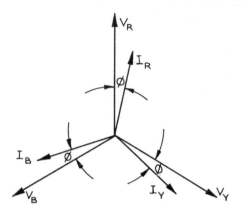

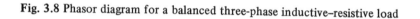

Fig. 3.8 Phasor diagram for a balanced three-phase inductive–resistive load

Since $V_{ph} = V_L/\sqrt{3}$ and $I_{ph} = I_L$
an alternative expression is

$$\text{total power} = \frac{3V_L}{\sqrt{3}} I_L \cos \phi$$

$$= \sqrt{3}.V_L I_L \cos \phi$$

Example A balanced three-phase star-connected load has an inductive reactance of 16 Ω and a resistance of 12 Ω per phase. Calculate (a) the impedance per phase, (b) the phase and line currents, (c) the total power consumed when the network is connected to a 415 V 50 Hz three-phase supply.

a) Impedance per phase is given by

$$Z_{ph} = \sqrt{R_{ph}^2 + X_{ph}^2}$$

where $R_{ph} = 12\,\Omega$ and $X_{ph} = 16\,\Omega$

∴ $Z_{ph} = \sqrt{(12\,\Omega)^2 + (16\,\Omega)^2} = 20\,\Omega$

b) $I_{ph} = V_{ph}/Z_{ph}$

where $V_{ph} = V_L/\sqrt{3} = (415\,\text{V})/\sqrt{3} = 240\,\text{V}$ and $Z_{ph} = 20\,\Omega$

∴ $I_{ph} = \dfrac{240\,\text{V}}{20\,\Omega} = 12\,\text{A}$

Also $I_L = I_{ph} = 12\,\text{A}$

74

c) Power consumed per phase $= V_{ph} I_{ph} \cos \phi$

where $\quad V_{ph} = 240\,\text{V} \qquad I_{ph} = 12\,\text{A}$

and $\quad \cos \phi = \dfrac{R}{Z} = \dfrac{12\,\Omega}{20\,\Omega} = 0.6$

$\therefore \quad$ power per phase $= 240\,\text{V} \times 12\,\text{A} \times 0.6$

$$= 1728\,\text{W}$$

$\therefore \quad$ total power consumed $= 3 \times$ power per phase

$$= 3 \times 1728\,\text{W}$$

$$= 5184\,\text{W} = 5.18\,\text{kW}$$

i.e. the impedance per phase is $16\,\Omega$, the phase and line currents are $12\,\text{A}$, and the total power consumed is $5.18\,\text{kW}$.

3.6 Delta-connected three-phase systems
Another method of connecting the three coils of the three-phase alternator is the delta connection. This is also sometimes referred to as the mesh connection.

In the delta connection, the three phase windings are connected as shown in fig. 3.9(a). The 'finish' of one winding is connected to the 'start' of the next (R' to Y, Y' to B, and B' to R). The corresponding voltage phasor diagram is shown in fig. 3.9(b).

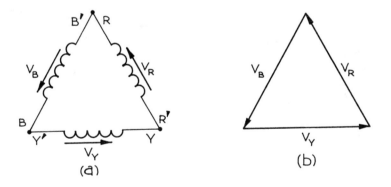

Fig. 3.9 A delta-connected three-phase supply and its voltage phasor diagram

Since the voltages are all shown as acting in the same direction around the mesh, it may at first be thought that a circulating current would flow. However, this is not the case. The explanation is as follows.

If we consider the voltage waveforms shown in fig. 3.2(b), then at any instant some are positive and some are negative. The resultant of the voltages around the loop at any instant is in fact zero. This may be seen by adding the magnitudes of the voltages at any instant in fig. 3.2(b). If the resultant voltage around the loop is zero then there will be no circulating current. This fact may also be seen by considering the phasor diagram of fig. 3.9(b). It is apparent that addition of the three phasors is zero, and hence there is no resultant voltage around the loop. This does not mean that the phase voltages are zero, but only that the resultant voltage around the loop is zero.

The delta connection is normally made inside the generator, and the terminal voltages are brought out through three slip rings. Notice that there is no neutral point in the delta connection and therefore it is only possible to connect this arrangement to a three-wire system.

3.7 Delta-connected resistive loads
A delta-connected resistive load is shown in fig. 3.10. Notice that in this case the line voltage is the same as the phase voltage:

$$V_L = V_{ph}$$

However, the line currents and phase currents are not the same.

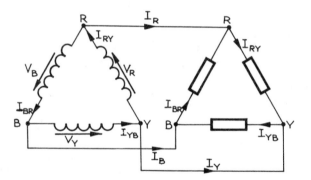

Fig. 3.10 A three-phase delta-connected load

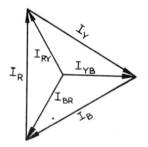

Fig. 3.11 The current phasor diagram for a delta-connected load.

The phasor representation of the currents is shown in fig. 3.11. $I_{BR}, I_{RY},$ and I_{YB} are the phase currents and $I_R, I_Y,$ and I_B are the line currents. This diagram is similar to the voltage phasor diagram of fig. 3.5(b) for the star-connected system. By a similar analysis, we may say that

line current $= \sqrt{3} \times$ phase current

or $\qquad I_L = \sqrt{3}.I_{ph}$

Example Three resistances, each of 20 Ω, are connected in delta to a three-phase 415 V supply. Calculate (a) the phase current, (b) the line current, (c) the total power consumed.

a) $\quad I_{ph} = V_{ph}/R_{ph}$

where $\quad V_{ph} = V_L = 415\,\text{V}$ and $\quad R_{ph} = 20\,\Omega$

∴ $\quad I_{ph} = \dfrac{415\,\text{V}}{20\,\Omega} = 20.8\,\text{A}$

b) $\quad I_L = \sqrt{3}.I_{ph}$

$\qquad = \sqrt{3} \times 20.8\,\text{A} = 36.0\,\text{A}$

c) $\quad$ Power consumed per phase $= V_{ph}I_{ph}$

where $\quad V_{ph} = 415\,\text{V}$ and $\quad I_{ph} = 20.8\,\text{A}$

∴ $\quad$ power per phase $= 415\,\text{V} \times 20.8\,\text{A}$

$\qquad\qquad = 8630\,\text{W} = 8.63\,\text{kW}$

∴ $\quad$ total power consumed $= 3 \times$ power per phase

$\qquad\qquad = 3 \times 8.63\,\text{kW} = 25.9\,\text{kW}$

i.e. the phase current is 20.8 A, the line current is 36.0 A, and the total power consumed is 25.9 kW.

3.8 Delta-connected reactive loads
In cases where the delta-connected load is reactive and resistive, a similar procedure is adopted to that used for star-connected reactive loads. Since we are considering a balanced system, we may consider each phase separately.

As with the star-connected load,

$\qquad V_{ph} = I_{ph}Z_{ph}$

where $\quad Z_{ph} = \sqrt{R_{ph}^2 + X_{ph}^2}$

The power consumed by a balanced three-phase load is equal to three times the power consumed by each phase.

The power per phase is found from

$\qquad$ power per phase $= V_{ph}I_{ph} \cos \phi$

$\therefore$ total power $= 3V_{ph}I_{ph}\cos\phi$

Now $V_{ph} = V_L$ and $I_{ph} = I_L/\sqrt{3}$

$\therefore$ total power $= 3V_L\dfrac{I_L}{\sqrt{3}}\cos\phi$

$$= \sqrt{3}.V_LI_L\cos\phi$$

Notice that this is the same expression as for the case with star-connected loads.

Example   Three coils are connected in delta to a three-phase 415 V 50 Hz supply. Each coil has a resistance of 20 Ω and an inductive reactance of 15 Ω. Calculate (a) the impedance per phase, (b) the line current, and (c) the total power consumed.

a) $Z_{ph} = \sqrt{R_{ph}^2 + X_{ph}^2}$

where $R_{ph} = 20\,\Omega$ and $X_{ph} = 15\,\Omega$

$\therefore$ $Z_{ph} = \sqrt{(20\,\Omega)^2 + (15\,\Omega)^2} = 25\,\Omega$

b) $I_{ph} = V_{ph}/Z_{ph}$

where $V_{ph} = V_L = 415\,V$ and $Z_{ph} = 25\,\Omega$

$\therefore$ $I_{ph} = \dfrac{415\,V}{25\,\Omega} = 16.6\,A$

$I_L = \sqrt{3}.I_{ph}$

$= \sqrt{3} \times 16.6\,A = 28.75\,A$

c)   Total power consumed $= \sqrt{3}.V_LI_L\cos\phi$

where $V_L = 415\,V$ $I_L = 28.75\,A$

and $\cos\phi = \dfrac{R}{Z} = \dfrac{20\,\Omega}{25\,\Omega} = 0.8$

$\therefore$ total power consumed $= \sqrt{3} \times 415\,V \times 28.75\,A \times 0.8$

$$= 16\,530\,W = 16.53\,kW$$

i.e. the impedance per phase is 25 Ω, the line current is 28.75 A, and the total power consumed is 16.53 kW.

3.9 Use of star and delta connections

The normal consumer three-phase line voltage is 415 V line-to-line, and this is the voltage that is used to drive many of the three-phase induction motors used in industry.

For domestic use for heating, lighting, and small single-phase motors, this voltage is dangerously high and a lower voltage is required. If a three-phase star-connected system is used then the voltage between line and neutral is also available. This voltage is approximately 240 V and is more suitable for domestic use.

A three-phase four-wire system is used for electricity distribution. Since any single-phase consumer would only be connected between any one line and neutral, it is usual to arrange the loading on each phase so that a similar load is taken by each phase. A fairly balanced three-phase system is thus achieved.

For the *transmission* of a three-phase supply, a four-wire system would not be economical on cable cost, and therefore a three-wire delta-connected system is used. Transmission is, of course, carried out at a high voltage, and three-phase step-down transformers are used to transform the voltage down to a level suitable for distribution. This requires the use of delta-to-star step-down transformers.

3.10 Power, V A, and V Ar in three-phase systems

The a.c. load for a three-phase system is usually stated in terms of kV A and power factor, just as for single-phase systems.

For a balanced system, the power factor is given by

$$\text{power factor} = \frac{\text{total power (watts)}}{\text{total V A}}$$

$$= \frac{\sqrt{3}.V_L I_L \cos \phi}{\text{total V A}}$$

But power factor $= \cos \phi$

$\therefore$ total V A $= \sqrt{3}.V_L I_L$

Similarly, in a balanced three-phase system the V Ar is given by

V Ar $= \sqrt{3}.V_L I_L \sin \phi$

Example A balanced three-phase delta-connected load consumes 5 k VA at a power factor of 0.8. If the line voltage is 415 V, calculate (a) the total power consumed, (b) the phase current, (c) the line current.

a) Total power consumed $=$ kV A $\times$ power factor

$$= 5\,\text{kV A} \times 0.8 = 4\,\text{kW}$$

b) $I_{ph} = \dfrac{\text{V A per phase}}{V_{ph}}$

where V A per phase $= (5\,\text{kV A})/3 = 1.67\,\text{kV A} = 1670\,\text{V A}$

and $V_{ph} = V_L = 415\,\text{V}$

$\therefore$ $I_{ph} = \dfrac{1670\,\text{V A}}{415\,\text{V}} = 4\,\text{A}$

c) $I_L = \sqrt{3}.I_{ph}$

$\quad = \sqrt{3} \times 4\,A = 6.93\,A$

i.e. the total power consumed is 4 kW, the phase current is 4 A, and the line current is 6.93 A.

3.11 Unbalanced three-phase systems

So far we have considered only *balanced* three-phase systems in which the line currents are all the same. If these conditions do not apply, as may be the case under certain loading or fault conditions, then the system is said to be *unbalanced*. In normal circumstances there is always some degree of imbalance in a three-phase system.

Consider the case of an unbalanced four-wire star-connected load as shown in fig. 3.12(a). We will assume that the line impedance supplying the load is negligible and therefore the line and phase voltages are equal in magnitude (i.e. a symmetrical system). Each phase may therefore be treated separately. The phase voltages are equal in magnitude and 120° apart, as shown in the phasor diagram of fig. 3.12(b).

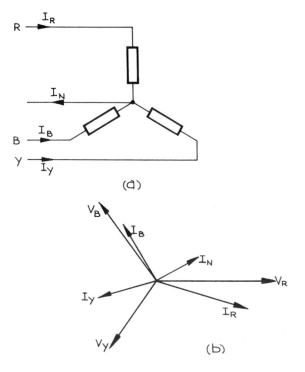

Fig. 3.12 An unbalanced four-wire star-connected three-phase load

The current in each line (or phase) is shown for a case where the loads are reactive and not all the same. The neutral current is now the resultant of the phasor addition of these three line currents as shown. The currents may be added graphically or by taking horizontal and vertical components.

Example A workshop is provided with a 440 V 50 Hz three-phase four-wire supply and feeds the following loads between each of the three separate phases and neutral:

a) four single-phase induction motors each rated at 1 kW and with a lagging power factor of 0.8 connected to the red phase,
b) a lighting load of 2 kW at unity power factor connected to the yellow phase,
c) a heating load of 4 kW at unity power factor connected to the blue phase.

Calculate the current in each line and the neutral current. Assume that the phase voltage is 250 V.

a) Total motor load $= 4 \times 1\,\text{kW}$

$$= 4\,\text{kW}$$

$\therefore$ motor kV A $= \dfrac{\text{kW}}{\text{power factor}} = \dfrac{4\,\text{kW}}{0.8} = 5\,\text{kV A}$

$I_{\text{ph}} = \dfrac{\text{kV A}}{V_{\text{ph}}} = \dfrac{5\,\text{kV A}}{250\,\text{V}} = 20\,\text{A}$

phase angle $= \text{arcos}\,(-0.8) = -36.9°$

$\therefore$ $I_{\text{R}} = 20\,\text{A at } 36.9°\,\text{lagging}$

b) Lighting load $= 2\,\text{kW at unity power factor}$

$\therefore$ $I_{\text{Y}} = \dfrac{2\,\text{kW}}{250\,\text{V}} = 8\,\text{A}$

c) Heating load $= 4\,\text{kW at unit power factor}$

$\therefore$ $I_{\text{B}} = \dfrac{4\,\text{kW}}{250\,\text{V}} = 16\,\text{A}$

The phasor diagram is shown in fig. 3.13. From this diagram, $I_{\text{N}} = 6.4\,\text{A}$ at an angle of 52° lagging the red voltage phasor.

3.12 Power measurement in three-phase systems
At first sight it would appear that the simplest method of measuring power in three-phase systems is to insert a wattmeter in each line. This is the method used in fig. 3.14 to measure the power in a four-wire system. Each wattmeter measures the power in that particular phase, and the total power consumed is given by

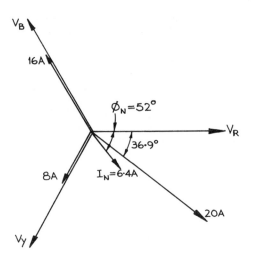

Fig. 3.13

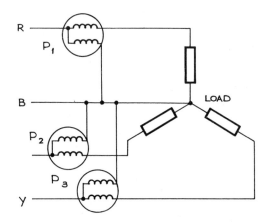

Fig. 3.14 Power measurement in a three-phase four-wire star-connected load

$$P_T = P_1 + P_2 + P_3$$

In the case of a three-wire system there is no neutral wire and the watt-meter voltage coils are connected together to a common point as shown in fig. 3.15. The total power consumed is again the sum of the three wattmeter readings.

For a three-phase three-wire system there is a simpler method of measuring power which uses only two wattmeters. This is referred to as the 'two-watt-

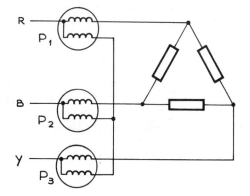

Fig. 3.15 Power measurement in a three-phase three-wire delta-connected load

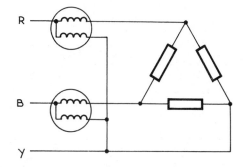

Fig. 3.16 The two-wattmeter method

meter method' and uses wattmeter connections as shown in fig. 3.16. The wattmeters have their current coils connected in two of the lines, while their voltage coils are connected between each of these lines and the third line. The total power consumed is given by

$$P_T = P_1 + P_2$$

(The proof for this method can be found in a more advanced text.)

The methods described so far are suitable for balanced or unbalanced loads which may be resistive or reactive. If the reading on any of the wattmeters is negative then this indicates that the voltage and current through that wattmeter are more than 90° out of phase. In this case the connections of the voltage coil of that particular wattmeter should be reversed to give a reading up the scale, and this reading is then subtracted from the total rather than added.

83

For measurement of power in balanced three-phase systems, then, one wattmeter is sufficient. The wattmeter reads the power in one of the phases and the total power is given by

$$P_\mathrm{T} = 3P_\mathrm{ph}$$

The arrangement for four-wire and three-wire systems is shown in fig. 3.17(a) and (b). Notice that in the three-wire system an artificial star point (neutral) must be set up using resistors, with the value R of the two resistors equal to the total resistance in the voltage circuit of the wattmeter (i.e. $R = R_V$ + voltage-coil resistance).

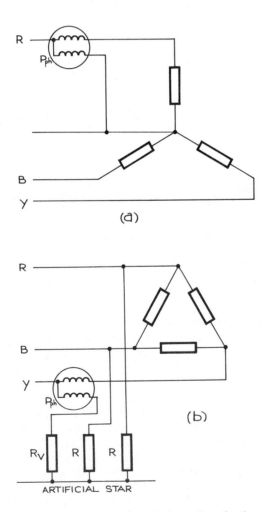

Fig. 3.17 Power measurement in balanced three-phase loads

A simpler method for a balanced three-wire system is shown in fig. 3.18. Wattmeter readings are taken with the switch in position 1 (P_1) then in position 2 (P_2) and the total power consumed is given by

$$P_T = P_1 + P_2$$

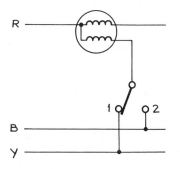

Fig. 3.18 A simple method of power measurement in a balanced three-wire system.

Exercises on chapter 3

1 a) Show that, for both star-connected and delta-connected balanced loads, the total power is given by $\sqrt{3}.\ V_L I_L \cos\phi$, where V_L and I_L are the values of line voltage and current respectively and ϕ is the angle between the phase voltage and current.

b) Three coils, each having an inductance of 0.05 H and a resistance of 20 Ω, are connected in star to a 415 V 50 Hz three-phase supply. Calculate (i) the line current and (ii) the total power. [9.44 A; 5.34 kW]

2 a) With the aid of a phasor diagram, show that in a balanced star-connected three-phase load $V_L = \sqrt{3}.\ V_{ph}$, where V_{ph} and V_L are the phase and line voltages respectively.

b) A balanced three-phase star-connected load has a resistance per phase of 9 Ω and an inductive reactance per phase of 12 Ω. When the network is connected to a 415 V 50 Hz three-phase supply, calculate (a) the line current, (b) the phase current, (c) the total power consumed. [16 A; 16 A; 2.30 kW]

3 a) With the aid of a phasor diagram, show how in a balanced star-connected load the neutral wire may be removed without affecting the current flow.

b) A 660 V three-phase supply is connected across a balanced inductive load. The line current is 1 A and the total power consumed is 571 W. Calculate the resistance and reactance per phase if the load is (i) star-connected, (ii) delta-connected. [330 Ω, 190 Ω; 989 Ω, 573 Ω]

4 Explain why in a symmetrical delta-connected three-phase alternator there is no circulating current in the coils.

A balanced three-phase delta-connected load is fed from a 415 V 50 Hz three-phase supply and takes 60 kW at a power factor of 0.8 lagging. Calculate the line and phase currents.   [181 A; 104 A]

5   a) Explain the following terms when used to refer to a three-phase supply: (i) symmetrical, (ii) balanced, (iii) positive sequence.

b) Each phase of a delta-connected three-phase load consists of an 0.02 H inductor and a 4 Ω resistor in series. The load is connected to a 440 V 50 Hz supply. Calculate (i) the phase current, (ii) the line current, (iii) the total power, (iv) the apparent power.   [59 A; 102 A; 24.2 kW; 44.9 kV A]

6   State the reasons why electricity is transmitted using a three-phase supply system. Explain how it is possible to arrange for a single-phase distribution system.

A delta-connected three-phase load has a resistance and inductive reactance per phase of 20 Ω and 15 Ω respectively. The load is fed from a three-phase 500 V star-connected alternator. Calculate (a) the alternator phase current, (b) the active power in kW delivered by the alternator, (c) the apparent power in kV A.   [34.6 A; 13.8 kW; 17.3 kV A]

7   An 11 kV three-phase alternator is rated at 20 MV A and supplies full load at a lagging power factor of 0.6. Assuming that the earning capacity is proportional to the active power supplied (in kW), calculate the percentage increase in earning capacity if the power factor is raised to 0.85.   [41.7%]

8   A 33 kV three-phase alternator supplies a load of 20 MW at a power factor of 0.8 lagging. Calculate the current in the windings if the alternator is (a) star-connected, (b) delta-connected.   [757 A; 437 A]

9   Each phase of a three-phase star-connected load consists of a 28 μF capacitor *in parallel* with a 100 Ω resistor. Calculate (a) the line current, (b) the power absorbed, (c) the total kV A, (d) the power factor when connected to a 415 V three-phase 50 Hz supply.   [3.19 A; 0.99 kW; 0.75]

10   With the aid of a circuit diagram, show how power is measured in a three-phase three-wire system using the two-wattmeter method.

A three-phase balanced load takes a current of 7.4 A from a 415 V 50 Hz three-phase supply. The power consumed is measured by the two-wattmeter method, the wattmeters indicating 3 kW and 2 kW. Calculate (a) the total power consumed, (b) the power factor.   [5 kW; 0.94]

4　D.C. transients

4.1 Introduction

In electrical circuits we are often concerned with the response of a network to a sudden change (a step change) of voltage or current. We call the response to a step change the *transient response*.

In a purely resistive network, for example, the response to a step change of voltage would be almost instantaneous, with the current changing in the same way that the voltage changed. With networks which contain capacitors or inductors, the response is not instantaneous. This is due to the time taken to cause a change in the energy stored in these components.

In this chapter we shall consider the transient response of simple R-C and R-L networks.

4.2 Transient response of an R-C network

The arrangement of fig. 4.1 shows an R-C network connected to a d.c. supply via a switch. Initially the switch is open and the capacitor is uncharged.

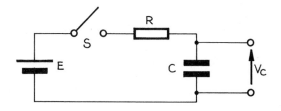

Fig. 4.1 Circuit for transient response of R-C network

At the instant that the switch is closed, current flows into the capacitor, and the capacitor begins to charge. The current continues to flow until the capacitor is charged to the same level as the d.c. supply voltage. It is important to realise that the current is not flowing through the capacitor, which has an insulating dielectric between its plates, but rather that the upper plate is accumulating a positive charge while the lower plate is accumulating an equal and opposite negative charge.

The way in which the current varies with time from the moment of switch-on is shown in fig. 4.2(a). Initially the capacitor is uncharged, and the full supply voltage is developed across the resistor. The initial current is thus given by

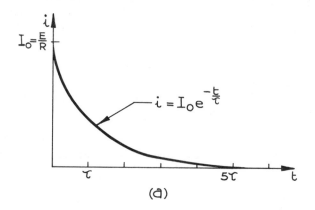

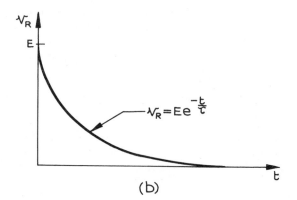

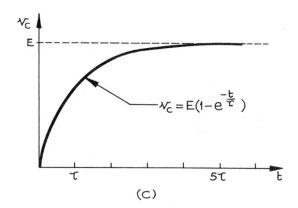

Fig. 4.2 Transient responses of an $R–C$ network

88

$$I_0 = \frac{E}{R}$$

As the capacitor charges, a voltage is developed across the capacitor, and therefore a smaller voltage remains across the resistor. The charging current thus becomes smaller and smaller as the capacitor voltage increases. The current continues to fall until the voltage across the capacitor is equal to the supply voltage.

The shape of the current waveform is referred to as *exponential*, and the charging current thus exhibits an exponential decay with time, from its initial value I_0.

The reason that the curve is exponential is because the current at any instant is in proportion to the *voltage difference* across the resistor. Thus the rate at which the capacitor charges is in proportion to this voltage difference. In other words, the rate of change of voltage across the capacitor is in proportion to the voltage difference $(E - V_C)$. As V_C gets closer to E, the rate of change of V_C decreases. This causes the current to decrease exponentially with time.

The mathematical equation which describes this exponential decay of current is

$$i = I_0 e^{-t/\tau} = \frac{E}{R} e^{-t/\tau}$$

where I_0 is the initial value of current. The constant τ (tau) in this equation is referred to as the circuit *time constant*. This time constant is given by $\tau = CR$, where C is the capacitance in farads and R is the resistance in ohms. The units of τ are seconds.

Figure 4.2(b) shows the variation of voltage v_R across the resistor. The equation of this voltage is given by

$$v_R = E e^{-t/\tau}$$

Notice that this waveform is the same shape as the current waveform.

The curve which shows the variation of voltage v_C across the capacitor is shown in fig. 4.2(c). The shape of this curve is referred to as an *exponential rise*. The equation of this voltage is given by

$$v_C = E(1 - e^{-t/\tau}) \tag{i}$$

where $\tau = CR$.

The capacitor voltage v_C takes a theoretically infinite time to reach the supply voltage. In fact, in a time equal to 5τ the capacitor voltage has achieved 99.3% of the final value, and this is generally considered to be sufficiently close for most purposes.

Also after a time equal to 5τ, the current has fallen to 0.007 of its initial value, therefore

at $t = 5\tau$, $\quad v_C = 0.993E$

and $\qquad\qquad i = 0.007I_0$

Thus the current and voltage may be assumed to have reached their final (or steady-state) value after a time equal to 5τ.

Differentiating equation (i) with respect to time gives

$$\frac{dv_C}{dt} = \frac{E}{\tau}e^{-t/\tau}$$

From this equation, when $t = 0$ then

$$\frac{dv_C}{dt} = \frac{E}{\tau}$$

This is the slope of the curve at $t = 0$.

In the exponential curve of fig. 4.3(a), a line is drawn tangential to the exponentially rising curve at $t = 0$. This line will therefore have a slope of E/τ as shown. Thus the time constant of the circuit may be defined as the time taken for the voltage to reach its final steady-state value if it were to maintain its initial rate of rise of voltage.

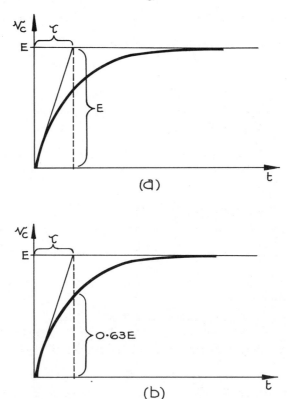

Fig. 4.3 Exponential rise and time constant

From equation (i) it may be seen that, when $t = \tau$,

$$v_C = E(1 - e^{-1}) = 0.63E$$

i.e. when $t = \tau$ the voltage across the capacitor has reached 63% of its final value, as shown in fig. 4.3(b).

Example A $0.2\,\mu F$ capacitor is connected in series with a $10\,k\Omega$ resistor across a 10 V a.c. supply. Calculate (a) the circuit time constant, (b) the initial rate of change of voltage across C, (c) the initial charging current, (d) the initial voltage across the $10\,k\Omega$ resistor.

a) $\tau = CR$

where $C = 0.2\,\mu F = 0.2 \times 10^{-6}\,F$ and $R = 10\,k\Omega = 10 \times 10^3\,\Omega$

$\therefore$ $\tau = 0.2 \times 10^{-6}\,F \times 10 \times 10^3\,\Omega$

$= 2 \times 10^{-3}\,s = 2\,ms$

b) The initial rate of change of voltage is given by

$$\left.\frac{dv_C}{dt}\right|_{t=0} = \frac{E}{\tau}$$

where $E = 10\,V$ and $\tau = 2\,ms$

$\therefore$ $\left.\dfrac{dv_C}{dt}\right|_{t=0} = \dfrac{10\,V}{2\,ms} = 5\,V/ms$

c) The initial charging current is given by

$$I_0 = E/R$$

where $E = 10\,V$ and $R = 10\,k\Omega = 10 \times 10^3\,\Omega$

$\therefore$ $I_0 = \dfrac{10\,V}{10 \times 10^3\,\Omega}$

$= 1 \times 10^{-3}\,A = 1\,mA$

d) The initial voltage across the $10\,k\Omega$ resistor is the total supply voltage of 10 V.

i.e. the time constant is 2 ms, the initial rate of change of capacitor voltage is 5 V/ms, the initial charging current is 1 mA, and the initial voltage across the $10\,k\Omega$ resistor is 10 V.

4.3 Discharging a capacitor

Now let us look at how a capacitor discharges.

Consider the circuit of fig. 4.4(a). Assuming the capacitor is initially charged to a voltage E, when the switch is closed the capacitor will discharge through the resistor with a current waveform as shown in fig. 4.4(b). This waveform is an exponential decay with the equation.

$$i = I_0 e^{-t/\tau} = \frac{E}{R} e^{-t/\tau}$$

where $\tau = CR$ seconds and I_0 is the initial discharge current.

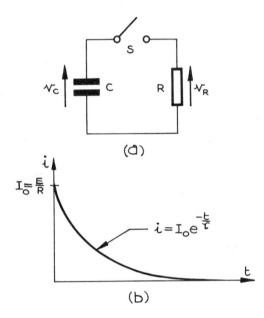

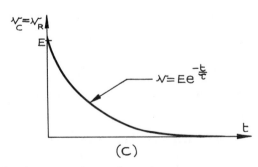

Fig. 4.4 Discharging a capacitor and transient responses

The voltage waveform follows the same shape, as shown in fig. 4.4(c), with the equation

$$v_C = v_R = Ee^{-t/\tau} \qquad (ii)$$

The initial rate of decay of voltage is found by differentiating equation (ii) with respect to time:

$$\frac{dv_C}{dt} = -\frac{E}{\tau}e^{-t/\tau}$$

When $t = 0$,

$$\left.\frac{dv_C}{dt}\right|_{t=0} = -\frac{E}{\tau}$$

Example In the circuit of fig. 4.5, the switch is suddenly moved from position 1 to position 2. Calculate (a) the circuit time constant, (b) the initial discharging current, (c) the initial rate of decay of voltage.

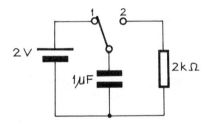

Fig. 4.5

a) $\tau = CR$

where $C = 1\,\mu\text{F} = 1\times10^{-6}\,\text{F}$ and $R = 2\,\text{k}\Omega = 2\times10^3\,\Omega$

$\therefore \quad \tau = 1\times10^{-6}\,\text{F} \times 2\times10^3\,\Omega$

$\qquad = 2\times10^{-3}\,\text{s} = 2\,\text{ms}$

b) $I_0 = E/R$

where $E = 2\,\text{V}$ and $R = 2\,\text{k}\Omega = 2\times10^3\,\Omega$

$\therefore \quad I_0 = \dfrac{2\,\text{V}}{2\times10^3\,\Omega} = 1\,\text{mA}$

c) $\left.\dfrac{dv_C}{dt}\right|_{t=0} = -\dfrac{E}{\tau}$

where $E = 2\,\text{V}$ and $\tau = 2\,\text{ms}$

$$\therefore \quad \left.\frac{\mathrm{d}v_C}{\mathrm{d}t}\right|_{t\,=\,0} = -\frac{2\,\text{V}}{2\,\text{ms}} = -1\,\text{V/ms}$$

i.e. the time constant is 2 ms, the initial discharge current is 1 mA, and the initial rate of decay of voltage is 1 V/ms.

4.4 Graphical determination of variation of current and voltage waveforms in an R–C network

One method of determining the growth and decay of current and voltage waveforms in a series R–C network is to calculate the values at various intervals of time using the equations in the previous sections.

Another method is to use a graphical procedure. One approach is based on the fact that an exponentially rising waveform reaches 50% of its final value after a period of time equal to 0.69τ (which may be approximated to 0.7τ).

Consider the circuit of fig. 4.1. When the switch is closed, the capacitor will charge to a voltage equal to $\frac{1}{2}E$ in a time of 0.7τ seconds, as shown in fig. 4.6. Furthermore, it will take another 0.7τ seconds to charge to 50% of the remainder (i.e. charge to $\frac{3}{4}E$) and so on. Thus the voltage levels at each 0.7τ second interval are $\frac{1}{2}E, \frac{3}{4}E, \frac{7}{8}E, \frac{15}{16}E, \frac{31}{32}E$, and so on, as shown in fig. 4.6.

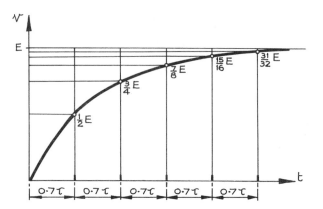

Fig. 4.6 Graphical determination of transient response

The current and voltage waveforms for charging and discharging the capacitor may be found using this method.

Example   In the circuit of fig. 4.7, the capacitor is initially uncharged. The switch S is switched to position 1 for 5 seconds then switched to position 2. Calculate the time constant for both positions and sketch the waveforms of the voltage across and of the current through the capacitor.

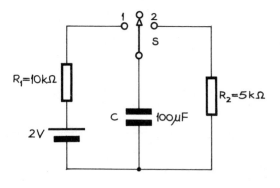

Fig. 4.7

Position 1:

$$\tau_1 = CR_1$$

where $C = 100\,\mu\text{F} = 100 \times 10^{-6}$ F and $R_1 = 10\,\text{k}\Omega = 10 \times 10^3\ \Omega$

$\therefore \quad \tau_1 = 100 \times 10^{-6}$ F $\times 10 \times 10^3\ \Omega$

$\qquad = 1\,\text{s}$

Position 2:

$$\tau_2 = CR_2$$

$$= 100 \times 10^{-6} \text{ F} \times 5 \times 10^3\ \Omega$$

$$= 0.5\,\text{s}$$

The initial charging current is given by

$$I_{01} = \frac{2\,\text{V}}{10\,\text{k}\Omega} = 0.2\,\text{mA}$$

The initial discharge current is given by

$$I_{02} = -\frac{2\,\text{V}}{5\,\text{k}\Omega} = -0.4\,\text{mA}$$

The voltage and current waveforms are shown in fig. 4.8.

4.5 Growth of current in a series R–L circuit

In inductive circuits, a similar form of transient response exists to that discussed so far with regard to capacitive circuits.

Consider the circuit of fig. 4.9(a) in which an inductor L is connected to a d.c. supply voltage E via a resistor R and a switch S.

In this case, when the switch is closed the current rises exponentially to the final value

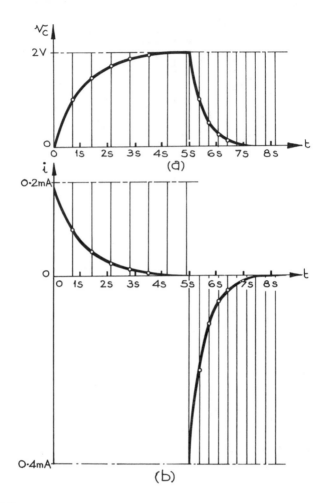

Fig. 4.8

$$I_F = \frac{E}{R}$$

as shown in fig. 4.9(b).

The current cannot rise instantaneously, due to the inductive effect. As the current in the inductor starts to increase, an opposing e.m.f. is generated (Lenz's law) which opposes the change of current. The current thus increases exponentially.

The voltages v_L and v_R across the inductor and across the resistor are as shown in fig. 4.9(c), with the initial voltage across the inductor equal to E.

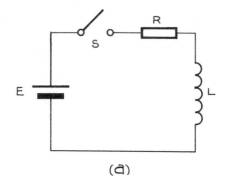

(a)

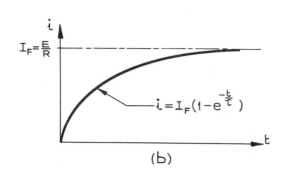

$$i = I_F(1 - e^{-\frac{t}{\tau}})$$

$$I_F = \frac{E}{R}$$

(b)

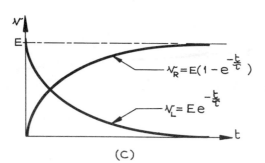

$$v_R = E(1 - e^{-\frac{t}{\tau}})$$

$$v_L = E e^{-\frac{t}{\tau}}$$

(c)

Fig. 4.9 Transient responses of an R–L network

Notice that at any instant the sum of v_L and v_R is equal to the supply voltage E.

The equation for the variation of current i with time is given by

$$i = I_F (1 - e^{-t/\tau}) = \frac{E}{R}(1 - e^{-t/\tau})$$

where $\tau = L/R$.

If L is the inductance in henrys and R is the resistance in ohms, then τ is measured in seconds.

In fig. 4.10, the tangent is drawn to the exponential curve at $t = 0$. We know that the time constant is defined as the time taken for the current to reach the final value, assuming that it were to maintain its initial rate of change,

$$\therefore \quad \text{initial rate of rise of current} = \frac{I_F}{\tau}$$

$$= \frac{E}{R\tau}$$

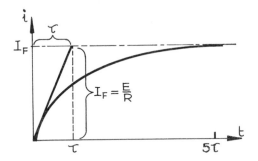

Fig. 4.10

The equations for the voltages across the inductor and across the resistor are given respectively by

$$v_L = Ee^{-t/\tau} = Ee^{-Rt/L}$$

and $\quad v_R = E(1 - e^{-t/\tau}) = E(1 - e^{-Rt/L})$

Example 1 A coil of inductance 20 mH and resistance 10 Ω is connected to a 5 V supply. Calculate (a) the time constant of the circuit, (b) the initial rate of change of current, (c) the maximum value of current that will be reached.

a) $\quad \tau = L/R$

where $\quad L = 20\,\text{mH} = 20 \times 10^{-3}$ H $\quad$ and $\quad R = 10\,\Omega$

$$\therefore \quad \tau = \frac{20 \times 10^{-3}\,\text{H}}{10\,\Omega} = 2 \times 10^{-3}\,\text{s} = 2\,\text{ms}$$

b) $\quad \left.\dfrac{di}{dt}\right|_{t=0} = \dfrac{I_F}{\tau} = \dfrac{E}{R\tau}$

where $\quad E = 5\,\text{V} \qquad R = 10\,\Omega \quad$ and $\quad \tau = 2 \times 10^{-3}\,\text{s}$

98

$$\therefore \quad \frac{di}{dt}\bigg|_{t=0} = \frac{5\text{ V}}{10\ \Omega \times 2 \times 10^{-3}\text{ s}} = 250\text{ A/s}$$

c) $I_F = \dfrac{E}{R} = \dfrac{5\text{ V}}{10\ \Omega} = 0.5\text{ A}$

i.e. the time constant is 2 ms, the initial rate of change of current is 0.5 A/s, and the maximum current is 0.5 A.

Example 2 A coil of inductance 15 H and resistance 10 Ω is connected to a d.c. supply. At the instant of closing the switch, the rate of increase of current is 5 A/s. Calculate (a) the applied voltage, (b) the rate of growth of current 3 s after the switch is closed.

a) $\tau = \dfrac{L}{R} = \dfrac{15\text{ H}}{10\ \Omega} = 1.5\text{ s}$

      Initial rate of rise of current $= \dfrac{I_F}{\tau} = \dfrac{E}{R\tau} = 5\text{ A/s}$

$\therefore$ $E = 5\text{ A/s} \times R\tau$

where $R = 10\ \Omega$ and $\tau = 1.5\text{ s}$

$\therefore$ $E = 5\text{ A/s} \times 10\ \Omega \times 1.5\text{ s}$

        $= 75\text{ V}$

b) The equation for current growth is

$$i = I_F(1 - e^{-t/\tau}) = \frac{E}{R}(1 - e^{-t/\tau})$$

$$\therefore \quad \frac{di}{dt} = \frac{E}{R} \cdot \frac{1}{\tau} e^{-t/\tau}$$

where $E = 75\text{ V}$ $R = 10\ \Omega$ and $\tau = 1.5\text{ s}$

When $t = 3\text{ s}$,

$$\frac{di}{dt} = \frac{75\text{ V}}{10\ \Omega} \times \frac{1}{1.5\text{ s}} e^{-3/1.5}$$

$$= 5\,e^{-2}\text{ A/s}$$

$$= 5 \times 0.135\text{ A/s}$$

$$= 0.68\text{ A/s}$$

i.e. the applied voltage is 75 V and the rate of growth of current after 3 s is 0.68 A/s.

4.6 Decay of current in a series $R-L$ circuit

Consider the circuit of fig. 4.11. Let us assume that the switch has been in position 1 for a period of time long enough for the current to reach its steady-state value of $I = E/R_1$. Now move the switch to position 2. The magnetic field surrounding the coil will collapse, causing a current to flow in the resistor R_2. The energy stored in the coil will gradually dissipate in the resistance.

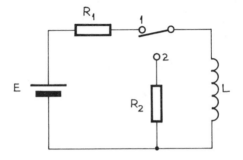

Fig. 4.11

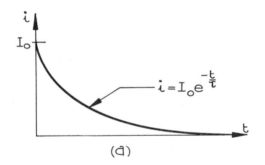

(a)

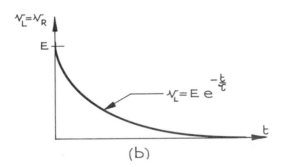

(b)

Fig. 4.12

The shape of the current and voltage waveforms will be a decaying exponential, as shown in fig. 4.12(a) and (b).

The equation for the current is given by

$$i = I_0 \, e^{-t/\tau} = \frac{E}{R_1} e^{-t/\tau}$$

where $\tau = L/R_2$.

The equation for the voltage waveform is

$$v_L = v_R = E \, e^{-t/\tau}$$

Example 1   The R–L circuit shown in fig. 4.13 is energised when the switch is moved to position 1. Ten seconds later the switch is moved to position 3. Sketch a curve showing how the current in the coil varies over a period of about 20 s. On the sketch, mark values of maximum current and time constants.

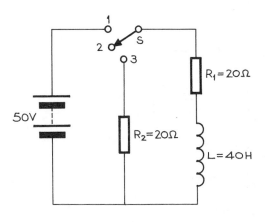

Fig. 4.13

In position 1,

$$I_{\text{max.}} = \frac{E}{R_1} = \frac{50 \text{ V}}{20 \, \Omega} = 2.5 \text{ A}$$

$$\tau_1 = \frac{L}{R_1} = \frac{40 \text{ H}}{20 \, \Omega} = 2 \text{ s}$$

In position 3, the energy in the coil is dissipated in the resistors:

$$\tau_2 = \frac{L}{R_1 + R_2} = \frac{40 \text{ H}}{40 \, \Omega} = 1 \text{ s}$$

The curve which shows how the current varies with time is shown in fig. 4.14.

101

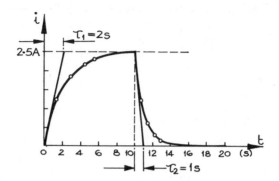

Fig. 4.14

Example 2 In the circuit of fig. 4.15, the relay contacts close when the current in the coil reaches 0.3 A. Calculate the time, from the moment of closing the switch S, for the capacitor to charge to 6 V.

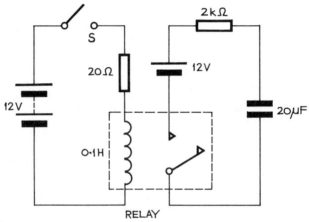

Fig. 4.15

The time constant of the inductor circuit is given by

$$\tau_1 = L/R$$

where $L = 0.1\,\mathrm{H}$ and $R = 20\,\Omega$

$$\therefore \quad \tau_1 = \frac{0.1\,\mathrm{H}}{20\,\Omega} = 5\,\mathrm{ms}$$

The final coil current is given by

$$I_F = \frac{E}{R} = \frac{12\,\mathrm{V}}{20\,\Omega} = 0.6\,\mathrm{A}$$

102

The equation for the rise of current in the coil is given by

$$i = I_F(1 - e^{-t/\tau_1})$$

When $\quad i = 0.3\,\text{A} \quad$ let $\quad t = t_1$

$\therefore \qquad 0.3\,\text{A} = 0.6\,\text{A}\,(1 - e^{-t_1/\tau_1})$

$\therefore \quad e^{-t_1/\tau_1} = 0.5$

$$t_1 = 0.69\,\tau_1$$
$$= 0.69 \times 5\,\text{ms}$$
$$= 3.45\,\text{ms}$$

The time constant of the capacitor circuit is given by

$$\tau_2 = CR$$

where $\quad C = 20\,\mu\text{F} = 20 \times 10^{-6}\,\text{F} \quad$ and $\quad R = 2\,\text{k}\Omega = 2 \times 10^3\,\Omega$

$\therefore \quad \tau_2 = 20 \times 10^{-6}\,\text{F} \times 2 \times 10^3\,\Omega$

$$= 0.040\,\text{s} = 40\,\text{ms}$$

The equation for the rise of voltage across the capacitor is

$$v_C = E(1 - e^{-t/\tau_2})$$

When $\quad v_C = 6\,\text{V} \quad$ let $\quad t = t_2$

$\therefore \qquad 6\,\text{V} = 12\,\text{V}\,(1 - e^{-t_2/\tau_2})$

$\therefore \quad e^{-t_2/\tau_2} = 0.5$

$\therefore \qquad t_2 = 0.69\,\tau_2$

$$= 0.69 \times 40\,\text{ms}$$
$$= 27.6\,\text{ms}$$

i.e. the total time for the capacitor to charge to 6 V from the moment of closing the switch is 3.45 ms + 27.6 ms = 31.05 ms.

4.7 Care when switching inductive circuits

If the current flowing in a coil is suddenly interrupted, say by opening a switch, then the current will decay to zero in a very short time. In this case the induced e.m.f. may be dangerously large, due to the rapid rate of change of current.

This effect is used in a motor-car ignition system to generate a sufficiently large voltage to cause a spark from only a 12 V battery, a coil, and a switch (the contact breaker).

The large induced e.m.f. can cause problems due to sparking across switch contacts. Also, if the current in a coil is being switched on and off by a transistor, the high-voltage 'spike' generated at switch-off can damage the transistor.

Example A coil of inductance 0.2 H and resistance 6 Ω is supplied via a switch from a 12 V battery. Calculate (a) the steady-state current when the switch is closed, (b) the induced e.m.f. if the current is uniformly reduced to zero in 2 ms.

a) $I = \dfrac{E}{R} = \dfrac{12\,V}{6\,\Omega} = 2\,A$

b) $e = -L\dfrac{\Delta I}{\Delta t}$

where $L = 0.2\,H$ and $\dfrac{\Delta I}{\Delta t} = \dfrac{2\,A}{2\,ms} = 1\,A/ms$

∴ $e = -0.2\,H \times 1 \times 10^3\ A/s$

  $= -200\,V$

i.e. the steady-state current when the switch is closed is 2 A, and the induced e.m.f. when the switch opens is 200 V.

4.8 Effect of circuit time constant on a square wave
A square wave is a very convenient test signal with which to test the transient response of a circuit. Since it is a repetitive waveform, a steady trace may be obtained when displaying the waveform on an oscilloscope.

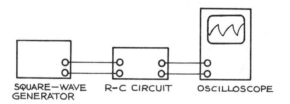

SQUARE–WAVE   R–C CIRCUIT   OSCILLOSCOPE
GENERATOR

Fig. 4.16 Testing the transient response of an R–C network

    A typical test arrangement is shown in fig. 4.16. The precise shape of the waveform displayed is determined by the circuit time constant. For example, the R–C network of fig. 4.17(a) has a square-wave test signal applied to its input. The output waveform will be somewhere between that shown in fig. 4.17(b) (short time constant) and fig. 4.17(c) (long time constant).
    With the R–C network of fig. 4.18(a), the output waveform will be somewhere between fig. 4.18(b) (long time constant) and fig. 4.18(c) (short time constant).

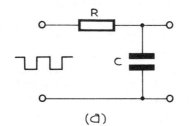

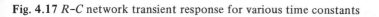

Fig. 4.17 *R–C* network transient response for various time constants

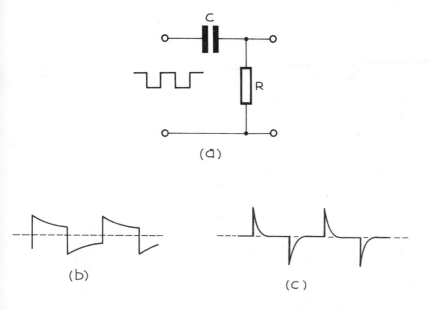

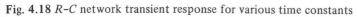

Fig. 4.18 *R–C* network transient response for various time constants

Exercises on chapter 4

1   a) Define the terms (i) transient response, (ii) time constant.

b) A $0.1\,\mu F$ capacitor is connected in series with a $10\,k\Omega$ resistor across a $100\,V$ d.c. supply. Calculate (i) the time constant, (ii) the initial charging current, (iii) the initial rate of change of voltage across the capacitor, (iv) the initial voltage across the resistor.   [1 ms; 10 mA; 100 V/ms; 10 V]

2   Sketch graphs for the charging of a capacitor through a resistor when connected to a d.c. supply, showing (a) the voltage across the capacitor, (b) the current, (c) the voltage across the resistor. Show the time constant on graph (a).

A $10\,\mu F$ capacitor is charged through a series resistor from a $50\,V$ d.c. supply. Calculate the value of resistor which will give a circuit time constant of $0.1\,s$, and calculate the charge on the capacitor after $0.2\,s$.   [10 kΩ; 432 μC]

3   A $2\,\mu F$ capacitor is connected via a $2\,M\Omega$ resistor and a switch to a $100\,V$ d.c. supply. Sketch curves to show how the charging current and the voltage across the capacitor vary with time when the switch is closed. Indicate the circuit time constant on the sketch.

When the capacitor is fully charged, it is disconnected from the supply and discharged via a $3\,M\Omega$ resistor. Calculate (a) the time to discharge to approximately zero (within 2%), (b) the energy dissipated in the $3\,M\Omega$ resistor during the complete discharge.   [24 s; 0.01 J]

4   Explain the purpose of connecting a diode across a relay coil which is to be switched from a transistor, and sketch the circuit diagram.

A coil has an inductance of $200\,mH$ and a resistance of $120\,\Omega$ and is fed from a $12\,V$ d.c. supply. Calculate the induced e.m.f. in the coil if the current is uniformly reduced to zero in $0.001\,s$.   [20 V]

5   Explain why it is undesirable suddenly to open a switch which connects an iron-cored choke to a d.c. supply.

A coil has an inductance of $8\,H$ and takes a current of $0.3\,A$ when connected across a $20\,V$ d.c. supply. Calculate the time constant of the choke.   [0.12 s]

6   A capacitor is initially charged from a d.c. supply. Sketch waveforms to show how the voltage across it varies when the capacitor is discharged through a resistor.

A $2\,\mu F$ capacitor with negligible leakage resistance is used to measure the leakage resistance of a cable. It is charged to $200\,V$ and then connected across the terminals of the cable. If the voltage drops to $180\,V$ in $30\,s$, calculate the cable leakage resistance.   [150 MΩ]

7   A coil has an inductance of $15\,H$ and a resistance of $10\,\Omega$. It is connected to a d.c. supply via a switch, and at the instant of closing the switch the current increases at a rate of $5\,A/s$. Calculate (a) the applied voltage, (b) the rate of increase of current when $4.5\,A$ flows in the circuit, (c) the stored energy when the current has reached a steady value.   [75 V; 3 A/s; 422 J]

8   A coil of inductance $15\,H$ and resistance $8\,\Omega$ is connected in parallel with a $22\,\Omega$ resistor across a $40\,V$ supply. The supply is suddenly disconnected.

Calculate (a) the voltage across the 22 Ω resistor, (i) initially and (ii) after 0.4 s; (b) the initial rate of change of current.   [110 V, 49.4 V; 10 A/s]

9   The leakage resistance of an 8 μF capacitor is calculated by charging it to 100 V and allowing it to discharge through its own leakage resistance. The capacitor voltage is measured on a high-impedance voltmeter of impedance 10 MΩ, and after a period of 7 s the voltage reads 80 V. Calculate the leakage resistance of the capacitor.   [2.5 MΩ]

10   A 10 μF capacitor is fully charged by connecting it via a 10 kΩ resistor to a 12 V supply. The supply is then removed and a 20 kΩ resistor is connected across the series combination. Calculate (a) the time constants during charging and discharging, (b) the energy dissipated in the 20 kΩ resistor during the complete discharge period.   [0.1 s, 0.3 s; 0.48 mJ]

11   A coil has an inductance of 5 H and carries a current of 6 A. Calculate (a) the induced e.m.f. in the coil if the current is uniformly reduced to zero in 0.05 s, (b) the value of the discharge resistor which must be connected in parallel with the field winding on opening the switch so that the maximum voltage across the winding does not exceed 400 V.   [600 V; 66.7 Ω]

12   A 0.1 μF capacitor is connected across a 25 V supply via a 5 MΩ resistor. Calculate the time for the capacitor to charge to 20 V.

When the voltage across the capacitor reaches 20 V, the supply is removed and a second, imperfect, capacitor is connected in parallel with the first. The p.d. falls instantly to 15 V and then decays to 10 V in 25 s. For the imperfect capacitor, determine (a) the capacitance, (b) the leakage resistance.   [0.8 s; 0.03 μF; 460 MΩ]

13   A sawtooth-waveform generator consists of a 1 kΩ resistor connected in series with a 1 μF capacitor across a 150 V d.c. supply. A gas-discharge tube is connected across the capacitor and has a striking voltage of 70 V. The operation is as follows: the capacitor charges up with a time constant dependent on the capacitor and resistor until its voltage reaches the discharge voltage of the discharge tube. The tube then discharges the capacitor to approximately zero volts in a negligible time, and the operation is repeated. Sketch the waveform and calculate its period and frequency.   [0.63 ms; 1.6 kHz]

5   Single-phase transformers

5.1 Introduction
The transformer is one of the most commonly used electrical devices whose operation depends on electromagnetic induction. It is used in all branches of electrical engineering where alternating currents are involved and it has no moving parts.

Its principal use is in converting an alternating voltage from one value to another value at either a higher or a lower voltage level. (When a transformer is described as 'step-up' or 'step-down', it is always the voltage that is being referred to.)

Some transformers are designed to handle voltages of the order of several millivolts, while others are designed to handle tens of thousands of volts. Similarly, current-handling capacities range between several milliamperes and several hundred amperes.

5.2 Transformer principle
The principle of operation of the transformer is explained with reference to fig. 5.1, where a laminated soft-iron core is wound with a primary and a secondary winding.

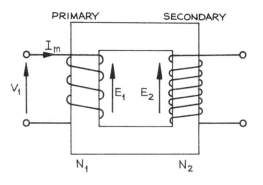

Fig. 5.1 Transformer schematic diagram

Consider the case shown, where the secondary winding is open circuit. The supply voltage V_1 is connected across the primary winding and causes an alternating current to flow. This alternating current produces an alternating magnetic flux in the core which links with the primary windings and causes an induced e.m.f. E_1 which opposes the primary applied voltage (Lenz's law). This induced e.m.f. is almost equal to the applied voltage V_1, and therefore only a small current flows in the primary winding. This current is just sufficient to maintain the magnetisation of the core and is referred to as the 'magnetising current', I_m.

The alternating magnetic flux in the core also links with the secondary windings and induces an alternating e.m.f. E_2.

If we neglect magnetic leakage, then the same flux links with the primary and the secondary turns.

By Faraday's law of electromagnetic induction, the magnitudes of the e.m.f.'s in the primary and secondary coils are given by the equations

$$e_1 = N_1 \frac{d\phi}{dt}$$

and $\quad e_2 = N_2 \frac{d\phi}{dt}$

where e_1 and e_2 represent the instantaneous values of primary and secondary induced e.m.f. and $d\phi/dt$ represents the rate of change of flux in the core.

Taking E_1 and E_2 as the r.m.s. values, we may say

$$E_1 = kN_1$$

and $\quad E_2 = kN_2$

where k represents the rate of change of flux.

$$\therefore \quad \frac{E_1}{E_2} = \frac{N_1}{N_2} \tag{i}$$

In this equation, E_1/E_2 is referred to as the *voltage ratio* and N_1/N_2 as the *turns ratio*,

$\therefore \quad$ voltage ratio = turns ratio

Notice that, if we neglect the very small difference between the applied voltage V_1 and the primary induced e.m.f. E_1, we may say

$$\frac{E_1}{E_2} = \frac{V_1}{E_2} = \frac{N_1}{N_2}$$

In fact there is a small difference in voltage between the applied voltage V_1 and the primary induced e.m.f. E_1, due to the magnetising current flowing through the resistance of the coil of the primary winding. To make the above equation approximately true, we must arrange that the winding resistance is small and also that the magnetic leakage is negligibly small. To keep magnetic leakage small, the transformer coils are wound either as a sandwich or as concentric coils as discussed in section 5.9.

The ratio of the voltage across a transformer winding to the number of turns of that winding is called the *volts per turn*.

The volts per turn of the primary winding is E_1/N_1, while that of the secondary winding is E_2/N_2.

Notice that, since $E_1/E_2 = N_1/N_2$, we may say

$$\frac{E_1}{N_1} = \frac{E_2}{N_2}$$

i.e. in an ideal transformer the volts per turn is the same for both the primary and the secondary windings.

Example A transformer is required to step down from 1320 V to 240 V at 50 Hz and to have 1.5 V per turn. Calculate (a) the turns ratio, (b) the number of turns required on both the primary and secondary windings.

a) Turns ratio $= N_1/N_2 = E_1/E_2$

where $E_1 = 1320$ V and $E_2 = 240$ V

$\therefore \quad \dfrac{N_1}{N_2} = \dfrac{1320 \text{ V}}{240 \text{ V}} = 5.5$

b) Volts per turn on secondary $= E_2/N_2 = 1.5$

$\therefore \qquad\qquad\qquad\qquad N_2 = E_2/1.5$

where $E_2 = 240$ V

$\therefore \quad N_2 = \dfrac{240 \text{ V}}{1.5 \text{ V/turn}} = 160$ turns

Now $N_1/N_2 = 5.5$

$\therefore \quad N_1 = 5.5 \times N_2$

$\qquad\quad = 5.5 \times 160 = 880$ turns

i.e. the turns ratio is 5.5 and the number of turns is 880 on the primary and 160 on the secondary.

5.3 No-load phasor diagram

In the transformer shown in fig. 5.1, the secondary turns are open circuit and therefore no secondary current flows. This is the condition of 'no load'.

Consider first the case for an *ideal transformer* in which the resistance and magnetic leakage of the coil winding are ignored and in which transformer core losses are considered negligible (core losses are discussed in section 5.8).

The *ideal* no-load phasor diagram is shown in fig. 5.2, which shows the r.m.s. alternating voltages and core flux.

Since we are neglecting losses, the primary circuit is purely inductive.

The magnetic flux Φ is at right angles to the applied voltage V_1.

The average power taken by the transformer is zero (i.e. energy fed into the primary on one part of the voltage waveform is fed back into the supply

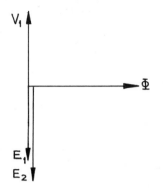

Fig. 5.2 Ideal no-load phasor diagram for a transformer

on another part of the waveform). The primary induced e.m.f. E_1 is exactly equal and opposite to the applied voltage V_1. The secondary induced e.m.f. E_2 is in the same direction as E_1 and has a magnitude given by

$$E_2 = E_1\left(\frac{N_2}{N_1}\right)$$

In practice the transformer is not ideal and the magnetising current I_m and core losses are taken into consideration.

The magnetising current I_m is required to produce the magnetising flux. The magnetising current may be represented on the no-load phasor diagram as being in phase with the magnetising flux. Since core losses (section 5.8) constitute a power loss, they may be taken account of on the no-load phasor diagram by the addition of a component of current I_w in phase with the voltage. This current is referred to as the iron-loss current. The no-load phasor diagram now looks as shown in fig. 5.3.

The resultant of the two currents I_w and I_m is referred to as the no-load current I_0.

Example A 450 V/150 V step-down power transformer takes a no-load current of 2 A and has a power loss of 135 W. Calculate (a) the iron-loss current, (b) the magnetising current, (c) the no-load power factor

a) $I_w = \dfrac{\text{power loss}}{\text{supply volts}}$

$\quad\ \ = \dfrac{135\,\text{W}}{450\,\text{V}} = 0.3\,\text{A}$

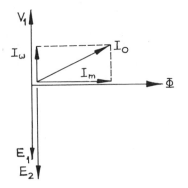

Fig. 5.3 Practical no-load phasor diagram

b) $\quad I_0{}^2 = I_m{}^2 + I_w{}^2$

$\therefore \quad I_m = \sqrt{I_0{}^2 - I_w{}^2}$

where $\quad I_0 = 2\,A \quad$ and $\quad I_w = 0.3\,A$

$\therefore \quad I_m = \sqrt{(2\,A)^2 - (0.3\,A)^2} = 1.98\,A$

c) $\quad$ Power factor $= \dfrac{I_w}{I_0} = \dfrac{0.3\,A}{2\,A} = 0.15$

i.e. the iron-loss current is 0.3 A, the magnetising current is 1.98 A, and the no-load power factor is 0.15.

5.4 Transformer on load

Consider the arrangement of fig. 5.4, in which a load resistance R_L is connected across the secondary coil of the transformer. Since there is an e.m.f. E_2

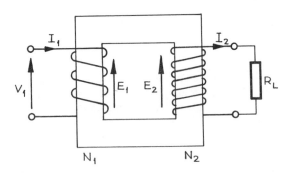

Fig. 5.4 Transformer on load

across the secondary turns, a current I_2 will flow in the load resistance. This secondary current will give rise to an opposing magnetic flux in the core which will tend to reduce the primary and secondary induced e.m.f.'s E_1 and E_2. It only requires the primary induced e.m.f. E_1 to be reduced slightly below the primary applied voltage V_1 to cause a relatively large current I_1 to flow in the primary winding. This primary current will tend to maintain the magnetic flux in the core.

For the primary induced e.m.f. E_1 to be maintained approximately equal to the applied voltage V_1, the m.m.f. (magnetomotive force) $N_1 I_1$ in the primary must be equal to the opposing m.m.f. $N_2 I_2$ in the secondary,

$$N_1 I_1 = N_2 I_2$$

or
$$\frac{I_2}{I_1} = \frac{N_1}{N_2} \qquad \text{(ii)}$$

I_2/I_1 is referred to as the *current ratio*. Thus we may say, for a transformer on load,

current ratio = turns ratio

This is true only provided the magnetising current I_m is small in comparison with the primary current I_1. The magnetising current is kept small by using a core material which has a high permeability.

From equations (i) and (ii) we have

$$\frac{E_1}{E_2} = \frac{N_1}{N_2} \quad \text{and} \quad \frac{I_1}{I_2} = \frac{N_2}{N_1}$$

If we multiply these together, we have

$$\frac{E_1 I_1}{E_2 I_2} = \frac{N_1 N_2}{N_1 N_2} = 1$$

or $\quad E_1 I_1 = E_2 I_2$

Thus for a transformer on load, we have,

primary volt amperes = secondary volt amperes

Remember that this is true only if we ignore the winding resistance and flux leakage and also ignore the magnetising current and the core losses. We refer to this as an *ideal transformer*.

5.5 Phasor diagram for a transformer on load

The phasor diagram for the transformer on load is shown in fig. 5.5 for the case with a resistive load. In this diagram, the voltage drop across the winding resistance and the magnetic leakage have been ignored.

The induced e.m.f.'s E_1 and E_2 act in the same direction, with E_1 approximately equal and opposite to V_1. The secondary current I_2 is in phase with E_2, since the load is purely resistive.

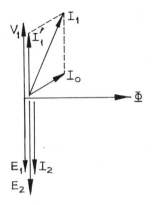

Fig. 5.5 Phasor diagram for transformer with resistive load

The primary current I_1 is the phasor addition of the primary load current I_1' (where $I_1'/I_2 = N_2/N_1$) and the no-load current I_0. Thus I_1 is not quite in phase with the applied voltage V_1. In power transformers this phase difference is very small, due to the relatively small value of I_m.

Example   A single-phase 750 V/250 V step-down transformer takes a no-load current of 1 A at a power factor of 0.2 lagging. The secondary is connected to a resistive load taking 24 A. Draw to scale a phasor diagram and hence find (a) the current taken by the primary, (b) the power factor at which the transformer operates, (c) the power taken from the supply. (Neglect the impedance of the transformer windings.)

The phasor diagram is as shown in fig. 5.6.

$$\frac{I_1'}{I_2} = \frac{E_2}{E_1} = \frac{250 \text{ V}}{750 \text{ V}} = \frac{1}{3}$$

$$\therefore \quad I_1' = \frac{I_2}{3} = \frac{24 \text{ A}}{3} = 8 \text{ A}$$

$$\phi_{\text{no-load}} = \arccos 0.2 = 78.5°$$

Drawing the diagram to scale gives

a) $I_1 = 8.3$ A

b) $\phi = 6.8°$

$\therefore$ power factor $= \cos 6.8° = 0.99$

114

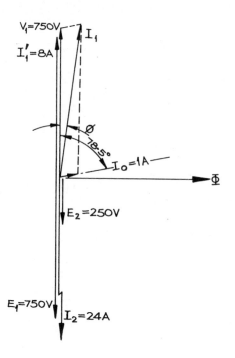

Fig. 5.6

c) Power $= V_1 I_1 \cos \phi = V_1 I_1'$

where $V_1 = 750\,\text{V}$ and $I_1' = 8\,\text{A}$

∴ Power $= 750\,\text{V} \times 8\,\text{A}$

$\qquad\qquad = 6000\,\text{W} = 6\,\text{kW}$

i.e. the primary current is 8.3 A, the power factor is 0.99, and the power taken from the supply is 6 kW.

If the secondary load is not purely resistive, then the secondary current I_2 will be out of phase with the secondary e.m.f. E_2. The most common type of load is inductive – such as a.c. motors etc. – but capacitive loads do occur.

5.6 Transformer efficiency
We have seen that in an ideal transformer the input power is equal to the output power. Transformer efficiency η (eta) is defined as

$$\eta = \frac{\text{output power}}{\text{input power}}$$

115

where   output power $= E_2 I_2 \cos \phi_2$

and   input power $= V_1 I_1 \cos \phi_1$

Also,   transformer losses = input power − output power

In practice transformers are very efficient, with efficiencies better than 95%.

Example   A 2:1 step-down transformer whose output is rated at 5 kV A, 250 V, 50 Hz delivers its full-load current to a 250 V induction motor at a power factor of 0.8 lagging. The transformer has a no-load primary current of 2 A and a no-load power loss of 150 W. Draw a phasor diagram to scale and hence find (a) the primary current, (b) the power factor on load, (c) the power taken from the supply, (d) the full-load efficiency.

The phasor diagram is shown in fig. 5.7, drawn to scale.

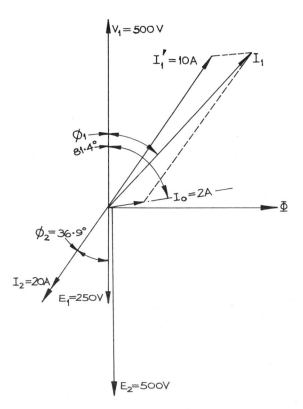

Fig. 5.7

116

$$\text{Secondary current } I_2 = \frac{\text{secondary V A}}{E_2}$$

$$= \frac{5000 \text{ V A}}{250 \text{ V}} = 20 \text{ A}$$

$$\frac{I_1'}{I_2} = \frac{N_2}{N_1} = \frac{1}{2}$$

$$\therefore \quad I_1' = \frac{I_2}{2} = \frac{20 \text{ A}}{2} = 10 \text{ A}$$

The phase angle θ of the no-load current is found from

$$\text{no-load power} = V_1 I_0 \cos \theta$$

$$\therefore \quad \cos \theta = \frac{\text{no-load power}}{V_1 I_0}$$

where   no-load power = 150 W $V_1 = 500 \text{ V}$ and $I_0 = 2 \text{ A}$

$$\therefore \quad \cos \theta = \frac{150 \text{ W}}{500 \text{ V} \times 2 \text{ A}} = 0.15$$

$$\therefore \quad \theta = 81.4°$$

The phase angle of the secondary load is given by

$$\phi_2 = \arccos 0.8 = 36.9°$$

Drawing the diagram to scale gives

a) $I_1 = 11.5 \text{ A}$

b) $\phi_1 = 44°$

$\therefore$ primary power factor on load = $\cos 44° = 0.72$

c)   Power taken from supply = $V_1 I_1 \cos \phi$

$$= 500 \text{ V} \times 11.5 \text{ A} \times 0.72$$

$$= 4140 \text{ W} = 4.14 \text{ kW}$$

d)   Efficiency = $\dfrac{\text{output power}}{\text{input power}}$

where   output power = $5 \text{ kV A} \times 0.8 = 4 \text{ kW}$

and   input power = 4.14 kW

117

$$\therefore \quad \text{Efficiency} = \frac{4\,\text{kW}}{4.14\,\text{kW}} = 0.97 \text{ per unit}$$

$$= 97\%$$

i.e. the primary current is 11.5 A, the power factor on load is 0.72, the power taken from the supply is 4.14 kW, and the efficiency on full load is 97%.

5.7 The transformer equation

The transformer equation relates the induced e.m.f. in the windings to the magnetic flux in the transformer core. Since there are two windings – primary and secondary – we can write two equations:

$$E_1 = 4.44\,\Phi_m\,fN_1$$

and $\quad E_2 = 4.44\,\Phi_m\,fN_2$

where E_1 and E_2 are the r.m.s. values of the primary and secondary induced e.m.f.'s, Φ_m is the peak value of the flux on the core, f is the frequency of the supply, and N_1 and N_2 are the numbers of turns on the primary and secondary windings.

The equations are derived from Faraday's law as follows.

The instantaneous magnitude of the e.m.f. induced in any winding is given by

$$e = N\frac{d\phi}{dt} \quad \text{(ignoring the minus sign)}$$

If the variation of flux in the transformer core is sinusoidal, then

$$\phi = \Phi_m \sin 2\pi ft$$

$$\therefore \quad \frac{d\phi}{dt} = \Phi_m\,2\pi f\cos 2\pi ft$$

$$\therefore \quad e = N\Phi_m\,2\pi f\cos 2\pi ft$$

$$= E_m \cos 2\pi ft$$

where $\quad E_m = 2\pi\Phi_m fN$

Now $\quad E_{\text{r.m.s.}} = \dfrac{E_m}{\sqrt{2}}$

$$\therefore \quad E_{\text{r.m.s.}} = \frac{2\pi\Phi_m fN}{\sqrt{2}}$$

$$\therefore \quad E_{\text{r.m.s.}} = 4.44\,\Phi_m fN$$

Example 1   A 4800 V/300 V 50 Hz single-phase transformer is to have an approximate e.m.f. per turn of 12 V and operate with a maximum flux

118

density of 1.5 tesla. Calculate (a) the number of primary and secondary turns,
(b) the net cross-sectional area of the core.

a)   Volts per turn $= \dfrac{E_1}{N_1} = \dfrac{E_2}{N_2} = 12$

$\therefore \quad N_1 = \dfrac{E_1}{12} = \dfrac{4800\,\text{V}}{12\,\text{V/turn}} = 400 \text{ turns}$

and $N_2 = \dfrac{E_2}{12} = \dfrac{300\,\text{V}}{12\,\text{V/turn}} = 25 \text{ turns}$

b) $E_1 = 4.44\,\Phi_m f N_1$

$\therefore \quad \Phi_m = \dfrac{E_1}{4.44 f N_1}$

where $E_1 = 4800\,\text{V} \qquad f = 50\,\text{Hz} \quad$ and $\quad N_1 = 400$

$\therefore \quad \Phi_m = \dfrac{4800\,\text{V}}{4.44 \times 50\,\text{Hz} \times 400} = 0.054\,\text{Wb}$

Now $B_m = \Phi_m / A$

where B_m = maximum flux density   and A = cross-sectional area of core

$\therefore \quad A = \dfrac{\Phi_m}{B_m} = \dfrac{0.054\,\text{Wb}}{1.5\,\text{T}}$

$= 0.036\,\text{m}^2 = 360\,\text{cm}^2$

i.e. the number of primary and secondary turns are 400 and 25 and the cross-
sectional area of the core is $360\,\text{cm}^2$.

Example 2   A single-phase 50 Hz 440 V/110 V transformer has an effective
cross-sectional area of $40\,\text{cm}^2$ and a maximum core flux density of 1.2 tesla.
Calculate the primary and secondary turns.

$E = 4.44\,\Phi_m f N$

$\therefore \quad N = \dfrac{E}{4.44\,\Phi_m f}$

Now $\Phi_m = B_m A$

where B_m = maximum flux density = $1.2\,\text{T}$

and A = cross-sectional area = $40\,\text{cm}^2 = 0.004\,\text{m}^2$

$\therefore \quad \Phi_m = 1.2\,\text{T} \times 0.004\,\text{m}^2$

$= 0.0048\,\text{Wb}$

For the primary, $E_1 = 440\,\text{V}$

$$\therefore \quad N_1 = \frac{440\,\text{V}}{4.44 \times 0.0048\,\text{Wb} \times 50\,\text{Hz}} = 413 \text{ turns}$$

For the secondary, $E_2 = 110\,\text{V}$

Now $N_2/N_1 = E_2/E_1$

$$\therefore \quad N_2 = N_1 \frac{E_2}{E_1} = 413 \times \frac{110\,\text{V}}{440\,\text{V}} = 103 \text{ turns}$$

i.e. the primary and secondary turns are 413 and 103.

Notice that we calculate the number of turns to the nearest full or half turn.

5.8 Transformer core losses

As well as the losses associated with the windings of the transformer, there are also losses associated with the core of the transformer. The requirements of the core of a transformer are that it should easily be magnetised and demagnetised (i.e. have a low magnetic reluctance) and that it should have a low iron loss (i.e. low hysteresis and eddy-current losses).

Low magnetic reluctance is achieved by constructing the core of a material with a high permeability. Iron loss occurs in the core because the magnetising flux in the core is alternating at the same frequency as the supply.

Iron loss is made up of two components: hysteresis loss and eddy-current loss.

Hysteresis loss

This is the energy loss incurred in magnetising and demagnetising the core. The energy loss per cycle is proportional to the area of the B-H loop of the core material, and this area should therefore be as small as possible. Hysteresis loss is also proportional to the maximum flux density attained and to the frequency of the supply. A material with a high permeability and a low hysteresis loss is Stalloy (a silicon–iron alloy).

Eddy-current loss

This is the energy loss incurred due to the circulating currents in the transformer core. Due to the changing magnetic flux in the core, e.m.f.'s are induced in the iron and, since iron is a good conductor, circulating currents flow in the core. These give rise to heating of the core and corresponding energy loss. This loss must be kept as small as possible by making the resistance of the conducting paths large. This is done by constructing the core from thin sheets (laminates) as shown in fig. 5.8.

5.9 Transformer construction

The three aspects to consider in the construction of a transformer are the core, the windings, and the method of cooling.

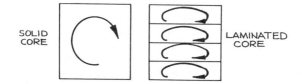

Fig. 5.8 Effect of laminations on eddy currents

The core is made up of thin sheets (or laminates) as already discussed, to reduce eddy-current loss and thus keep heat generation to a minimum. The sheets are insulated from each other by a coating of varnish on one side. The core material is a steel of a high permeability with some silicon content to reduce hysteresis loss. The two most common types of construction are shell-type, as shown in fig. 5.9(a), where the windings are on the centre limb, and core-type, as shown in fig. 5.9(b), where half of the primary winding and half of the secondary winding are on each outer limb. (Primary on one limb and secondary on the other is not used, due to the inefficient magnetic coupling.)

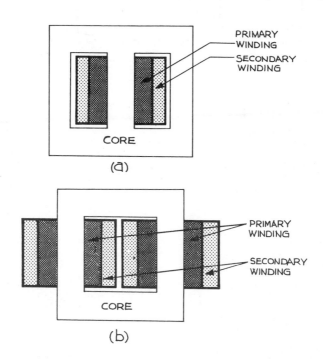

Fig. 5.9 Transformer construction: (a) shell type, (b) core type

The windings are copper wire with a cross-sectional area sufficient to handle the required load current without overheating and thus keep winding losses down. The wire is covered with varnished cotton or paper strip for insulation. The primary and secondary windings require to be tightly coupled and are thus interleaved to reduce magnetic leakage. The form of the windings may be either the concentric-winding type, as shown in fig. 5.10(a), or the sandwich-winding type as shown in fig. 5.10(b).

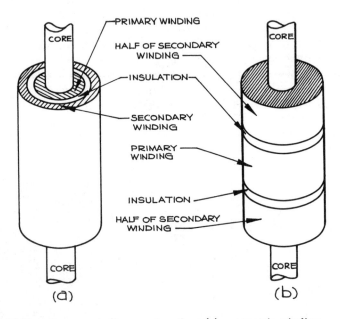

Fig. 5.10 Transformer winding construction: (a) concentric winding, (b) sandwich winding

The concentric type has one winding placed over the top of the other with thin paper insulation on each winding, the primary and secondary being well insulated from each other. The low-voltage winding is nearest to the core, to reduce insulation problems.

The sandwich type has the advantage that it reduces flux leakage. The high-voltage winding is split as shown in fig. 5.10(b), with the primary winding sandwiched in the middle.

Some form of cooling is required in a transformer, due to the heat generated by the hysteresis and eddy-current losses in the core and the I^2R loss in the windings. In small transformers, natural air cooling is sufficient; but in larger transformers oil cooling is used, the transformer being immersed in oil in a steel tank. The oil circulates by convection, and this provides satisfactory cooling in most cases. The tank is often corrugated or has cooling tubes to assist in cooling the circulating oil.

Oil is a good cooling liquid since it is a good heat conductor and a good electrical insulator and suitable for use with high-voltage transformers. In some cases a pump is required to circulate the oil.

The transformer construction considered so far is used in the construction of power and low-frequency transformers (see figs 5.11 and 5.12). In the case of transformers which are to be used at high frequencies for audio- and radio-frequency work, the laminated-core construction is not satisfactory due to the eddy-current and hysteresis losses, which are both frequency-dependent. Instead, the iron cores for radio work are constructed from powdered iron dust, compacted together with wax into a solid core and called simply 'dust cores'. These do not give as high a permeability as laminated iron cores, but the iron loss is much reduced.

Another material used for cores at high frequencies is ferrite. This is made from iron oxide with part of the iron replaced by nickel or manganese. This material has a high permeability while also having a low iron loss. A number of examples of ferrite cores are shown in fig. 5.13.

Fig. 5.11 Two low-power transformers and two chokes

Fig. 5.12 A 800 MV A, 345/26 kV, three-phase, 50 Hz transmission transformer being made ready for placing in its tank before testing (*top*) and leaving
the factory on its trailer (*below*). Stripped for transporting, the transformer
weighed 310 tonnes and was 8.81 m long, 5 m wide, and 5.3 m high.

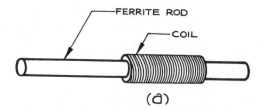

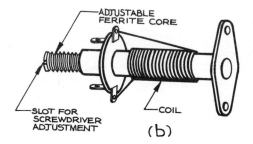

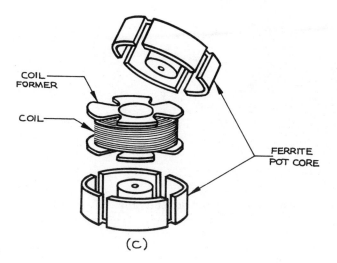

Fig. 5.13 Ferrite cores

5.10 Transformer matching

A transformer may be used to 'match' a load resistance to a signal source to ensure maximum power transfer as discussed in chapter 1. The transformer is usually assumed to be ideal, and the losses are therefore ignored.

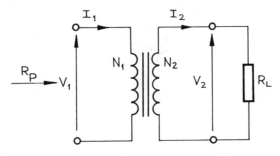

Fig. 5.14

Consider the arrangement of fig. 5.14, in which the load resistance R_L is connected across the secondary winding of the transformer. Assuming an ideal transformer,

$$\frac{V_1}{V_2} = \frac{N_1}{N_2} \quad \text{and} \quad \frac{I_2}{I_1} = \frac{N_1}{N_2}$$

Multiplying the equations together gives

$$\frac{V_1}{I_1} \cdot \frac{I_2}{V_2} = \left(\frac{N_1}{N_2}\right)^2$$

$$\therefore \qquad \frac{V_1}{I_1} = \left(\frac{N_1}{N_2}\right)^2 \cdot \frac{V_2}{I_2}$$

Now $\dfrac{V_2}{I_2} = R_L$ and $\dfrac{V_1}{I_1} = R_p$

where R_p is the resistance seen looking into the primary.

$$\therefore \quad R_p = \left(\frac{N_1}{N_2}\right)^2 R_L$$

By choice of the turns ratio N_1/N_2, we can match a load resistance to a source resistance for maximum power transfer.

Example A 3.9 kΩ load resistor is to be matched to a source of internal resistance 23 Ω so that maximum power is transferred into the load. Calculate the transformer turns ratio.

For maximum power to be transferred into the load, the resistance R_p seen looking into the transformer primary should match the source resistance R_S,

$$\therefore \quad R_p = R_S = 23\,\Omega$$

Also $\quad R_p = (N_1/N_2)^2 R_L$

where $\quad R_p = 23\,\Omega \quad$ and $\quad R_L = 3.9\,\text{k}\Omega = 3900\,\Omega$

$$\therefore \quad \left(\frac{N_1}{N_2}\right)^2 = \frac{23\,\Omega}{3900\,\Omega} \approx \frac{1}{169}$$

$$\therefore \quad \frac{N_1}{N_2} = \frac{1}{\sqrt{169}} = \frac{1}{13}$$

i.e. the turns ratio is 1:13.

5.11 Regulation

The voltage regulation of a transformer is the change in terminal voltage between no load and full load at a given power factor. If we define the no load and full load voltages as V_2 and V_2' then the 'per-unit regulation' is given by

$$\text{voltage regulation p.u.} = \frac{V_2 - V_2'}{V_2}$$

Example A 10 kV A 3300 V/240 V single-phase transformer has no-load and full-load secondary voltages of 240 V and 235 V respectively. Calculate the per-unit regulation

$$V_2 = 240\,\text{V} \quad \text{and} \quad V_2' = 235\,\text{V}$$

$$\therefore \quad \text{regulation p.u.} = \frac{V_2 - V_2'}{V_2}$$

$$= \frac{240\,\text{V} - 235\,\text{V}}{240\,\text{V}} = 0.021$$

i.e. the voltage regulation is 0.021 per unit or 2.1 percent.

Exercises on chapter 5

1 An ideal transformer has primary and secondary turns of 100 and 25 respectively. The supply voltage is 200 V, and the secondary load dissipates 1 kW at unity power factor. Calculate the primary and secondary currents. [5 A; 20 A]

2 An ideal 50 kV A, 1000 V/250 V, 50 Hz single-phase transformer has 500 turns on the primary. Calculate (a) the number of secondary turns, (b) the primary and secondary full-load currents, (c) the maximum value of core flux. [125; 50 A, 200 A; 9 mWb]

3 A 440 V/110 V 4 kV A transformer has iron losses of 80 W and its primary and secondary winding resistances are 0.6 Ω and 0.05 Ω respectively. Determine the full-load efficiency (a) at unity power factor, (b) at a power factor of 0.8 lagging.   [95%; 94%]

4 A 3300 V/415 V transformer takes a primary current of 2 A when the secondary winding is open circuit and a wattmeter connected across the primary reads 660 W. Sketch the no-load phasor diagram and calculate the no-load power factor and the magnetising current.   [0.1; 1.99 A]

5 The primary winding of a 110 V/220 V transformer is connected to a 50 Hz supply. When the secondary winding is open circuit, the primary current and power are 0.9 A and 35 W respectively. A load having an inductance of 0.25 H and resistance 50 Ω is connected across the secondary winding. Sketch the phasor diagram and hence calculate the total primary current, neglecting the impedance of the windings.   [5.6 A]

6 A 500 V/250 V single-phase step-down transformer takes a no-load current of 1 A at a power factor of 0.2 lagging. The secondary is connected to a load taking 40 A at a power factor of 0.707 *leading*. Draw to scale a phasor diagram and hence find (a) the current taken by the primary, (b) the power factor at which the transformer operates, (c) the power taken from the supply. The impedance of the transformer windings may be neglected.   [19.5 A; 0.74; 7.2 kW]

7 Sketch labelled phasor diagrams for a transformer with a one-to-one ratio supplying (a) a unity-power-factor load, (b) a load with a lagging current, (c) a load with a leading current. The impedance of the transformer windings may be neglected.

8 a) Derive the e.m.f. equation of a transformer.

b) A single-phase transformer has 400 primary and 1000 secondary turns. The net cross-sectional area of the core is 60 cm^2. If the primary winding is connected to a 500 V 50 Hz supply, calculate (i) the peak value of the flux density in the core, (ii) the voltage induced in the secondary winding. [0.94 T; 1250 V]

9 A 400 kV A transformer has a copper loss on full load of 3 kW. Calculate the copper loss when the transformer supplies a load of (a) 200 kV A, (b) 200 kW at 0.7 power factor lagging.   [0.75 kW; 1.53 kW]

10 A 25 kV A transformer has an iron loss of 350 W. Estimate the full load copper loss if the full-load efficiency is 97% at unity power factor.   [400 W]

11 A 100 kV A, 50 Hz, 3300 V/250 V single-phase transformer has 4 V induced per turn and operates at a peak flux density of 1.2 T. Calculate the cross-sectional area of the core and the number of primary and secondary turns. If the transformer is to be used on a 60 Hz system, determine the new value of core flux density for the same voltages.   [150 cm^2; 825; 62.5; 1 T]

12 A single-phase transformer has 400 primary turns and 200 secondary turns. Calculate the supply current and power factor when the primary is connected to a 240 V 50 Hz supply and the secondary is connected to a load of inductive reactance 7 Ω and resistance 10 Ω. The magnetising current is 0.5 A and the effect of resistance and reactance of the transformer windings may be neglected.   [5.24 A; 0.77 lagging]

13 A transformer is used to match a 300 Ω load to the output stage of a transistor amplifier. If the output resistance of the transistor is 10 kΩ, calculate the most appropriate transformer turns ratio for maximum power transfer.   [5.5]

6   Electric machines

6.1 Introduction

Electric motors and generators are both referred to as electric machines. The electrical engineer is most frequently concerned with electric motors, due to their extensive application.

The electric motor must be one of man's most useful inventions. In the manufacturing industries they are used in large numbers to drive lathes, drilling and milling machines, conveyors, and steel-rolling equipment. In the process industries they are used to pump liquids and gases. They are used in transport to provide electric drive such as for electric trains, automobiles, and ships, and to drive cranes, hoists, lifts, fans, etc.

In domestic situations they find wide application in washing machines, electric drills, fridges, food mixers, vacuum cleaners, clocks, etc. You can probably think of many more examples.

Why are electric motors so popular? Well, they are compact, reliable, relatively cheap, need little attention, and are convenient to use since they only need a cable to supply the electricity. They can be provided in a wide range of sizes and can be designed to have different characteristics for various different applications. Also there is a readily available supply of electricity.

6.2 Motoring and generating

Electric machines may be regarded as energy converters.

The *electric motor* is supplied with electrical energy and provides mechanical energy as an output as shown in fig. 6.1 (a). The motor thus produces rotational torque at its output shaft.

The *electric generator*, on the other hand, is supplied with mechanical energy as an input and provides electrical energy as an output as shown in fig. 6.1 (b). The generator input drive shaft is driven by an external source.

In both cases there is some loss of energy in the conversion process.

This motor–generator duality means that the construction of motors and generators are very similar. In the case of d.c. machines, the same machine may be used either as a motor or as a generator, depending on the requirement.

6.3 Classification of electric machines

Motors and generators are classified in various ways. For example, motors may be classified as a.c. or d.c. motors, depending on the nature of the supply that they require. Similarly, generators may be of the a.c. (alternator) type or the d.c. type, depending on the nature of the supply that they produce.

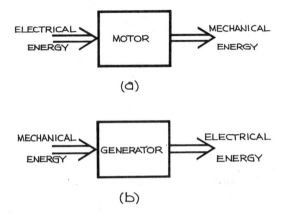

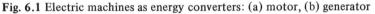

Fig. 6.1 Electric machines as energy converters: (a) motor, (b) generator

Machines many also be classified by their power rating. Motor ratings range from the miniature motors of a few watts used in clocks, through the 'fractional horse-power' motors, to large machines of the order of tens of megawatts. Generators range in size from small portable petrol-driven generators to the large 600 megawatt alternators ('sets') used in large power stations.

Machines are also classified by the way in which the field winding is connected (see sections 7.3 and 8.3).

6.4 Structure of rotating electric machines

Why do we use *rotating* electric machines? As regards the principle of operation of the electric motor, for example, there is no reason why it should not use linear motion, as for example in the linear-motor drive of the 'tracked hovercraft'.

However, most of the requirements of a mechanical drive are that it should provide rotational drive. It is therefore fixed in one place and is able to drive some mechanical system via gears. These requirements are of course met by the conventional structure of rotating electric motors.

The basic feature of electric motors is that they depend for their operation on the interaction between two magnetic fields. Generally, both of these magnetic fields are produced by electric current flowing through windings of copper wire (although some small machines use a permanent magnet to provide one of the fields).

One of the windings is wound on the fixed (or stationary) part of the machine called the *stator*. The other is wound on the movable (or rotating) part of the machine called the *rotor*. The stator is a hollow cylinder and is fixed. The rotor is a solid cylinder and is free to rotate inside the fixed stator as shown in fig. 6.2. The rotor therefore needs to be supported by end

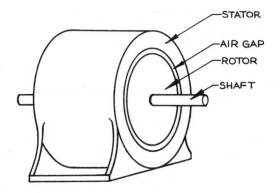

Fig. 6.2 Structure of a rotating electric machine

bearings at both ends of the shaft. This rotor–stator construction is used both in motors and in generators.

There are two methods of arranging the windings in electric machines. One method is to lay the coils in slots in the core. This allows for a small air gap and provides good support for the windings. Figure 6.3(a) shows the structure of the stator of a typical a.c. motor with the windings situated in slots, while fig. 6.3(b) shows a typical wound rotor.

An alternative arrangement is the use of *salient poles* in which the core is designed to have parts which *stand out* and on which the winding is placed. Figure 6.4(a) shows the structure of the stator or a typical d.c. motor with pole shoes, and fig. 6.4(b) shows a salient-pole rotor as used in one type of a.c. synchronous motor.

Figure 6.5 shows the flux pattern produced by the field winding of a d.c. machine with a salient-pole stator. Both a two-pole and a four-pole arrangement are shown.

Almost all of the magnetic flux produced by the winding m.m.f. exists in the rotor and stator *cores*. Together they constitute the magnetic circuit of the machine. They must both therefore provide a magnetic circuit which is short and fat so that the magnetic circuit has a low reluctance.

Due to the flux changes that occur in rotating machines, the cores must also be laminated to reduce eddy-current loss in the core (see section 5.8).

Since the magnetic circuit consists of a rotor rotating within a stator, the two parts must be physically separate and there must therefore be a small air gap between the two. To keep the reluctance of the magnetic circuit low, this air gap must be as small as possible (see fig. 6.2).

The two windings are referred to as the *armature winding* and the *field winding*. The armature winding is the main winding and carries the larger of the two currents. The field winding produces the field flux and carries the smaller current.

131

Fig. 6.3(a) Stator of a large a.c. motor (18 500 kW, six-pole, 1200 rev/min, 13 200 V, three-phase, 60 Hz, synchronous motor)

Fig. 6.3(b) Armature assembly typical of a d.c. machine

Fig. 6.4(a) Frame and poles of a four-pole d.c. machine showing interpoles

Fig. 6.4(b) A salient-pole rotor (two double rotors of large synchronous motors, each rated at 3450/1800 kW, 24/48 pole, 6 kV for compressor drives)

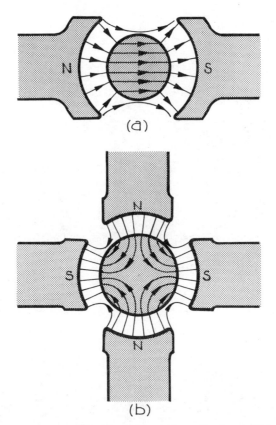

Fig. 6.5 Flux pattern produced by field winding of a d.c. machine: (a) two-pole, (b) four-pole

In a d.c. machine, the stator usually carries the field winding while the rotor carries the armature (main) winding.

6.5 Machine equations
A d.c. electric motor may be driven either as a motor or as a generator. This motor–generator duality extends also to their basic equations. The following equations thus apply to both motors and generators.

We shall consider two equations. The first gives the magnitude of the *e.m.f.* generated in the armature of a rotating machine. The second gives the magnitude of the *torque* produced at the drive shaft of a rotating machine.

E.M.F. equation
Consider the diagram of fig. 6.6 which shows a conductor of length l m moving at a velocity v m/s through a magnetic field of flux density B tesla.

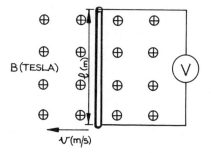

Fig. 6.6 E.M.F. induced in a conductor cutting through a magnetic flux

The magnitude of induced e.m.f. e volts in the conductor is given by

$$e = Blv$$

Now in the rotating electric machine the conductor is one of the coil sides of the armature winding, as shown in fig. 6.7. The velocity of motion of the winding through the magnetic field is in proportion to the rotational speed N rev/min.

$$\therefore \quad v \propto N$$

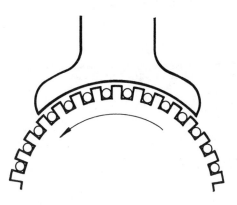

Fig. 6.7

Also the flux density B is proportional to the total flux Φ produced.

Since the other parameters are constant, the e.m.f. E in the armature winding may be expressed as

$$E = K_e N\Phi$$

where K_e is a constant for a given machine.

135

Now the magnetic flux Φ is produced by a field current I_f flowing in the field winding. Assuming that the field core is not saturated with magnetic flux, then

$$\Phi \propto I_f$$

and we may write

$$E = k_e N I_f$$

where k_e is a constant.

i.e. the e.m.f. E volts induced in the armature winding of a rotating machine is proportional to the rotational speed N rev/min and to the field current I_f amperes.

Example 1 A d.c. generator produces an e.m.f. of 200 V when rotating at 1000 rev/min. Assuming that the field current remains constant, calculate the e.m.f. generated when the speed is increased to 1500 rev/min.

$$E = k_e N I_f$$

We can use this equation by comparing the values at two different conditions.

Condition 1:

$$E_1 = 200 \text{ V at } N_1 = 1000 \text{ rev/min.}$$

Condition 2:

Calculate E_2 when $N_2 = 1500$ rev/min.

The field current I_f is the same in both conditions.

We have $\quad E_1 = k_e N_1 I_f \quad$ and $\quad E_2 = k_e N_2 I_f$

therefore we may say

$$\frac{E_2}{E_1} = \frac{k_e N_2 I_f}{k_e N_1 I_f}$$

$$\therefore \quad E_2 = E_1 \frac{N_2}{N_1}$$

where $\quad E_1 = 200 \text{ V} \qquad N_1 = 1000 \text{ rev/min} \quad$ and $\quad N_2 = 1500 \text{ rev/min}$

$$\therefore \quad E_2 = 200 \text{ V} \times \frac{1500 \text{ rev/min}}{1000 \text{ rev/min}} = 300 \text{ V}$$

i.e. the generated e.m.f. is 300 V.

Notice that the constant k_e cancels because we are taking the *ratio* of two conditions. This method will be used frequently in calculations on machines.

Torque equation

Consider fig. 6.8, which shows a current-carrying conductor of length l m carrying a current I amperes and situated in a magnetic field of flux density B tesla. The force F newtons on the conductor is given by

$$F = BIl$$

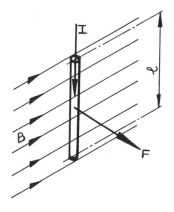

Fig. 6.8 Force on a current-carrying conductor in a magnetic field

In the case of the rotating electric motor, the current-carrying conductor is the armature winding carrying the armature current I_a. Also, the flux density B is proportional to the total flux Φ. Since the other coefficients are constant, the torque T produced is given by

$$T = K_t \Phi I_a$$

where K_t is constant for a given machine. Now, since the flux Φ is proportional to the field current I_f, we may write

$$T = k_t I_a I_f$$

i.e. the torque T newton metres produced at the shaft of a rotating electric motor is proportional to the armature current I_a amperes and to the field current I_f amperes.

Example 2   A d.c. motor produces a torque of 20 N m when the armature current is 4 A. Assuming that the field current remains unchanged, calculate the armature current required to produce a torque of 25 N m.

We have $T = k_t I_a I_f$

When $I_{a1} = 4\,\text{A}, T_1 = 20\,\text{N m}$

Calculate I_{a2} to produce a torque $T_2 = 25\,\text{N m}$.

The field current I_f remains constant; thus

$$\frac{T_2}{T_1} = \frac{k_t I_{a2} I_f}{k_t I_{a1} I_f}$$

$$\therefore \quad I_{a2} = I_{a1} \frac{T_2}{T_1}$$

where $I_{a1} = 4\,\text{A}$ $T_2 = 25\,\text{N m}$ and $T_1 = 20\,\text{N m}$

$$\therefore \quad I_{a2} = 4\,\text{A} \times \frac{25\,\text{N m}}{20\,\text{N m}} = 5\,\text{A}$$

i.e. the required armature current is 5 A.

Exercises on chapter 6
1   For a d.c. machine, (a) state the equation which relates generated e.m.f. E, field current I_f, and rotational speed N; (b) state the equation which relates torque T, field current I_f, and armature current I_a.
2   With the aid of sketches, show two methods of arranging the windings in electric machines.
    State one disadvantage of having the armature winding situated on the rotor and the field winding on the stator of a d.c. motor. Explain why the opposite is not the usual arrangement. How does the a.c. motor overcome this disadvantage?
3   A closed-circuit 500 turn coil of resistance 100 Ω and negligible inductance is wound on a square frame of 40 cm side. The frame is pivoted at the mid-points of two opposite sides and is rotated at 4 rev/s in a uniform magnetic field of 0.06 T. The field direction is at right angles to the axis of rotation.

a) Derive an expression for the instantaneous value of the e.m.f. induced in the 500 turn coil in terms of the speed of rotation, and calculate the e.m.f. for the instant that it has its maximum value.
b) Given that the force acting on a conductor situated in and at right angles to a uniform magnetic field is Bil newtons, where B (tesla) is the magnetic flux density, i (amperes) is the current, and l (metres) is the length of the conductor, derive an expression for the instantaneous value of the torque of the coil in terms of the speed of rotation and the resistance of the coil. Calculate the torque for the instant that the e.m.f. is maximum.
c) Verify that the mechanical power supplied balances the electrical power produced. [120 V; 5.76 N m]
4   A coil rotates at constant speed in a uniform magnetic field, the axis of rotation being perpendicular to the direction of the magnetic field. Derive from first principles an expression for the voltage induced in the coil in terms of flux density, the coil area, the number of turns, and the angular velocity. Hence obtain an expression for the torque exerted on the coil

138

when it carries a current, stating in which direction the torque acts (a) if the coil is rotated mechanically and (b) if the current is supplied to the coil from an external source.

5   A d.c. generator running at its normal speed with a field current of 2 A generates an e.m.f. of 350 V. Calculate the field current required to generate 250 V, assuming a linear relationship between flux and field current.
[1.43 A]

6   A d.c. motor takes an armature current of 20 A when producing a torque of 36 N m. If the armature current is reduced to 12 A, calculate the torque produced, assuming that the field current remains constant.   [21.6 N m]

7   D.C. generators

7.1 Introduction

You will have already considered the simple a.c. generator consisting of a
single-turn coil rotating in a magnetic field, with the ends of the coil connected to brushes via two *slip rings*. The voltage induced in the coil is
sinusoidal and reverses its direction each time the coil passes through the
vertical plane.

The only way in which we can obtain d.c. from this generator is to
convert the generated a.c. to d.c. by some means. One way of doing this is
to use a *switch* which reverses the connections to the load each time the
polarity of the e.m.f. changes inside the generator. By this means the voltage
applied to the load will always have the same polarity, and the current
flowing through the resistor will not reverse direction, although it will rise
and fall in value as the coil rotates.

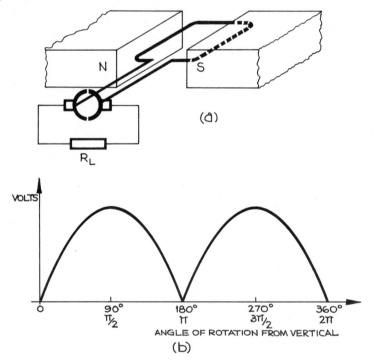

Fig. 7.1 A simple generator with a split-ring commutator and its waveform

A manually controlled switch would be impractical, but a solution is found by using the arrangement shown in fig. 7.1(a). The ends of the coil are connected to the load via a ring which is *split* along its axis, one coil end being connected to each segment of the ring.

The two segments are insulated from each other and from the shaft, the entire split ring being known as a *commutator*. The brushes make contact with the rotating commutator and, each time the coil passes through the vertical, the brushes are effectively 'switched' from one segment to the other. The resulting voltage waveform produced across the load is shown in fig. 7.1(b). The action of the commutator is one of *rectification*.

Now, although the waveform in fig. 7.1(b) is unidirectional, it is still pulsating. Let us consider how we can more closely approximate to a d.c. waveform. In the arrangement of fig. 7.2(a) there are two coils which rotate in the magnetic field as shown. These coils are connected to a commutator which has four sections. As the coils rotate, the e.m.f. that is produced across the load is as shown in fig. 7.2(b).

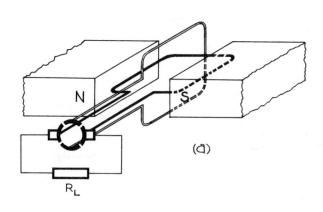

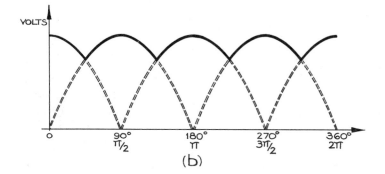

Fig. 7.2 Coils connected to a four-section commutator and the waveform

141

This waveform approximates more closely to a direct constant voltage. At each quarter of a revolution of the coils the commutator switches the brush connection from one coil to the other. This means that the load is always connected to a coil which is producing e.m.f. and therefore the e.m.f. across the load never falls to zero.

By simply extending this principle we arrive at a generator which has many coils evenly spaced around the rotor, each connected to a commutator segment. The voltage waveform is almost d.c., with only a small ripple voltage as the commutator switches from one coil to the other.

However, we can improve on this arrangement. So far we have only connected the brushes across the coil which is *directly under the pole shoe*. But almost all of the other coils will at any instant have an e.m.f. induced in them. (Only the coil which is moving parallel to the flux will not have an e.m.f. induced in it.) A better arrangement is therefore to connect the coils together end to end, by connecting adjacent coil ends to the same commutator segment. This is shown schematically in fig. 7.3 for an eight-segment commutator. By this means, all of the coils are contributing to the resultant voltage across the brushes.

The arrangement may now best be understood by imagining it as shown in fig. 7.4. The e.m.f. in each coil is shown separately. All of the e.m.f.'s contribute to the voltage which appears across the brushes. As may be seen from fig. 7.4, both the generator voltage and the current drive capacity are improved by this arrangement. The commutator ensures that as different coils move under the pole shoes, they are always contributing to the resultant voltage across the brushes.

A typical commutator and brushgear for a d.c. machine is shown in fig. 7.5 and the brushgear arrangement in fig. 7.6.

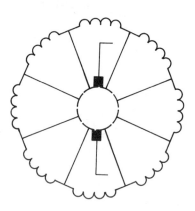

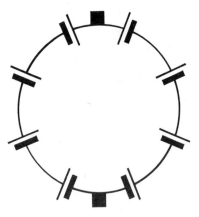

Fig. 7.3 Schematic representation of multi-coil winding with commutator and brushes

Fig. 7.4 How the e.m.f. in each coil in fig. 7.3 contributes to the resultant e.m.f. across the brushes

Fig. 7.5 Commutator and brushgear assembly of a large d.c. generator

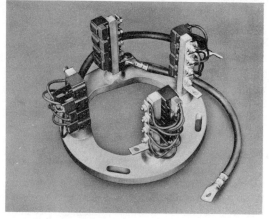

Fig. 7.6 Brushgear assembly

7.2 A practical d.c. generator

The relationship of the various parts that make up a small d.c. generator is shown in fig. 7.7.

Fig. 7.7 Construction of a small d.c. machine (motor/generator), showing the end frame (*top left*); the armature (*top right*); the frame shell, containing the field core (*bottom left*); and the end frame containing the brushgear (*bottom right*). (The armature and field windings have not yet been inserted.)

The field coils are mounted on the field-core pole shoes. The armature winding is situated in the slots in the armature. (The slots are skewed to provide a smooth starting torque.) The ends of the coil connect to the commutator segments. The armature is inserted between the field poles and is supported at each end by bearings situated in an end housing. The brushgear assembly is mounted in the end housing at the commutator end of the machine. The magnetic field of the stator is produced by current flowing in field coils situated around the stator poles.

The field winding may have its current supplied from a separate source. In this case the generator is referred to as 'separately-excited'. Alternatively, the generator may supply its own field current, using the generator e.m.f. as its source. In this case it is referred to as 'self-excited'. The field current is only a small proportion of the full-load armature current, and so self-excitation is the usual arrangement.

The generator will have different characteristics, depending on the way in which the field is connected.

The schematic representation of a generator is as shown in fig. 7.8. The armature winding is represented by the voltage-source symbol with open-circuit e.m.f. E as shown. The resistance of the armature winding is R_a and is shown as being is series with the armature. This is in fact the Thévenin equivalent circuit.

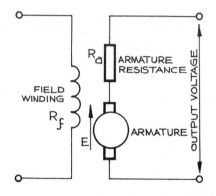

Fig. 7.8 Schematic representation of a d.c. generator

The armature resistance is the internal resistance of the armature winding and has a magnitude of the order of only several ohms. The field winding is shown with a field resistance R_f.

When the generator is running on no-load (i.e. with an open circuit across the terminals), the terminal voltage is the same as the open-circuit e.m.f. E.

When the generator is delivering current I_a, a voltage is dropped across the internal resistance R_a. The terminal voltage V is then given by

$$V = E - I_a R_a$$

Example 1 The d.c. separately-excited generator shown in fig. 7.8 produces an open-circuit e.m.f. E of 220 V. Calculate the terminal voltage V when the generator supplies a current of 10 A. The armature resistance is 1 Ω.

$$V = E - I_a R_a$$

where $E = 220\,\text{V}$ $I_a = 10\,\text{A}$ and $R_a = 1\,\Omega$

$$\therefore \quad V = 220\,\text{V} - 10\,\text{A} \times 1\,\Omega$$
$$= 220\,\text{V} - 10\,\text{V}$$
$$= 210\,\text{V}$$

i.e. the terminal voltage is $210\,\text{V}$.

We have seen in chapter 6 that, assuming the field core is not saturated, the open-circuit e.m.f. E volts is given by

$$E = k_e N I_f$$

where N = speed in rev/min

and I_f = field current in amperes

Example 2   A d.c. generator produces an open-circuit e.m.f. of $200\,\text{V}$ at a speed of 1000 rev/min with a field current of $1\,\text{A}$. Calculate the open-circuit e.m.f. if the field current is increased to $1.5\,\text{A}$. Assume the speed remains constant.

$$E = k_e N I_f$$

We have $E_1 = 200\,\text{V}$ when $I_{f1} = 1\,\text{A}$

Calculate E_2 when $I_{f2} = 1.5\,\text{A}$.

$$\frac{E_2}{E_1} = \frac{k_e N I_{f2}}{k_e N I_{f1}}$$

$$\therefore \quad E_2 = E_1 \times \frac{I_{f2}}{I_{f1}}$$

$$= 200\,\text{V} \times \frac{1.5\,\text{A}}{1.0\,\text{A}} = 300\,\text{V}$$

i.e. the open-circuit voltage is $300\,\text{V}$.

7.3 Generator classification
D.C. generators may be classified according to the way in which the field winding is connected. They may be separately-excited or self-excited. The way in which the field winding is connected determines the characteristics of the particular machine.

The characteristics with which we are most concerned in d.c. generators are

a) the variation of the open-circuit e.m.f. E with field current I_f (the open-circuit characteristic);

b) the variation of the terminal voltage V with load current I_a (the load characteristic).

146

7.4 Separately-excited generator

This method uses a separate source of e.m.f. to supply the field current, as shown in fig. 7.9.

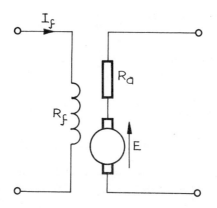

Fig. 7.9 Separately-excited d.c. generator

The *open-circuit characteristic* is shown in fig. 7.10(a), with the test circuit in fig. 7.10(b). It may be seen that with zero field current there is a small e.m.f. This is due to the residual magnetisation of the field core. As the field current I_f is increased, the open-circuit e.m.f. E increases until the field core begins to saturate with magnetic flux and the characteristic therefore begins to level off, as shown in fig. 7.10(a).

The *load characteristic* is shown in fig. 7.11(a) for a constant field current, with the corresponding test circuit in fig. 7.11(b). When the load current is zero, the terminal voltage V is equal to the open-circuit e.m.f. E. As the load current increases, the terminal voltage falls due to the voltage drop across the internal resistance R_a of the generator. For the generator on load, we have

$$V = E - I_a R_a$$

Example A separately-excited d.c. generator produces an open-circuit voltage of 250 V with a field current of 1.5 A. If the field current is increased to 2 A, calculate (a) the new open-circuit e.m.f., (b) the terminal voltage if the generator supplies a current of 5 A. Assume armature resistance = 0.8 Ω and the speed remains constant.

a)   Since the speed is constant,

$$\frac{E_2}{E_1} = \frac{I_{f2}}{I_{f1}}$$

where $E_1 = 250\,\text{V}$ $I_{f1} = 1.5\,\text{A}$ and $I_{f2} = 2\,\text{A}$

147

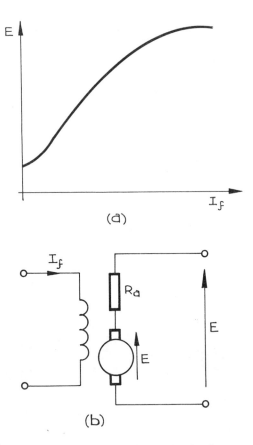

(d)

(b)

Fig. 7.10 Open-circuit characteristic and test circuit of separately excited d.c. generator

$$\therefore \quad E_2 = 250\,\text{V} \times \frac{2\,\text{A}}{1.5\,\text{A}} = 333\,\text{V}$$

b) $V = E - I_a R_a$

where $E = 333\,\text{V}$ $\quad I_a = 5\,\text{A}$ and $\quad R_a = 0.8\,\Omega$

$$\therefore \quad V = 333\,\text{V} - 5\,\text{A} \times 0.8\,\Omega$$

$$= 333\,\text{V} - 4\,\text{V}$$

$$= 329\,\text{V}$$

i.e. the new open-circuit e.m.f. is 333 V and the terminal voltage is 329 V.

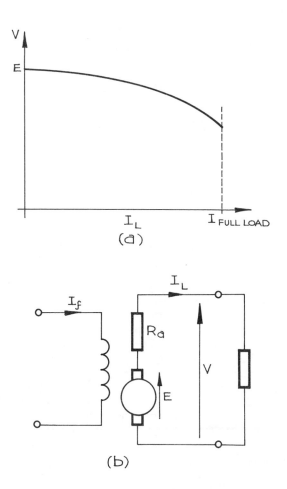

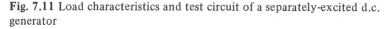

Fig. 7.11 Load characteristics and test circuit of a separately-excited d.c. generator

7.5 Self-excited generators

There are several possible ways in which a generator may be designed for self-excitation. They are referred to as shunt-wound, series-wound, and compound-wound.

7.6 Shunt-wound generator

In the shunt-wound generator the field winding is connected in parallel with the armature as shown in fig. 7.12. The generator thus supplies its own field current. The question is, 'How does the generator ever build up its voltage from start-up?' With no field current we would expect no generated e.m.f.

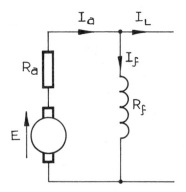

Fig. 7.12 Shunt-wound d.c. generator

With no e.m.f. there would be no field current. The answer is that the e.m.f. builds up due to the small residual magnetisation in the field core as we saw on the graph for the separately-excited generator.

When the armature rotates, a small e.m.f. is generated. This in turn provides the field current. As the generator e.m.f. builds up, so does the field current.

The curve showing the variation of e.m.f. with field current is given in fig. 7.13 (a). The curve is the same as that of the self-excited generator. On the same graph is drawn the characteristic of the resistance of the field winding. This is of course a straight line with a slope equal to R_f.

The voltage which the generator produces is the voltage at which the two characteristics cross (E_{oc} in fig. 7.13 (a)). At this point the open-circuit e.m.f. and field current satisfy both characteristics.

The load characteristic is as shown in fig. 7.13 (b) and is similar to the case for separately-excited. The terminal voltage falls slightly with increasing load current.

Example A separately-excited d.c. generator has the following open-circuit characteristic:

Field current (A)	0	0.2	0.4	0.6	0.8	1.0	1.2
E.M.F. (V)	8	31	64	97	126	145	158

If the machine is connected as a shunt generator with a field-circuit resistance of $150\,\Omega$, find the e.m.f. generated.

The characteristic is shown in fig. 7.14. The field-resistance line is shown on the same graph. The point at which the two cross is 140 V, i.e. the open-circuit voltage of the shunt generator is 140 V.

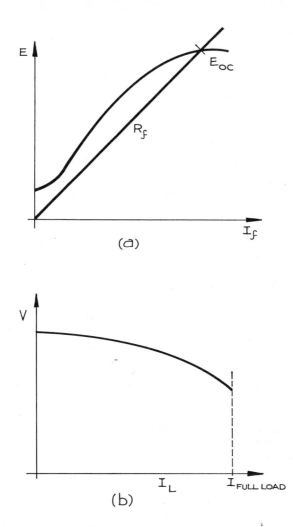

(a)

(b)

Fig. 7.13 Open-circuit and load characteristic of shunt-wound d.c. generator

7.7 Series-wound generator
In the series-wound generator, the field winding is connected in series with the armature winding as shown in fig. 7.15. For field current to flow, there must be a load connected across the generator terminals. The field resistance must be low, since there would otherwise be a significant internal voltage drop.

The characteristic is shown in fig. 7.16. It is similar to the characteristic for the shunt motor but in this case the resistance slope is $R_f + R_L$. This is in fact the load characteristic as well, since the series generator will not run on open-circuit, otherwise there would be no current in the field winding.

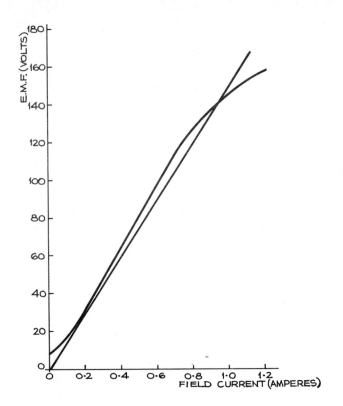

Fig. 7.14

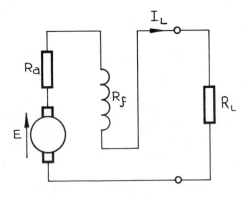

Fig. 7.15 Series-wound d.c. generator

152

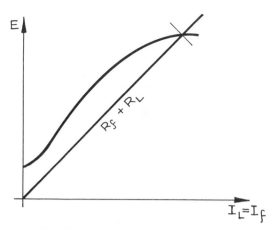

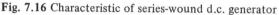

Fig. 7.16 Characteristic of series-wound d.c. generator

As with the shunt-wound generator, the actual voltage produced is the point on the graph where the generator curve and the resistance characteristic cross. In this case we have

$$V = E - I_a(R_a + R_f)$$

Example A separately-excited d.c. generator has an open-circuit characteristic as shown in fig. 7.17. When the machine is connected as a series generator, the armature resistance and series field resistance are 0.5 Ω and 0.2 Ω respectively. Calculate the terminal voltage (V_T) and the load current (I_L) when the load resistance is (a) 20 Ω, (b) 15 Ω.

The load-resistance slope is drawn on the graph for both cases. In fact it is the slope of the load resistance plus the field and armature resistance.

a) With $R_L = 20\,\Omega$, $E = 127\,\text{V}$ and $I_a = I_f = 6.14\,\text{A}$

$\therefore\quad V_T = E - I_a(R_a + R_f)$

$\qquad = 127\,\text{V} - 6.14\,\text{A}(0.5\,\Omega + 0.2\,\Omega)$

$\qquad = 123\,\text{V}$

$\quad I_L = I_f = 6.14\,\text{A}$ (see graph)

b) With $R_L = 15\,\Omega$, $E = 174\,\text{V}$ and $I_a = I_f = 11.07\,\text{A}$

$\therefore\quad V_T = 174\,\text{V} - 11.07\,\text{A}(0.5\,\Omega + 0.2\,\Omega)$

$\qquad = 166\,\text{V}$

$\quad I_L = I_f = 11.07\,\text{A}$ (see graph)

i.e. with $R_L = 20\,\Omega$ the terminal voltage is 123 V and the load current is 6.14 A. With $R_L = 15\,\Omega$ the values are 166 V and 11.07 A.

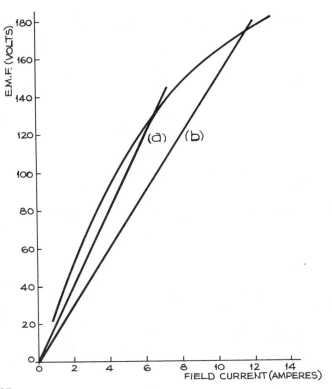

Fig. 7.17

Notice that in the series-wound generator the terminal voltage is very dependent on the value of the load resistance.

7.8 Compound-wound generator

It is common for generators to be constructed with a combination of both shunt and series field windings. This provides a composite characteristic and the shape of the load characteristic may be chosen from a variety of possible options, depending on the proportions of shunt and series winding.

The compound generator may be arranged as either a 'short shunt' (fig. 7.18(a)) or a 'long shunt' (fig. 7.18(b)).

Also, the series winding may be arranged to aid the effect of the shunt field (cumulative compound) or to oppose the shunt field (differential compound).

The range of load characteristics available is shown in fig. 7.19. In the case of cumulative compounding, the voltage between no load and full load may be arranged to increase (over compounding), stay level, or fall off (under compounding). With differential compounding, the voltage falls off considerably between no load and full load.

154

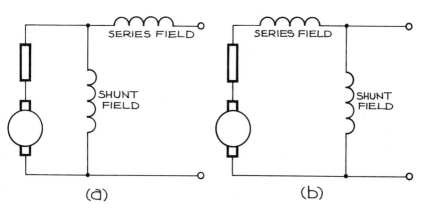

Fig. 7.18 Compound-wound d.c. generator: (a) short-shunt, (b) long-shunt

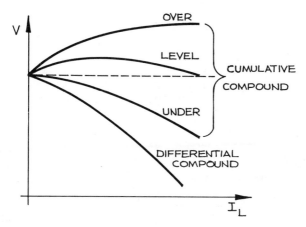

Fig. 7.19 Range of load characteristics for a compound-wound d.c. generator

It should be noted that once a compound machine has been designed for a particular characteristic, it cannot be modified to any other without rewinding.

Example A short-shunt compound-wound d.c. generator has armature, series field, and shunt-field resistances of $0.2\,\Omega$, $0.1\,\Omega$, and $100\,\Omega$ respectively. It delivers a full-load current of 50 A with a terminal voltage of 220 V. Calculate (a) the armature current, (b) the generated e.m.f. on full load.

The generator circuit is shown in fig. 7.20.

155

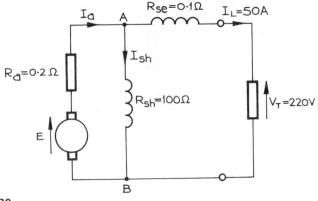

Fig. 7.20

a) The voltage across AB is given by

$$V_{AB} = \cdot V_T + I_L R_{se}$$

where V_T = terminal voltage = 220 V I_L = 50 A

and R_{se} = series field resistance = 0.1 Ω

$\therefore$ V_{AB} = 220 V + 50 A × 0.1 Ω

$\qquad$ = 220 V + 5 V = 225 V

The current in the shunt field is given by

$$I_{sh} = \frac{V_{AB}}{R_{sh}}$$

where R_{sh} = shunt field resistance = 100 Ω

$\therefore$ $I_{sh} = \dfrac{225 \text{ V}}{100 \text{ Ω}}$ = 2.25 A

$\therefore$ $I_a = I_L + I_{sh}$

$\qquad$ = 50 A + 2.25 A

$\qquad$ = 52.25 A

b) $E = V_{AB} + I_a R_a$

$\qquad$ = 225 V + 52.25 A × 0.2 Ω

$\qquad$ = 225 V + 10.45 V

$\qquad$ = 235.45 V

i.e. the armature current is 52.25 A and the full-load generated e.m.f. is 235.45 V.

7.9 Generator losses and efficiency

The types of losses in a generator may be divided into mechanical, electrical, and magnetic as shown:

mechanical – (a) friction
     (b) windage

electrical – (a) copper losses in field winding
   (b) copper losses in armature winding

magnetic (iron loss) – (a) hysteresis
       (b) eddy-current loss

The relationship between the input and output power and the losses is shown in fig. 7.21:

shaft input power = electrical output power + losses

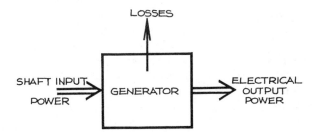

Fig. 7.21 Relationship between generator input and output power and losses

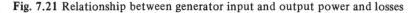

Now the mechanical input power is given by

mechanical input power P = rate of change of energy input

$$= \frac{\text{energy change}}{\text{time}}$$

where energy = torque × angular rotation = $T\theta$

$\therefore$ mechanical input power $P = \dfrac{T\theta}{t} = T\omega$

where ω = angular velocity in rad/s

and T = torque in N m

Now $\omega = 2\pi n$

where n = speed in rev/s

therefore mechanical input power in watts is given by

$$P = 2\pi Tn$$

The efficiency η (eta) is defined as

$$\text{efficiency } \eta = \frac{\text{electrical output power}}{\text{mechanical input power}} \text{ per unit}$$

$$= \frac{\text{electrical output power}}{\text{mechanical input power}} \times 100\%$$

$$= \frac{VI_L}{2\pi Tn} \times 100\%$$

$$\text{Also} \quad \eta = \frac{\text{electrical output power}}{\text{electrical output power + losses}} \times 100\%$$

Example A 250 V d.c. shunt-wound generator delivers a full-load output of 15 kW. The resistances of the armature and shunt field circuits are 0.5 Ω and 125 Ω respectively. The full-load speed is 16 rev/s, and the mechanical and iron losses total 750 W. Calculate (a) the efficiency of the generator, (b) the torque on the drive shaft of the generator at full load.

The circuit is shown in fig. 7.22.

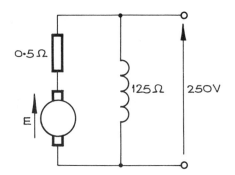

Fig. 7.22

a) The mechanical and iron losses = 750 W

The copper losses are calculated as follows:

$$\text{field current } I_f = \frac{V_T}{R_f} = \frac{250 \text{ V}}{125 \text{ }\Omega} = 2 \text{ A}$$

158

$$\text{load current } I_L = \frac{P}{V} = \frac{15\,000\,\text{W}}{250\,\text{V}} = 60\,\text{A}$$

$\therefore$ armature current $I_a = I_L + I_f = 60\,\text{A} + 2\,\text{A} = 62\,\text{A}$

Armature and field losses are given by

$$\begin{aligned}
\text{copper losses} &= I_a{}^2 R_a + I_f{}^2 R_f \\
&= (62\,\text{A})^2 \times 0.5\,\Omega + (2\,\text{A})^2 \times 125\,\Omega \\
&= 1922\,\text{W} + 500\,\text{W} \\
&= 2422\,\text{W}
\end{aligned}$$

Total losses $= 2422\,\text{W} + 750\,\text{W} = 3172\,\text{W}$

$$\begin{aligned}
\text{Efficiency} &= \frac{\text{output power}}{\text{output power} + \text{losses}} \times 100\% \\
&= \frac{15\,000\,\text{W}}{15\,000\,\text{W} + 3172\,\text{W}} \times 100\% \\
&= 82.5\%
\end{aligned}$$

b) Shaft input power = output power + losses

$$= 15\,000\,\text{W} + 3172\,\text{W} = 18\,172\,\text{W}$$

Now $P = 2\pi T n$

where $n = 16$ rev/s

$\therefore$ $18\,172\,\text{W} = 2\pi T \times 16$ rev/s

$\therefore$ $T = \dfrac{18\,172\,\text{W}}{2\pi \times 16\ \text{rev/s}} = 181\,\text{N\,m}$

i.e. the generator efficiency is 82.5% and the torque at the drive shaft on full load is 181 N m.

7.10 Reasons for failure to excite

A generator may fail to excite (fail to build up the voltage) for a variety of reasons:

a) The field winding may be open-circuit.
b) The shunt field resistance (or the control resistance in series with the shunt field) may be too high. If this resistance exceeds the 'critical resistance', then the machine will not self-excite (see example below).
c) The field core may have become demagnetised by some means so that there is no residual magnetism.
d) The field-winding connection may have become reversed.

159

Example When a particular shunt generator is started up from rest, it is observed that its terminal voltage does not build up to its normal rated value. Explain the possible reasons for this by reference to the characteristic curve and show the slope of the critical resistance. State the remedy necessary to build the terminal voltage up to its normal value.

Answer Additional resistance is often inserted in series with the field winding of a shunt generator to give some control over the terminal voltage.

A typical open-circuit generator characteristic is shown in fig. 7.23. Two conditions are shown for the value of the field plus control resistance at A and B.

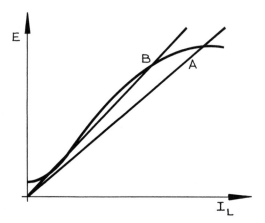

Fig. 7.23 Shunt-wound generator characteristic with field resistance below and above the critical value

It is evident that, for a shunt generator with field and control resistance of condition A, the generator voltage will build up. At condition B, however, the generator voltage will only build up to the point where the resistance line crosses the generator characteristic. A low voltage will be generated but it will *not* build up to its normal rated voltage. The value of field plus control resistance where the generator voltage just fails to build up is referred to as the *critical resistance*. This fault can be overcome by reducing the control resistance such that the voltage is allowed to build up.

Exercises on chapter 7
1   With the aid of circuit diagrams, describe three methods of excitation used in d.c. generators. For each case sketch a graph of terminal voltage against load current.
2   A d.c. generator is operated over a region where the flux per pole is proportional to the field current. When the generator is run at its normal

speed with a field current of 4 A, the generated e.m.f. is 400 V. Calculate the field current required for the generator to produce 300 V if it is run at half its normal speed.   [6 A]

3   A separately-excited d.c. generator has its field current supplied via a potential-divider. With the aid of a sketch, show the generator arrangement and give two reasons for using this method of control.

4   Sketch the terminal-voltage/load-current characteristic for a d.c. shunt generator. Label the axes and state any constant factors assumed.

5   A self-excited shunt generator supplies a load of 10 kW at 200 V. The armature resistance is 0.2 Ω and the field resistance is 100 Ω. Calculate the generated e.m.f.   [209.6 V]

6   A shunt generator is rebuilt and it is found that on starting-up it fails to excite. Give three possible reasons for this and describe how the faults could be rectified.

7   Sketch the graph of terminal voltage against load current for a d.c. generator in which the field winding is (a) series-connected, (b) shunt-connected. Explain the reasons for the shape of the two characteristics.

For the shunt generator, explain how the load characteristic may be predicted from the open-circuit characteristic.

8   Sketch the terminal-voltage/load-current characteristics for a compound-wound d.c. generator showing the effect of over, level, and under compounding. Briefly explain and account for the shape of these characteristics.

Sketch a circuit diagram showing how the generator is connected to a load, and include a shunt field regulator.

9   A test on a d.c. shunt generator produced the following results:

Field current (A)	0.1	0.2	0.3	0.4	0.5	0.6
D.C. voltage (V)	76	142	174	189	198	204

Plot the graph and use it to determine the terminal voltage and field current if the armature current is 20 A. The armature and field resistance are 1 Ω and 400 Ω respectively. Assume the speed remains constant throughout the test. (Hint: the terminal voltage is 20 V less than the open-circuit voltage.) [170 V; 0.42 A]

10   Sketch and explain the curves connecting (a) e.m.f. and speed at constant excitation, (b) e.m.f. and excitation at constant speed for a separately-excited generator.

The curve of induced e.m.f. for a separately-excited generator when run at 1300 rev/min on open circuit is given by

E.M.F. (V)		12	44	73	98	133	122	127
Exciting current (A)	0	0.2	0.4	0.6	0.8	1.0	1.2

Draw the curve of e.m.f. against excitation when the generator is running separately-excited at 1000 rev/min.

To what voltage will the generator build up on no load when shunt-excited and running at 1000 rev/min, if the total field resistance is 100 Ω? [90 V]

11 A separately-excited d.c. generator is run at 1000 rev/min and has an open-circuit characteristic given by the following:

Field current (A)	0.1	0.2	0.3	0.4	0.5	0.6
Open-circuit voltage (V)	40	66	81	90	96	100

The speed is increased to 1200 rev/min and the machine is run as a self-excited generator. Determine (a) the open-circuit voltage if the field resistance is 250 Ω, (b) the critical field resistance.   [112 V; 480 Ω]

12 A d.c. generator has a shunt field resistance of 100 Ω and an armature resistance of 0.1 Ω. It supplies a 20 kW load at a terminal voltage of 250 V. Determine (a) the armature current, (b) the generated e.m.f., (c) the power absorbed by the armature and field windings.   [82.5 A; 258.3 V; 1.3 kW]

13 Sketch a circuit diagram which shows how the field of a shunt generator is connected to the armature. Show how a variable resistor may be used as a regulator to control the e.m.f. generated by this machine. Sketch on the same axes the load characteristic of the above machine when the regulator is set to (a) its maximum value, (b) its minimum value.

14 The following table gives the open-circuit voltages for different values of field current in a shunt-connected d.c. generator driven at constant speed:

Open-circuit voltage (V)	120	240	334	400	440	470
Field current (A)	0.5	1.0	1.5	2.0	2.5	3.0

Plot a graph of open-circuit voltage against field current and derive from the graph the generated e.m.f. when the machine is operated as a self-excited shunt generator with a field resistance of (a) 160 Ω, (b) 210 Ω.

Find also the critical resistance of the shunt circuit.   [460 V; 370 V; 240 Ω]

15 Draw a circuit diagram of a compound-wound d.c. generator connected to a load. The circuit should also include a shunt field regulator.

Sketch the terminal-voltage/load-current characteristics, showing the effect of over, level, and under compounding. Briefly explain and account for the shape of these three characteristics.

16 Explain why the terminal voltage of a d.c. shunt-excited generator falls as the current supply load of the machine is increased.

The open-circuit characteristic of a separately-excited d.c. generator driven at constant speed is given by the following table:

Field current (A)	1	2	3	4	5	6	7
Voltage (V)	120	240	276	290	298	302	304

The resistance of the armature circuit is 0.2 Ω. The machine is now driven at the same speed as before but connected as a shunt generator with a total field circuit of 55 Ω. Find (a) the open-circuit voltage, (b) the load current when the terminal voltage is 280 V. Neglect the effect of armature reaction.
[300 V; 95 A]

8   D.C. motors

8.1 Introduction

A simple but inefficient d.c. motor may be constructed as shown in fig. 8.1.
It is similar to the simple d.c. generator and consists of a single-turn coil
situated in a magnetic field. Current is fed to the coil via a split-ring
commutator.

The current in the coil interacts with the magnetic field to produce a
torque. Applying Fleming's left-hand rule to fig. 8.1(a), the torque produced
is in an anticlockwise direction. In fig. 8.1(a) the coil is almost in the position
of maximum torque, which occurs when the coil is horizontal.

When the coil has rotated to the position of fig. 8.1(b), where it is almost
vertical, the current in the coil is just about to change direction. This is
achieved by means of the *split-ring commutator*, which acts as a switch to
reverse the direction of the current in the coil each time the coil passes
through the vertical.

When the coil has moved to the position of fig. 8.1(c), it has rotated $180°$
from the position of fig. 8.1(a), but the torque is still arranged to be in an
anticlockwise direction. The commutator thus ensures that rotational motion
is produced.

Of course in a practical machine we require many coil sides and therefore
many commutator segments. The coils are joined end to end, and are spaced
around the rotor circumference just as in the case of the d.c. generator. This
constitutes the armature winding and is of course wound on a soft-iron core
to provide a good magnetic circuit.

A schematic diagram of a multi-coil armature is shown in fig. 8.2. The
current through the armature winding produces a magnetic field whose axis
is perpendicular to the stator magnetic field as shown. These two magnetic
fields attempt to line up, and an anticlockwise torque is therefore produced
on the rotor. The purpose of the commutator is to maintain the armature
field in a fixed vertical position relative to the stator as the armature rotates.

The magnetic field of the stator is produced by current flowing in the
field winding which is wound around the stator poles. The d.c. motor is
therefore of the same construction as the d.c. generator. In fact a d.c. motor
may be run as a generator and vice versa. The construction of a d.c. motor is
thus as shown in fig. 7.7.

The diagrammatic representation of a d.c. motor is shown in fig. 8.3. In
this diagram the generator symbol represents the armature winding, where E
is the back e.m.f. The armature resistance is shown as R_a and is of the order
of $1\ \Omega$, while the field winding is shown with resistance R_f. The voltage V is
the d.c. supply voltage applied to the terminals.

163

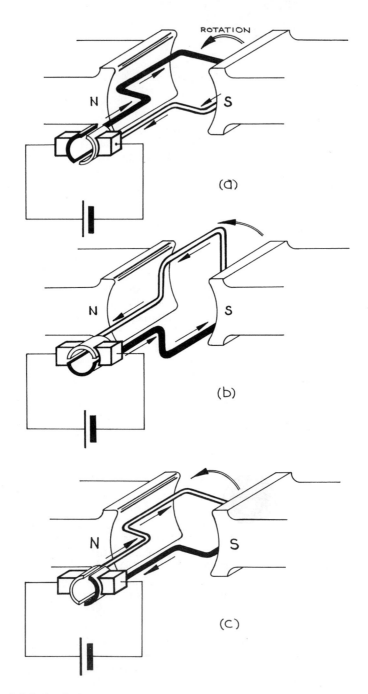

Fig. 8.1 A simple d.c. motor

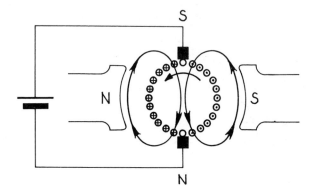

Fig. 8.2 Schematic diagram of d.c. motor with multi-coil armature

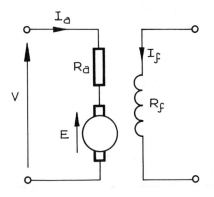

Fig. 8.3 Diagrammatic representation of a d.c. motor

When the motor is rotating, a back e.m.f. E is generated which opposes the supply voltage V. This back e.m.f. is just slightly less than the supply voltage, and, from the diagram of fig. 8.3, the corresponding armature current I_a is given by

$$I_a = \frac{V - E}{R_a}$$

∴ $V = E + I_a R_a$

Notice that this is a similar equation to that obtained for the d.c. generator (section 7.2), but with the sign changed.

Example   A d.c. motor is fed from a 230 V supply and runs at a speed such that the back e.m.f. is 220 V. If the armature resistance is 0.8 Ω, calculate the armature current.

$$I_a = \frac{V - E}{R_a}$$

where $V = 230\,\text{V}$ $\qquad E = 220\,\text{V}$ and $\qquad R_a = 0.8\,\Omega$

$$\therefore \quad I_a = \frac{230\,\text{V} - 220\,\text{V}}{0.8\,\Omega}$$

$$= \frac{10\,\text{V}}{0.8\,\Omega} = 12.5\,\text{A}$$

i.e. the armature current is 12.5 A.

8.2 Motor equations

Consider the parameters with which the engineer is concerned when choosing a motor; of course the price and the size, but primarily he is concerned with the power rating (or the current which it takes), the torque which it produces on full load, and the normal running speed. These latter three parameters are also the features of concern in the motor equations. We have already considered them in section 6.5. The equations are

$$E = k_e N I_f$$

i.e. the back e.m.f. E is proportional to the rotational speed N and the field current I_f;

also $\quad T = k_t I_a I_f$

i.e. the motor torque T is proportional to the armature current I_a and the field current I_f.

Both of these equations assume that the magnetic circuit is not saturated with flux.

Notice from the e.m.f. equation that the back e.m.f. E increases as the speed N increases, as we would expect. Also, the back e.m.f. E increases with increasing field current I_f, again as would be expected.

From the torque equation, it may seem that torque T increases both with field current I_f and armature current I_a.

Here are some typical examples of how the equations are used.

Example 1 A d.c. motor with a fixed field current produces a back e.m.f. of 180 V at a particular torque loading and runs at a speed of 2000 rev/min. If the torque loading is increased such that the back e.m.f. falls to 160 V, calculate the new rotational speed.

Notice that we are concerned with change of speed and therefore we use the equation

$$E = k_e N I_f$$

Consider the two conditions separately.

Condition 1:

$$E_1 = 180 \text{ V} \qquad N_1 = 2000 \text{ rev/min}$$

Condition 2:

$$E_2 = 160 \text{ V} \qquad N_2 = \text{unknown}$$

From the above,

$$\frac{E_2}{E_1} = \frac{k_e N_2 I_f}{k_e N_1 I_f}$$

$$\therefore \quad \frac{E_2}{E_1} = \frac{N_2}{N_1}$$

$$\therefore \quad N_2 = \frac{E_2}{E_1} N_1$$

$$= \frac{160 \text{ V}}{180 \text{ V}} \times 2000 \text{ rev/min} = 1778 \text{ rev/min}$$

i.e the new rotational speed is 1778 rev/min.

Example 2   A motor takes a fixed field current and requires an armature current of 10 A when providing a torque of 30 N m. Calculate the armature current when the torque loading is increased to 36 N m.

Since we are concerned with torque, we use the equation $T = k_t I_a I_f$.

There are two sets of conditions:

$$T_1 = 30 \text{ N m} \qquad I_{a1} = 10 \text{ A}$$

$$T_2 = 36 \text{ N m} \qquad I_{a2} = \text{unknown}$$

$$\therefore \quad \frac{T_2}{T_1} = \frac{k_t I_{a2} I_f}{k_t I_{a1} I_f}$$

$$= \frac{I_{a2}}{I_{a1}}$$

$$\therefore \quad I_{a2} = \frac{T_2}{T_1} I_{a1}$$

$$= \frac{36 \text{ N m}}{30 \text{ N m}} \times 10 \text{ A} = 12 \text{ A}$$

i.e. the new armature current is 12 A.

8.3 D.C. motor classification

D.C. motors are classified according to the way in which the field winding is connected. The field current may be supplied separately, in which case the motor is referred to as separately-excited. The more usual arrangement is for the field current to be supplied from the same supply source as the armature current; in this case the motor is referred to as self-excited. Each of the different arrangements has a different set of characteristics.

The characteristics with which the motor user is concerned are

a) variation of speed N with armature current I_a;
b) variation of torque T with armature current I_a;
c) variation of speed N with torque loading T.

8.4 Self-excited d.c. motors

There are three possible connections of the field winding with self-excited motors. These are

a) field winding in parallel with the armature winding (shunt-wound);
b) field winding in series with the armature winding (series-wound);
c) a combination of both the above (compound-wound).

The characteristics are shown on the same graphs in the following sections, for comparison.

8.5 Shunt-wound motor

The shunt-wound motor is shown in diagrammatic form in fig. 8.4.

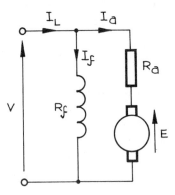

Fig. 8.4 Shunt-wound d.c. motor

Since the field winding is connected directly across the fixed supply voltage V, then the field current I_f is constant. The shunt motor is thus sometimes referred to as a constant-flux motor. Since the field current is constant, the speed and torque equations are modified as follows:

168

$$E \propto N$$

(i.e. the torque is proportional to the rotational current)

and $T \propto I_a$

(i.e. the torque is proportional to the armature current).

Notice also from fig. 8.4 that

$$I_L = I_a + I_f$$

and $V = E + I_a R_a$

The characteristics of the shunt-wound motor are shown in fig. 8.5.

As the torque demand on the drive shaft increases, the motor speed tends to fall (fig. 8.5(a)) and thus the back e.m.f. falls. This causes the armature current to increase which in turn provides a greater torque (fig. 8.5(c)). The speed thus falls only slightly with torque loading.

Example A 240 V d.c. shunt motor runs at a speed of 20 rev/s when the armature current is 40 A. Calculate the speed of the machine if the load is increased so that the armature current is 100 A. The armature resistance is 0.3 Ω.

We have $E \propto N$

but $E = V - I_a R_a$

$\therefore$ $\dfrac{E_2}{E_1} = \dfrac{V - I_{a2} R_a}{V - I_{a1} R_a} = \dfrac{N_2}{N_1}$

where $V = 240\,\text{V}$ $R_a = 0.3\,\Omega$ $I_{a1} = 40\,\text{A}$ $I_{a2} = 100\,\text{A}$

and $N_1 = 20$ rev/s

$\therefore$ $\dfrac{N_2}{20\,\text{rev/s}} = \dfrac{240\,\text{V} - 100\,\text{A} \times 0.3\,\Omega}{240\,\text{V} - 40\,\text{A} \times 0.3\,\Omega}$

$\therefore$ $N_2 = \left(\dfrac{210\,\text{V}}{228\,\text{V}} \right) \times 20\,\text{rev/s} = 18.4\,\text{rev/s}$

i.e. the new speed is 18.4 rev/s.

8.6 Series-wound motor

The series-wound motor is shown in diagrammatic form in fig. 8.6. Since the field winding is connected in series with the armature winding, the same current flows in each. The series field consists of a small number of turns of thick copper wire such that the field resistance R_f is small (of the order of a few ohms).

Although in the series motor the number of turns of the field winding is small, the field current is large, and thus the ampere-turns is of the same order as that of a similar-sized shunt motor.

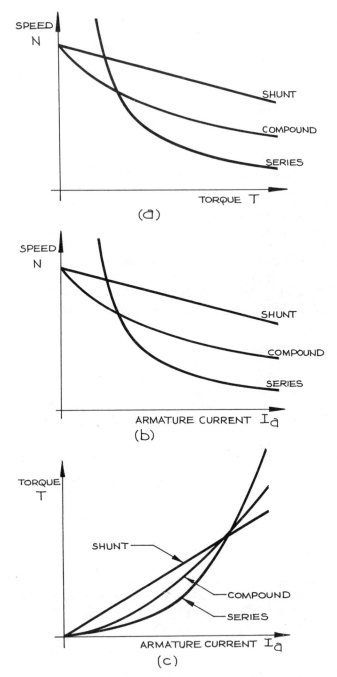

Fig. 8.5 D.C. motor characteristics: (a) speed/torque, (b) speed/armature-current, (c) torque/armature-current

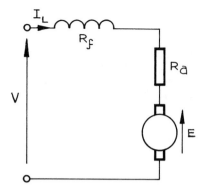

Fig. 8.6 Series-wound d.c. motor

Since $I_a = I_f$

then the equations for speed N and torque T become

$$E \propto NI_a$$

and $T \propto I_a^2$

also $V = E + I_a(R_a + R_f)$

The series-motor characteristics are shown in fig. 8.5. The speed/torque characteristic of fig. 8.5(a) shows that the series-motor speed falls off rapidly with torque loading of the motor shaft. It also shows that with very low torque loading the speed can become very high. In fact a series motor which is unloaded except for bearing friction etc. can gradually accelerate to a dangerously high speed, and larger motors can throw themselves to pieces under no-load conditions. Series motors should therefore never be run unloaded.

Figure 8.5(c) shows the square-law relationship between a series-motor torque and its armature current ($T \propto I_a^2$).

Example A 200 V series-wound d.c. motor takes a current of 10 A when producing a torque of 49 N m and runs at 1000 rev/min. If the torque loading is increased to 100 N m, calculate (a) the new armature current, (b) the new speed. The field and armature resistances are 2 Ω and 1 Ω respectively.

a) We have $T \propto I_a^2$

$\therefore \quad \dfrac{T_2}{T_1} = \left(\dfrac{I_{a2}}{I_{a1}}\right)^2$

where $T_1 = 49\,\text{N m}$ $\qquad T_2 = 100\,\text{N m}$ and $I_{a1} = 10\,\text{A}$

$$\therefore \quad \left(\frac{I_{a2}}{10\,\text{A}}\right)^2 = \frac{100\,\text{N m}}{49\,\text{N m}}$$

$$\therefore \quad \frac{I_{a2}}{10\,\text{A}} = \sqrt{\frac{100\,\text{N m}}{49\,\text{N m}}} = \frac{10}{7} = 1.43$$

$$\therefore \quad I_{a2} = 1.43 \times 10\,\text{A} = 14.3\,\text{A}$$

b) We have $E \propto NI_a$

$$\therefore \quad V - I_a(R_a + R_f) \propto NI_a$$

$$\therefore \quad \frac{V - I_{a2}(R_a + R_f)}{V - I_{a1}(R_a + R_f)} = \frac{N_2 I_{a2}}{N_1 I_{a1}}$$

where $V = 200\,\text{V}$ $I_{a1} = 10\,\text{A}$ $I_{a2} = 14.3\,\text{A}$

$N_1 = 1000\,\text{rev/min}$ and $R_a + R_f = 3\,\Omega$

$$\therefore \quad \frac{200\,\text{V} - 14.3\,\text{A} \times 3\,\Omega}{200\,\text{V} - 10\,\text{A} \times 3\,\Omega} = \frac{N_2 \times 14.3\,\text{A}}{1000\,\text{rev/min} \times 10\,\text{A}}$$

$$\therefore \quad \frac{200\,\text{V} - 42.9\,\text{V}}{200\,\text{V} - 30\,\text{V}} = \frac{N_2}{1000\,\text{rev/min}} \times 1.43$$

$$\therefore \quad N_2 = \left(\frac{157.1}{170 \times 1.43}\right) \times 1000\,\text{rev/min}$$

$$= 646\,\text{rev/min}$$

i.e. the armature current has increased to 14.3 A and the speed has fallen to 646 rev/min.

8.7 Compound-wound motor

The compound-wound motor is shown in fig. 8.7. It includes both shunt and series field windings.

The compound-motor characteristics are shown in fig. 8.5. These characteristics possess some of the properties of both the shunt and the series motors.

The speed/torque curve shows that, for the compound motor, the speed falls off more rapidly with torque loading than for the corresponding shunt motor. It does not however run up to dangerous speeds when unloaded. Figure 8.5(c) shows that the torque/armature-current characteristic lies somewhere between the shunt and series characteristics.

The precise shapes of the compound characteristics vary with the degree of compounding. The speed/torque curves of fig. 8.8 show conditions for

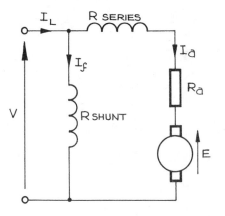

Fig. 8.7 Compound-wound d.c. motor

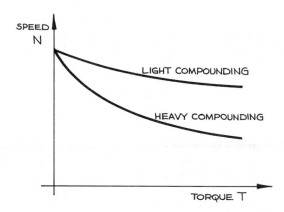

Fig. 8.8 Speed/torque curves for compound-wound d.c. motor

light compounding (only a small proportion of series field) and for heavy compounding (a large proportion of series field).

8.8 Separately-excited d.c. motors
The separately-excited d.c. motor is shown in diagrammatic form in fig. 8.9. The separately-excited motor is used in cases where the motor is to be controlled by variation of either field current I_f or armature current I_a. The most common application is as servo-motors for accurate speed and position control.

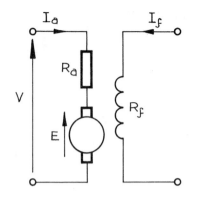

Fig. 8.9 Separately-excited d.c. motor

8.9 Speed control of d.c. motors

The speed of a d.c. motor may be controlled simply by addition of a variable resistance. The resistance is inserted in series or parallel with the armature and/or field winding as appropriate to the particular type of machine.

The reason is best seen by inspection of the e.m.f. equation. We have

$$N \propto \frac{E}{I_f}$$

$$\therefore \quad N \propto \frac{V - I_a R_a}{I_f}$$

From this equation it is evident that varying either the armature or field resistance will cause the speed to vary.

The method of varying the armature resistance is shown in fig. 8.10 for both the shunt and series motors. Increasing R_c will in both cases cause a decrease in speed. The disadvantage of this method of speed control is that it is wasteful of energy, due to the heat loss in the control resistor, and is unsuitable for large motors, which instead use control of the voltage supply.

The method of varying the field resistance is shown in fig. 8.11. In the shunt motor, increasing R_c reduces I_f and thus causes an increase in speed. In this method the heat loss generated in the control resistance is small, due to the small field current, and this method is therefore widely used. In the series motor, increasing R_c increases I_f and thus causes a decrease in speed.

8.10 Losses and efficiency of d.c. motors

The losses in d.c. motors are the same as those in d.c. generators. They consist of mechanical losses (friction and windage), copper losses (the $I^2 R$ loss in the armature and field windings), and iron losses in the magnetic circuit (hysteresis and eddy-current loss).

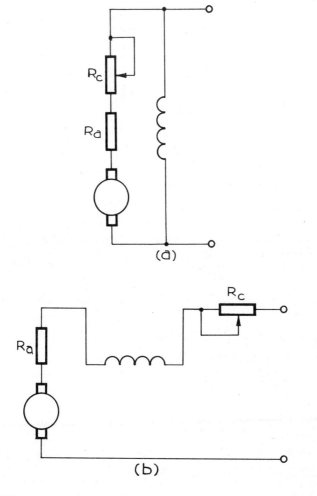

Fig. 8.10 Speed control by variation of resistance in the armature circuit: (a) shunt motor, (b) series motor

We may say that

output power = input power − total losses

Also, the motor efficiency is defined as

$$\text{efficiency } \eta = \frac{\text{mechanical output power}}{\text{electrical input power}} \times 100\%$$

$$= \frac{\text{mechanical output power}}{\text{mechanical output power + total losses}} \times 100\%$$

175

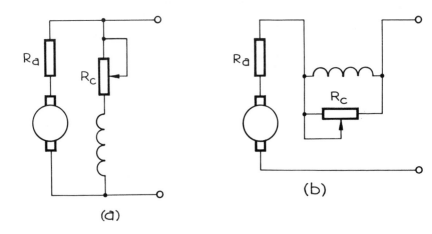

Fig. 8.11 Speed control by variation of resistance in the field circuit: (a) shunt motor, (b) series motor

The output is the power, P_o watts, available at the motor drive shaft and is given by

mechanical output power $P_o = T\omega$

where T = torque in N m

and ω = angular velocity in rad/s

Now $\omega = 2\pi n$

where n = rotational speed in rev/s

$\therefore$ $P_o = 2\pi Tn$

The input power, P_i watts, is given by

$P_i = VI_L$

where V = supply voltage

and I_L = load current

$\therefore$ efficiency $\eta = \dfrac{P_o}{P_i} \times 100\%$

$= \dfrac{T\omega}{VI_L} \times 100\%$

Example 1   A series motor takes 20 A from a 240 V d.c. supply. If the field and armature resistances are 1 Ω and 0.5 Ω respectively, calculate (a) the copper losses, (b) the efficiency if the mechanical and iron losses are 500 W.

a) For a series motor,

copper losses $= I_a^2(R_a + R_f)$

where $I_a = 20\,A$ and $R_a + R_f = 1.5\,\Omega$

∴ copper losses $= (20\,A)^2 \times 1.5\,\Omega$

$$= 600\,W$$

b) Input power $P_i = VI_L$

where $V = 240\,V$ and $I_L = 20\,A$

∴ $P_i = 240\,V \times 20\,A$

$$= 4800\,W = 4.8\,kW$$

Output power $P_o = P_i - \text{total losses}$

$$= 4.8\,kW - 0.5\,kW - 0.6\,kW$$

$$= 3.7\,kW$$

Efficiency $\eta = \dfrac{P_o}{P_i} \times 100\%$

$$= \dfrac{3.7\,kW}{4.8\,kW} \times 100\% = 77\%$$

i.e. the copper losses are 600 W and the efficiency is 77%.

Example 2   A d.c. shunt motor takes a current of 50 A at 240 V on full load. The resistances of the shunt field and armature windings are 120 Ω and 0.2 Ω respectively. The full-load speed is 16 rev/s, and the iron and mechanical losses at this speed total 250 W. Calculate (a) the copper losses at full load, (b) the full-load torque at the motor shaft, (c) the efficiency of the motor.

a) Copper losses $= I_a^2 R_a + I_f^2 R_f$

where $I_f = \dfrac{V}{R_f} = \dfrac{240\,V}{120\,\Omega} = 2\,A$

$I_a = I_L - I_f = 50\,A - 2\,A = 48\,A$

$R_a = 0.2\,\Omega$ and $R_f = 120\,\Omega$

∴ copper losses $= (48\,A)^2 \times 0.2\,\Omega + (2\,A)^2 \times 120\,\Omega$

$$= 460.8\,W + 480\,W$$

$$\simeq 941\,W$$

177

b)   Now   output power = input power − losses

∴ $P_o = VI_L - \text{losses}$

where $V = 240\,\text{V}$ $I_L = 50\,\text{A}$

and   losses $= 941\,\text{W} + 250\,\text{W} = 1191\,\text{W}$

∴ $P_o = 240\,\text{V} \times 50\,\text{A} - 1191\,\text{W}$

$\quad\quad = 12\,000\,\text{W} - 1191\,\text{W}$

$\quad\quad \simeq 10.8\,\text{kW}$

Now $P_o = T\omega$

∴ $T = \dfrac{P_o}{\omega}$

where $P_o = 10.8\,\text{kW}$ and $\omega = 16 \times 2\pi\,\text{rad/s}$

∴ $T = \dfrac{10.8 \times 10^3\,\text{W}}{2\pi \times 16\,\text{rad/s}} = 107\,\text{N m}$

c)   Efficiency $\eta = \dfrac{P_o}{P_i} \times 100\%$

where $P_o = 10.8\,\text{kW}$ and $P_i = 12\,\text{kW}$

∴ $\eta = \dfrac{10.8\,\text{kW}}{12\,\text{kW}} \times 100\% = 90\%$

i.e. the copper losses are 941 W, the full-load torque is 107 N m, and the efficiency is 90%.

Example 3   A 440 d.c. shunt motor has a full-load output rating of 7.5 kW when running at a speed of 12 rev/s. The armature and field resistances are 0.8 Ω and 1000 Ω respectively. The full-load efficiency of the motor is 87%. Calculate the combined mechanical and iron losses of the motor. (Assume that the field flux remains constant.)

$\quad$ Efficiency $\eta = \dfrac{P_o}{P_o + \text{total losses}} \times 100\%$

where $\eta = 87\%$ and $P_o = 7.5\,\text{kW}$

∴ $87\% = \dfrac{7.5\,\text{kW}}{7.5\,\text{kW} + \text{losses}} \times 100\%$

∴ $\dfrac{7.5\,\text{kW}}{7.5\,\text{kW} + \text{losses}} = 0.87$

$$\therefore \qquad \frac{7.5\,\text{kW}}{0.87} = 7.5\,\text{kW} + \text{losses}$$

$$\therefore \qquad 8.62\,\text{kW} = 7.5\,\text{kW} + \text{losses}$$

$$\therefore \qquad \text{total losses} = 1.12\,\text{kW}$$

Now $\quad$ copper losses $= I_a{}^2 R_a + I_f{}^2 R_L$

where $\quad I_f = \dfrac{440\,\text{V}}{1000\,\Omega} = 0.44\,\text{A} \quad$ and $\quad I_a = I_L - I_f$

But $\quad P_i = V I_L$

$$\therefore \qquad I_L = \frac{P_i}{V}$$

where $\quad P_i = \dfrac{7.5\,\text{kW}}{0.87} = 8.62\,\text{kW} \quad$ and $\quad V = 440\,\text{V}$

$$\therefore \qquad I_L = \frac{8.62\,\text{kW}}{440\,\text{V}} = 19.59\,\text{A}$$

$$\therefore \qquad I_a = 19.59\,\text{A} - 0.44\,\text{A} = 19.15\,\text{A}$$

$\therefore \quad$ copper losses $= (19.15\,\text{A})^2 \times 0.8\,\Omega + (0.44\,\text{A})^2 \times 1000\,\Omega$

$$= 293\,\text{W} + 194\,\text{W}$$

$$= 487\,\text{W}$$

$$\simeq 0.49\,\text{kW}$$

Mechanical and iron losses $=$ total losses $-$ copper losses

$$= 1.12\,\text{kW} - 0.49\,\text{kW}$$

$$= 0.63\,\text{kW}$$

i.e. the combined mechanical and iron losses are 630 W.

Example 4 A 440 V d.c. shunt motor takes a current of 3 A on no load. The resistances of the armature and shunt field circuits are 0.2 Ω and 220 Ω respectively. Assuming that the motor is fully loaded and taking an input current of 60 A, calculate (a) the mechanical power output, (b) the percentage change in speed between no load and full load.

Assume that mechanical and iron losses and field flux remain constant between no load and full load.

a) $\quad$ On no load,

$\qquad$ input power $=$ losses $= V I_L$

where $V = 440$ V and $I_L = 3$ A

$\therefore$ losses $= 440$ V $\times$ 3 A $= 1320$ W

Now no-load copper losses $= I_f^2 R_f + I_a^2 R_a$

where $I_f = \dfrac{440 \text{ V}}{220 \ \Omega} = 2$ A and $I_a = I_L - I_f = 3$ A $- 2$ A $= 1$ A

$\therefore$ no-load copper losses $= (2 \text{ A})^2 \times 220 \ \Omega + (1 \text{ A})^2 \times 0.2 \ \Omega$

$$= 880 \text{ W} + 0.2 \text{ W}$$

$$\simeq 880 \text{ W}$$

$\therefore$ mechanical and iron losses $= 1320$ W $- 880$ W $= 440$ W

On full load,

$$I_a = I_L - I_f = 60 \text{ A} - 2 \text{ A} = 58 \text{ A}$$

$\therefore$ copper losses $= (2 \text{ A})^2 \times 220 \ \Omega + (58 \text{ A})^2 \times 0.2 \ \Omega$

$$= 880 \text{ W} + 673 \text{ W}$$

$$= 1553 \text{ W}$$

$\therefore$ total losses $= 1553$ W $+ 440$ W

$$= 1993 \text{ W}$$

Now $P_o = VI_L -$ losses

where $V = 440$ V and $I_L = 60$ A

$\therefore$ $P_o = 440$ V $\times$ 60 A $- 1993$ W

$$= 24.4 \text{ kW}$$

b) Use the equation for a shunt motor:

$$E_2/E_1 = N_2/N_1$$

On no load,

$$E_1 = V - I_{a_1} R_a$$

$$= 440 \text{ V} - 1 \text{ A} \times 0.2 \ \Omega = 439.8 \text{ V}$$

On full load,

$$E_2 = V - I_{a_2} R_a$$

$$= 440 \text{ V} - 58 \text{ A} \times 0.2 \ \Omega = 428.4 \text{ V}$$

$\therefore$ $\dfrac{N_2}{N_1} = \dfrac{428.4 \text{ V}}{439.8 \text{ V}} = 0.97$

$$\therefore \quad \text{percentage change in speed} = \frac{N_1 - N_2}{N_1} \times 100\%$$

$$= \frac{N_1 - 0.97N_1}{N_1} \times 100\%$$

$$= \frac{0.03N_1}{N_1} \times 100\%$$

$$= 3\%$$

i.e. the output power at full load is 24.4 kW and the percentage change in speed from no load to full load is 3%.

8.11 Starting d.c. motors

A d.c. motor when stationary produces no back e.m.f. Also, the armature resistance is very small and of the order of 1 Ω. A d.c. motor should therefore *never* be started up from rest without the introduction of some series starting resistance, otherwise the current taken from the supply could be hundreds of amperes and therefore damage the motor windings or the connecting wires.

A typical d.c. motor starter arrangement is shown in fig. 8.12. It consists of a resistor with tapping points and a starter handle, which allows the resistance to be progressively reduced until the motor is running at full speed.

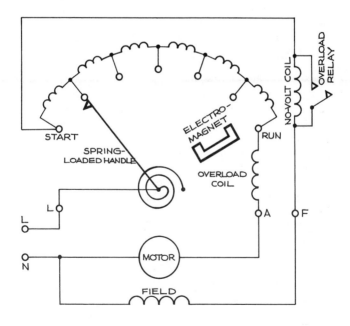

Fig. 8.12 A typical d.c. motor starter arrangement

181

Motor-protection circuits are also incorporated in the starter, these being a no-volt coil and an overload coil. The starter handle is spring-loaded, and would return to the starting position if it were not held in the running position by an electromagnet. This electromagnet holds the handle at the run position as long as current flows in the no-volt coil. If for any reason (such as power failure) the supply voltage falls to zero then the current in the no-volt coil will fall to zero, the starting handle will be released, and it will return to the starting position. The overload coil operates a relay whose contacts bypass the no-volt coil, so that in the event of overload current the starter handle is again released and returns to the starting position.

8.12 D.C. motor applications

D.C. motors are generally used in applications which require the control of speed and torque, since they are more suitable than a.c. motors for such applications. They are typically found in steel-rolling mills, lift drives, motor traction, and paper-making mills as well as in conveyor drives and aerial and radar-antennae position controllers. Small d.c. motors are also used for position control in applications such as computer tape and disc drives. Battery-driven vehicles of course use d.c. motors, and battery-operated motor cars become a more serious possibility as battery efficiency improves.

D.C. motors are more expensive than a.c. motors and of course need a d.c. supply. For this reason, a.c. motors are used in most domestic applications and in many of the industrial drives requiring constant speed.

The d.c. *shunt* motor is sometimes used for constant-speed drives, since its speed remains fairly constant with torque loading. This makes it suitable for lathes and milling and drilling machines, although a.c. motors are more commonly found in these applications. D.C. shunt motors are used in machine tools, pumps, and compressors, printing machinery, and steelworks drives.

The d.c. *series* motor produces a high starting torque which is useful for applications such as winches and cranes. Also with this machine, the speed falls if a heavy overload occurs. The series motor thus automatically adjusts for varying loads without taking an excessive current. D.C. series motors are used in cranes, hoists, heavy-duty traction, travelling gantries, fans, centrifugal pumps, and as automobile starter motors.

The d.c. *compound* motor may have a variety of characteristics and is therefore suitable for a wide range of drive requirements. The addition of the shunt winding prevents the motor from running away when unloaded, while the series winding aids the starting torque. D.C. compound motors are used in many applications including steel-rolling mills, lifts, heavy-duty machinery, flywheels, pumps, and compressors.

Exercises on chapter 8

1   Sketch the torque/load-current characteristic for a series d.c. motor and state why this type of motor should never be uncoupled from its load.

2   a) Draw clearly labelled circuit diagrams of (i) a shunt-wound d.c. motor, (ii) a compound-wound d.c. motor.

   b) Show how the direction of rotation may be reversed in each case.

3   A 220 V d.c. shunt motor has an armature resistance of 0.2 Ω. When running at 1470 rev/min it takes an armature current of 50 A. Calculate the back e.m.f. generated under these conditions.

If the load on the motor is reduced such that the armature current falls to 25 A, calculate the new speed. State any assumptions made.   [210 V; 1505 rev/min]

4   Sketch the characteristics of speed/armature-current and torque/armature-current for a d.c. shunt-wound motor and explain the reasons for their shape.

5   Compare briefly the d.c. series and shunt motors, giving one application of each type. State one advantage of each, and one disadvantage of the series motor. State a method of controlling the speed of a d.c. series motor.

A 200 V d.c. shunt motor takes a load current of 10 A and runs at a speed of 1000 rev/min. Calculate the new speed if the load torque is reduced to 50% of its original value. The armature and shunt field resistances are 0.5 Ω and 200 Ω respectively.   [1012 rev/min]

6   A 240 V d.c. shunt-wound motor takes an armature current of 10 A when running at a speed of 25 rev/s. When a load is applied, the speed falls to 80% of this value. Calculate the new armature current and state any assumptions made. The armature resistance is 2 Ω.   [32 A]

7   A variable resistance is connected in series with the shunt field winding of a d.c. machine. State the effect of decreasing the resistance if the machine is run as (a) a generator, (b) a motor.

8   A 240 V d.c. shunt-wound generator has an armature resistance of 2.5 Ω and when driven at 1200 rev/min produces an armature current of 10 A. At what speed would this generator run as a motor fed if from a 240 V supply with the shaft loaded such that the armature current is 10 A?   [974 rev/min]

9   A 250 V d.c. shunt-wound motor has an armature resistance of 0.2 Ω and takes an armature current of 60 A when running at a speed of 1500 rev/min. Calculate the back e.m.f. generated in the armature. If the load on the motor is reduced such that the armature current falls to 30 A, calculate the new speed. State any assumptions made.   [238 V; 1538 rev/min]

10   Sketch the speed/armature-current characteristic of a d.c. shunt-wound motor. Explain how the characteristic is modified by the addition of a series winding which is connected so as to increase the total flux.

11   a) Sketch the speed/load characteristic of a d.c. shunt motor and explain the reasons for its shape.

b) A 440 V d.c. shunt motor runs at a speed of 1000 rev/min when its armature current is 20 A. At what speed will it run when the armature current is 50 A if the armature resistance is 0.5 Ω?

c) At what speed will it run with the armature current remaining at 50 A if the field strength is now reduced to 80% of its original value?   [965 rev/min; 1206 rev/min]

12   State how the speed of a d.c. shunt wound motor may be (a) increased above and (b) decreased below its normal running speed. Show by means of circuit diagrams what modifications are required to produce these changes.

13 A 240 V d.c. series motor takes a current of 25 A when run at 800 rev/min. If a 0.6 Ω diverter is connected in parallel with the field winding and the load torque is reduced to 80% of its original value, calculate the new running speed. The armature and field resistances are 0.6 Ω and 0.4 Ω respectively and the field flux may be assumed to be proportional to the field current. [919 rev/min]

14 A 250 V d.c. shunt-wound motor takes a total current of 30 A when the speed is 1450 rev/min. If the combined mechanical and iron losses are 1200 W, calculate the load torque and the efficiency at this speed. The armature and field resistance are 0.2 Ω and 250 Ω respectively. [38.8 N m; 78.4%]

15 A 250 V shunt-connected d.c. machine when running unloaded as a motor takes a current of 4 A and runs at a speed of 20 rev/s. If the armature is driven as a generator at the same speed and with the same field current, estimate the efficiency when the armature current is 30 A. The armature and field resistances are 0.5 Ω and 250 Ω respectively. The effects of armature reaction may be ignored. [83%]

16 A 250 V series d.c. motor takes a current of 30 A. Calculate the resistance to be inserted in series with the armature to reduce the speed to 60% of its original value if the current at the new speed is 18 A. The armature and field resistances total 0.6 Ω and the flux may be assumed to be proportional to the current. [8.6 Ω]

17 A 240 V d.c. shunt-wound motor runs at a speed of 20 rev/s when the armature current is 25 A. If the load torque is constant and the field flux is reduced by 15%, determine the value of resistance to be connected in series with the armature in order that the speed should remain constant. The armature resistance is 0.3 Ω. [1.1 Ω]

18 Sketch graphs to show the variation in speed of a d.c. shunt-wound motor for variation in (a) the armature voltage with constant field current, (b) the field current with constant armature voltage.

19 a) A 200 V d.c. shunt motor runs at 3000 rev/min and takes an armature current of 10 A. Calculate the resistance to be added in series with the armature to reduce the speed to 2800 rev/min if the armature current remains the same.

b) With this additional resistance remaining in the armature circuit, calculate the resistance to be added in series with the field circuit to bring the speed back to 3000 rev/min, assuming the armature current remains at 10 A.

Armature resistance = 1 Ω. Field resistance = 200 Ω. The magnetic flux may be assumed to be proportional to field current. [1.3 Ω; 14.3 Ω]

20 A d.c. shunt motor takes 25 A when running from a 220 V supply at a speed of 1000 rev/min. The armature resistance is 0.1 Ω and the field resistance is 100 Ω. Calculate the speed at which the motor will run if the load torque is halved, a resistance of 50 Ω is inserted in the field circuit, and a resistance of 5 Ω is inserted in the armature circuit. Assume field flux to be proportional to the field current. [916 rev/min]

9   A.C. motors

9.1 Introduction

A.C. induction motors are the type of motor most commonly found in industrial and domestic applications. One reason is that the majority of electrical power available to the consumer is a.c. Another reason is that induction motors are generally cheaper and less troublesome to operate than d.c. motors, since they do not require a commutator; they do not therefore suffer from the commutation problems experienced with d.c. motors (such as sparking and commutator and brush wear).

A.C. motors are best suited to constant-speed applications, the speed of a particular machine being determined by the frequency of the a.c. supply fed to the motor. They can however be used as a variable-speed drive together with a suitable control circuit, and a.c. motors can duplicate the operation of d.c. motors in most applications.

A.C. motors can be designed to operate from a supply of any number of phases. Most industrial a.c. motors are three-phase induction motors, while most of the induction motors used in domestic appliances are single-phase. Examples of domestic applications are washing machines, refrigerators, fans, etc. Two-phase induction motors are also used in some control applications.

A.C. induction motors are robust, cheap, and simple to operate.

A.C. motors are classified as

a) induction motors;
b) synchronous motors.

Both have a stator and a rotor, as with any rotating electrical machine. Both have a distributed stator winding which fits in slots around the inner circumference of the stator core, as shown in fig. 9.1.

The a.c. supply is applied to the stator winding. This sets up a rotating magnetic field, which rotates at a speed determined by the frequency of the supply, as described in section 9.2. The speed of rotation of this magnetic field is referred to as the synchronous speed (n_s). As it sweeps past the conductors of the rotor winding, this rotating magnetic field induces currents in the rotor winding due to electromagnetic induction. These currents react with the stator magnetic field to produce torque. The torque produced causes the rotor to rotate in the same direction as the rotation of the stator field.

The induction motor does *not* have a supply of electricity connected to the rotor: it uses induced rotor current to produce torque (hence its name). It always runs at just less than synchronous speed (see section 9.5).

The synchronous motor *does* have a separate d.c. supply connected to the rotor, and therefore runs at synchronous speed (see section 9.6).

Fig. 9.1 Stator and stator winding of a three-phase induction motor (895 kW, 13 800 V, 60 Hz, two-pole, 3600 rev/min)

9.2 Production of a rotating magnetic field

It is often found surprising that supplying a three-phase alternating voltage to the windings of a *fixed* stator can produce a magnetic field which *rotates* in space. This is the basis of the operation of three-phase a.c. motors (induction motors and synchronous motors) and is the reason why no commutator is required.

The principle may be explained by considering a simple three-phase stator which has three separate coils physically spaced 120° apart and fed with a

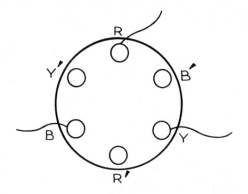

Fig. 9.2 Schematic representation of stator coils of a three-phase two-pole induction motor

three-phase alternating voltage. The three coils viewed end-on are shown schematically in fig. 9.2. The *starts* of the coils are represented as R (red), Y (yellow), and B (blue) and the *finishes* as R', Y', and B'.

If the three coils finishes are connected together as a 'common', then the motor may be connected to a conventional three-wire three-phase supply as a star-connected load.

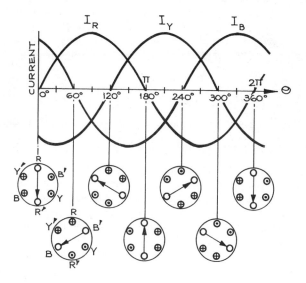

Fig. 9.3 Current waveforms in the stator coils of a three-phase two-pole motor

The corresponding current waveforms in the three phases are as shown in fig. 9.3. Notice that the currents rise and fall with a separation of 120° between their peaks.

Now consider the direction of the currents in the windings at different parts of the cycle. We shall consider them at 60° intervals as shown in fig. 9.3.

At 0°, current is flowing into B and out of B'. (The conventional representation is to show a cross for current flowing into a coil and a dot for current flowing out of a coil.) There is no current in R and R' (it is at zero). Current is flowing into Y' and out of Y. The direction of the magnetic field produced by the current in these coils will be vertically downwards as shown in the first diagram of fig. 9.3.

Now consider the condition at 60°. The current in the blue phase is zero. That in the red and yellow phases is as shown. The result is that the direction of the magnetic field has changed. It has rotated *physically* through 60°.

Continuing through the three-phase waveform at 60° intervals, it may be seen that, as the three-phase currents rise and fall, the magnetic field rotates in space. After one cycle, the field is back to its original direction. Remember that the stator does not move – only the magnetic field rotates.

Synchronous speed

The speed of rotation of the stator field is calculated as follows.

Consider the three-phase induction motor with three coils. Since each coil will produce a magnetic field when current flows through it, then each coil will produce its own north and south pole. This induction motor is therefore said to have one pole pair per phase (i.e. three pole pairs altogether).

Now we have seen that the resultant magnetic field for this induction motor completes one revolution in one cycle of the supply voltage. But

$$\text{1 cycle period } T = 1/f$$

where f = supply frequency

$\therefore$ speed of rotation of magnetic field = 1 revolution in $1/f$ seconds

$\therefore$ speed of rotation n_s = f rev/s

This is referred to as the *synchronous speed*.

It is evident that the synchronous speed depends on the frequency of the supply, f Hz, and on the number of pairs of poles per phase (p). Consider a three-phase induction motor with two pole pairs per phase (i.e. six pole pairs altogether). By a similar analysis to the above we find that the synchronous speed is halved (i.e. $n_s = f/2$).

In general, for an induction motor with p pole pairs per phase, the synchronous speed, n_s rev/s, is given by

$$n_s = \frac{f}{p}$$

Example 1   The stator winding of a three-phase induction motor has one pole pair per phase. If the frequency of the supply is 50 Hz, calculate the speed of rotation of the stator field.

$$n_s = f/p$$

where $f = 50\,\text{Hz}$ and $p = 1$

$\therefore$ $n_s = 50\,\text{rev/s}$

$ = 3000\,\text{rev/min}$

i.e. the speed of rotation of the stator field is 3000 rev/min.

Example 2   Calculate the number of pairs of poles of a three-phase induction motor which has a synchronous speed of 750 rev/min and is fed from a supply of frequency 50 Hz.

$$p = f/n_s$$

where $f = 50\,\text{Hz}$ and $n_s = 750\,\text{rev/min} = 12.5\,\text{rev/s}$

$\therefore$ $p = \dfrac{50\,\text{Hz}}{12.5\,\text{rev/s}} = 4$ pole pairs per phase

i.e. the motor has a total of 12 poles.

The synchronous speed of a 50 Hz three-phase induction motor for different numbers of poles per phase is given in Table 9.1.

Table 9.1 Synchronous speeds of a 50 Hz three-phase induction motor

Pole pairs per phase	n_s rev/s	N_s rev/min
1	50	3000
2	25	1500
3	16.67	1000
4	12.5	750
5	10	600
6	8.33	500

9.3 Types of rotor

The rotor of an induction motor consists of conductors mounted in slots on the surface of a laminated soft-iron core. The conductors in the slots may be one of two types: squirrel-cage or wound.

a) Squirrel-cage rotor

The squirrel-cage rotor consists of heavy uninsulated copper or aluminium bars equally spaced around the rotor periphery and connected together at each end by a copper or aluminium ring to form a closed circuit as shown in fig. 9.4. The induced currents flow in these bars as described in section 9.4. This type of construction is robust and cheap.

A typical squirrel-cage rotor for a large machine is shown in fig. 9.5.

b) Wound rotor

The wound rotor consists of coils of insulated wire wound in the rotor slots as shown in fig. 9.6. This method of construction is more expensive but allows for connection of the windings to external slip rings. External resistance can thus be introduced in series with the wound rotor to provide some degree of speed control and starting control.

The basic principle of operation is the same in both cases.

9.4 Induction-motor principle

In a three-phase induction motor, the stator winding is supplied with a three-phase alternating voltage. The currents in the windings set up a magnetic field which rotates in space in the manner described in section 9.3.

The induction-motor rotor is a self-contained unit and has no connection to and external source of current. Since no current is fed to the rotor, the question is, 'What produces the magnetic field of the rotor winding.' The answer is probably best shown by the following explanation.

Fig. 9.4 Cut-away view of a squirrel-cage rotor, which consists of aluminium cast directly into the core – the bars, and rings, and fan tips being formed at the same operation.

190

Fig. 9.5 Squirrel-cage rotor of a large induction motor

Fig. 9.6 Wound rotor for a three-phase induction motor, showing slip rings for speed control by introducing external resistance

Consider the rotating magnetic field produced by the currents in the stator winding. As it sweeps past the conductors of the rotor, currents are induced in the rotor circuit. (This is why the induction motor is so called.) This induced current in the rotor interacts with the field which is inducing it to produce a force and hence cause the rotor to turn. To find the direction of rotation, consider the diagram of fig. 9.7.

Figure 9.7(a) shows the magnetic field of the stator rotating in a clockwise direction, rather like the spokes of a wheel. As the field sweeps past the rotor conductors, an electric current is induced in them. The direction of the current is found by Fleming's right-hand rule. In this rule, the forefinger points in the direction of the magnetic field (downwards in this case). The

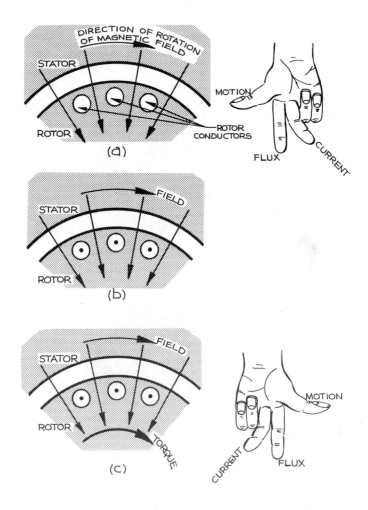

Fig. 9.7 Principles of operation of an induction motor

thumb points in the direction of motion of the *conductor relative to the magnetic field.* In this case, the fact that the field is moving means that we must consider the relative motion in order to apply Fleming's right-hand rule. The field moving clockwise past a stationary conductor gives the same effect as the conductor moving anticlockwise through the stationary field. The *relative* motion of the conductor is thus right to left. This produces a current out of the paper as shown by the dots on the conductors in fig. 9.7(b).

Now use Fleming's left-hand rule to find the direction of the force on the conductor. It is evident that the force is in a clockwise direction. The rotation of the rotor is thus in the same direction as that of the magnetic field. The rotor may be thought of rather as a cork floating in a whirlpool which is made to rotate in the same direction as the direction of rotation of the whirlpool.

9.5 Rotor speed and slip speed

The speed of rotation of an induction motor is referred to as the rotor speed, n_r. The rotor can never quite catch up with the rotating magnetic field, since there would then be no relative motion between the two. This would mean that the rotor conductors would not cut through the magnetic flux and hence no rotor current would be induced; therefore no torque.

The rotor speed n_r is always less than the synchronous speed n_s. The difference between the two is referred to as slip speed:

$$\text{slip speed} = n_s - n_r$$

The 'slip', s, is defined by

$$s = \frac{\text{slip speed}}{\text{synchronous speed}}$$

$$\therefore \quad s = \frac{n_s - n_r}{n_s}$$

Since this is a ratio, it is referred to as the 'fractional slip' or the 'per-unit slip'. The 'percentage slip' is given by

$$\text{percentage slip} = \frac{n_s - n_r}{n_s} \times 100\%$$

Typical values of full-load slip vary from about 4% for small motors to about 1.5% for large ones. The actual speed of the rotor is thus close to the synchronous speed.

As the torque loading on the shaft of an induction motor increases, the rotor speed falls. This means an increased slip speed, resulting in an increased current in the rotor and an increased supply current. The induction motor is thus able to provide a fairly constant speed with increased torque loading.

The speed/torque characteristic is shown in fig. 9.8. Notice that the speed falls off slightly with torque loading. Increasing the torque beyond the full-load limit will cause the motor to stall.

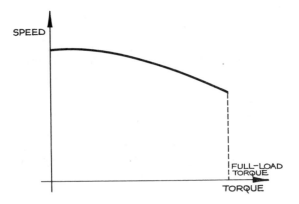

Fig. 9.8 Speed/torque characteristic for an induction motor

Example 1   A four-pole three-phase 50 Hz induction motor runs at 24 rev/s. Calculate (a) the synchronous speed, (b) the per-unit slip, (c) the percentage slip.

a)   A four-pole induction motor means four poles per phase or two pole pairs per phase.

$$\therefore \quad n_s = \frac{f}{p} = \frac{50\ Hz}{2} = 25\ rev/s$$

b) $$s = \frac{n_s - n_r}{n_s}$$

$$= \frac{25 - 24}{25} = 0.04\ per\ unit$$

c)   Percentage slip = $0.04 \times 100\%$

$$= 4\%$$

i.e. the synchronous speed is 25 rev/s, the per-unit slip is 0.04, and the percentage slip is 4%.

Example 2   A three-phase induction motor is fed from a 50 Hz supply and runs at 732 rev/min when the per-unit slip is 0.024. Calculate (a) the synchronous speed, (b) the total number of poles for which the machine is wound.

a)   732 rev/min = 12.2 rev/s

$$s = \frac{n_s - n_r}{n_s}$$

194

$$\therefore \quad sn_s = n_s - n_r$$

$$\therefore \quad n_r = n_s(1 - s)$$

$$n_s = \frac{n_r}{1 - s} = \frac{12.2 \text{ rev/s}}{1 - 0.024} = 12.5 \text{ rev/s}$$

b) $n_s = f/p$

$$\therefore \quad p = \frac{f}{n_s} = \frac{50 \text{ Hz}}{12.5 \text{ rev/s}} = 4 \text{ pole pairs per phase}$$

$\therefore$ total poles per phase = 8 poles per phase   or   24 poles total

i.e. the synchronous speed is 12.5 rev/s and the total number of poles is 24.

9.6 Synchronous motor

In the synchronous motor, the stator is fed with an a.c. supply which produces a rotating magnetic field just as in the case of the induction motor. The rotor, however, is always constructed as a wound rotor and has a separate d.c. supply fed to the winding via slip rings. This means that the rotor can run at synchronous speed and does not depend on induced rotor currents to produce torque. The synchronous-motor torque/speed characteristic is shown in fig. 9.9.

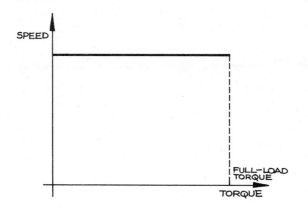

Fig. 9.9 Speed/torque characteristic for a synchronous motor

Notice that the speed remains constant with torque loading up to full-load, above which point it will stall.

Synchronous motors are highly efficient in converting electrical power into mechanical power, but they require an additional d.c. supply and are often more costly than induction motors. They are used in applications which require an improved economy of drive, but allowance must be made for their starting requirements. They are also used as an alternative to large capacitor banks for power-factor correction (see section 2.11). Small synchronous motors are used in electric clocks.

Exercises on chapter 9

1 Explain briefly the difference between a squirrel-cage rotor and a wound rotor of a three-phase induction motor, giving one advantage and one disadvantage of each type.

Explain briefly why induction motors are unsuitable for applications where a large speed variation is required.

A three-phase induction motor with two pole pairs per phase is supplied at 50 Hz. Calculate (a) the synchronous speed, (b) the fractional slip if the rotor speed is 1440 rev/min.   [1500 rev/min; 0.04]

2 Sketch on the same axes the speed/torque characteristics for d.c. series and shunt motors and for a three-phase induction motor. Compare the d.c. and a.c. motors with regard to speed range, cost, and application.

3 a) Explain with sketches how a rotating magnetic field may be produced with three-phase currents.

b) A three-phase four-pole induction motor runs at 1450 rev/min on a 50 Hz supply. What is the 'slip'? What would be the effect on slip and torque of introducing resistance into the rotor circuit?   [0.033]

4 Explain the principle of operation of a three-phase induction motor. Deduce an expression for its synchronous speed in terms of its number of poles per phase and the supply frequency. Why is the rotor speed always lower than the synchronous speed?

A certain motor is running at 24 rev/s with a slip of 4.0% on a 50 Hz supply. Calculate the total number of poles on the machine.   [12]

5 a) Given that a rotating magnetic field is produced by the stator, explain with the aid of a sketch how torque is produced in the rotor of an induction motor.

b) Explain why an induction motor running at synchronous speed cannot produce torque.

c) A three-phase induction motor runs at 1470 rev/min on a 50 Hz supply with a slip of 2%. Calculate the number of poles per phase and the frequency of the rotor currents.   [4; 1 Hz]

6 Define the terms 'synchronous speed' and 'per-unit slip' as applied to a three-phase induction motor.

A three-phase induction motor operates from a supply of 50 Hz frequency. The rotor speed is 16.3 rev/s when the per-unit slip is 0.024. Calculate the number of poles for which the machine is wound, and its synchronous speed. [18; 16.67 rev/s]

7 a) Show how a uniform rotating field may be produced by a two-phase supply.

b) Show that, if the fields produced by the two phases are $\Phi \sin \omega t$ and $\Phi \sin (\omega t - 90°)$, the resultant field has a constant value and rotates at synchronous speed. Indicate the direction of rotation.

c) What is the synchronous speed of a two-phase two-pole motor on a 50 Hz supply?   [3000 rev/min]

8   a) Show using waveforms how a rotating magnetic field may be produced by an a.c. supply with two phases separated by $90°$ and why this type of motor is particularly suitable for use as an a.c. servo-motor.

b) Calculate the slip and frequency of the rotor current of a three-phase six-pole induction motor running at 980 rev/min if its stator voltage is supplied at a frequency of 50 Hz.   [0.02; 1 Hz]

9   a) Explain why a synchronous motor cannot run at less than synchronous speed.

b) A four-pole synchronous motor runs at a speed of 1650 rev/min when connected to a three-phase a.c. supply. A six-pole induction motor having a full-load slip of 4% is connected to the same supply. Calculate (i) the rotor speed, (ii) the slip speed.   [1056 rev/min; 44 rev/min]

10   A 4 kW induction motor runs from a 250 V single-phase 50 Hz a.c. supply at a power factor of 0.8 lagging. Calculate (a) the current, (b) the reactive power taken by the motor, (c) the capacitance to be connected in parallel with the motor to improve the overall power factor to 0.95 lagging.   [20 A; 3 kV Ar; 86 μF]

10 Measuring instruments and measurements

10.1 Introduction
Measurement of electrical quantities is important in all branches of electrical and electronic engineering, and the electrical engineer must be capable of choosing the correct instrument to perform the required measurement.

The correct instrument is the one which performs the required measurement with the minimum amount of error, but of course it is quite possible to perform a measurement without realising that the reading is in error.

To perform accurate measurements it is necessary to become familiar with the limitations of the various measuring instruments, and also to be prepared to perform cross-checks using other instruments.

In this chapter we shall consider the limitations of direct-acting measuring instruments and discuss how the use of electronic instruments can overcome some of these limitations. We shall also consider the use of the cathode-ray oscilloscope (CRO) to measure frequency, phase, and waveform distortion; and the measurement of inductance, capacitance, and resistance using an a.c. bridge. Q-factor and dB measurement are also covered.

10.2 Measuring-instrument limitations
Since we are most concerned with measurement of voltage and current, we shall restrict this section to a discussion of the limitations of direct-acting voltmeters and ammeters, although the basic principles are applicable to all instruments.

You will have already considered the use of the moving-coil instrument, the moving-iron instrument, and the multimeter to measure voltage and current. It is useful to bear these instruments in mind when considering the features which must be taken into consideration when choosing a measuring instrument.

As a first step when using an instrument which is unfamiliar, you should read the information which is on the instrument itself. Useful information such as frequency limitations and loading effects is often available from this source. The second step is to read the operating instructions provided in the instrument manual.

As an example of the features which should be considered, the following features are relevant to voltage-measuring instruments.

a) Is the instrument suitable for measuring d.c. and a.c.?
An obvious question, but one to note. For example the rectifier/moving-coil instrument is calibrated only for a.c. measurements. It will given an approximate reading on d.c., but the reading will be in error.

b) What is the frequency limitation of the instrument?

Most a.c. voltmeters and multimeters are accurate only up to about 10 kHz or 20 kHz. This information is often provided on the instrument itself. Electronic voltmeters are available for high-frequency measurements.

c) What is the impedance of the instrument?

It is quite often not reliable to measure a d.c. or an a.c. voltage with a multimeter, due to the *loading* effect of the instrument resistance, even though in all other respects the instrument is satisfactory. Multimeters of either the analogue or digital type often have an input resistance of the order of only 20 kΩ on the 1 volt scale. The input resistance of oscilloscopes and electronic voltmeters is much higher – of the order of 10 MΩ.

The input resistance of a multimeter is specified on the instrument case. The value of input resistance depends on the range setting used, since each voltage range setting uses a different multiplier resistor in series with the meter. This means that the input resistance is higher on say the 10 V range than it is on the 1 V range (although the sensitivity is correspondingly reduced). For this reason the manufacturer specifies the instrument input resistance in terms of ohms per volt (Ω/V). To find the actual value of input resistance, the user must multiply the Ω/V by the voltage at full-scale deflection (f.s.d.) for the particular range chosen (*not* by the voltage being measured).

Example 1 The d.c. voltage between the points BC in fig. 10.1 is measured using a multimeter which is specified as having an input resistance of 20 kΩ/V. Calculate (a) the true voltage across BC, (b) the voltage that would be measured with the multimeter on the 10 V scale, and (c) the percentage error in the reading.

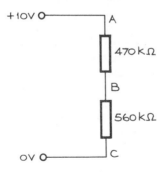

Fig. 10.1

a) True voltage $= \left(\dfrac{560\,\text{k}\Omega}{560\,\text{k}\Omega + 470\,\text{k}\Omega} \right) \times 10\,\text{V}$

$= 5.44\,\text{V}$

199

b)   On the 10 V range the multimeter input resistance is $20\,\mathrm{k\Omega/V} \times 10\,\mathrm{V} = 200\,\mathrm{k\Omega}$. This meter resistance is effectively in parallel with the $560\,\mathrm{k\Omega}$ resistor.

$$\text{Parallel combination} = \frac{560\,\mathrm{k\Omega} \times 200\,\mathrm{k\Omega}}{560\,\mathrm{k\Omega} + 200\,\mathrm{k\Omega}} = 147\,\mathrm{k\Omega}$$

$\therefore$ $\text{measured voltage} = \left(\dfrac{147\,\mathrm{k\Omega}}{147\,\mathrm{k\Omega} + 470\,\mathrm{k\Omega}}\right) \times 10\,\mathrm{V} = 2.38\,\mathrm{V}$

c) $\text{Percentage error} = \dfrac{5.44\,\mathrm{V} - 2.38\,\mathrm{V}}{5.44\,\mathrm{V}} \times 100\%$

$$= 56\%$$

i.e. the true voltage is 5.44 V and the measured voltage is 2.38 V, giving an error in the measurement of 56%.

d) What is the instrument range?
For measuring low voltages, less than say 1 V, an electronic voltmeter is generally chosen, since it provides for accurate measurement of voltages down to about $1\,\mu\mathrm{V}$.

For measuring high voltages, greater than say 500 V, a high-voltage multiplier may be used or an electrostatic voltmeter. Alternatively, a voltage step-down transformer may be used for a.c.

e) Does the instrument read true r.m.s. quantities?
Some instruments, such as the rectifier/moving-coil instrument, are calibrated only for use with purely sinusoidal waveforms. If the waveform is non-sinusoidal, such as a square or triangular waveform, or contains harmonics, then these instruments will give incorrect readings of the r.m.s. value of the waveform. They are said to suffer from 'waveform error'.

Other instruments, such as the thermocouple instrument or electronic equivalents called 'true r.m.s.' voltmeters, are specifically designed to measure r.m.s. values irrespective of the waveform.

Since many waveforms in practice have some harmonic content (see section 10.5), this feature should be considered when performing measurements.

f) Is the instrument accuracy sufficient?
The accuracy of an instrument is the closeness with which the measured value agrees with the true value of the quantity being measured. British Standard BS 89:1977 for 'direct-acting indicating electrical instruments and their accessories' specifies accuracy classes. Instruments may thus be classified according to the accuracy class to which they belong. These classes are specified as 0.05, 0.1, 0.2, 0.5, 1, 1.5, 2.5, and 5.

The accuracy class is in fact the maximum permissible percentage error of the instrument; for example, an instrument in accuracy class 0.5 may have an error not exceeding 0.5%, and so on. The accuracy class states the accuracy to which the instrument has been calibrated and is generally marked on the instrument dial.

Electronic instruments have accuracies specified by the manufacturer.

It is important that measuring instruments are regularly recalibrated. In some cases manufacturers will perform recalibration; alternatively, there are various companies throughout the country who specialise in instrument recalibration. Ideally, recalibration standards laboratories should be listed members of the British Calibration Service (BCS) scheme which issues approval certificates to satisfactory calibration organisations.

It is the responsibility of the instrument user to ensure that the instrument is recalibrated at least annually if measurements are to be at all reliable.

g) What is the instrument resolution?

Resolution is the fineness to which an instrument can be read. 'Pointer-on-dial' instruments generally have poorer resolution than 'digital-display' instruments. With a three-figure digital display the instrument can resolve to 1 in 999 (about 0.1%). With a pointer instrument it is difficult to resolve to better than 0.5%.

It should be realised that an instrument may resolve to 0.1% but only be accurate to say 0.5%.

The features of moving-coil and moving-iron instruments are given below. Table 10.1 shows the features of a variety of direct-acting indicating instuments.

Features of moving-coil instruments
 i) Measure d.c. only.
 ii) High sensitivity and low power consumption.
 iii) Linear scale.
 iv) Not much affected by stray magnetic fields.
 v) May be used as d.c. ammeter with shunt.
 vi) May be used as d.c. voltmeter with multiplier resistor.
 vii) Damping by eddy currents in the coil former.

Features of moving-iron instruments
 i) Measure d.c. and a.c. voltage and current.
 ii) Non-linear scale.
 iii) Robust and inexpensive.
 iv) Only accurate for frequencies below about 100 Hz.
 v) May be used as ammeter or voltmeter, but current shunts should not be used.
 vi) Theoretically true r.m.s., but errors occur with peaky waveforms.

Table 10.1 Features of direct-acting indicating instruments

Instrument	D.C./A.C.	Scale	Features
Moving-coil	D.C. only	Linear	High sensitivity
Moving-iron	D.C. and a.c. up to 100 Hz	Non-linear	Reads true r.m.s.
Dynamometer	D.C. and a.c. up to 60 Hz as a voltmeter	Non-linear	Reads true r.m.s.
Rectifier/ moving-coil	A.C. only, 25 Hz to 20 kHz	Linear	Average-responding
Thermocouple	D.C. and a.c., 50 Hz to 20 MHz	Non-linear	True r.m.s. Easily overloaded

Example 2 Five instrument specifications are to be matched with five instrument types. From the list of instruments, select the type most suitable for each specification.

Specifications:

1. a.c./d.c., non-linear scale, r.m.s.-responding, 25 Hz to 60 Hz
2. a.c. only, linear scale, average-responding, 25 Hz to 20 kHz
3. d.c. only, linear scale, high sensitivity
4. a.c./d.c. non-linear scale, r.m.s.-responding, 25 Hz to 100 Hz
5. a.c./d.c. non-linear scale, true r.m.s., 50 Hz to 20 MHz, easily overloaded

Instruments:

A moving-coil voltmeter
B moving-iron ammeter
C dynamometer ammeter
D thermocouple ammeter
E moving-coil/rectifier voltmeter

Answers: 1–C   2–E   3–A   4–B   5–D

10.3 Electronic voltmeters

Electronic voltmeters overcome some of the limitations experienced with direct-acting instruments. They are, of course, more expensive. In general they have a high frequency response and a high input resistance.

Various types of electronic voltmeter are available. They include general-purpose a.c./d.c. electronic voltmeters and electronic multimeters; radio-frequency electronic voltmeters for performing radio-frequency measurements; d.c. microvoltmeters for measurement of d.c. voltages down to microvolts range; differential d.c. voltmeters for very accurate measurement of d.c. voltages (0.02%), with high input resistance (100 MΩ); and true r.m.s. voltmeters for measurement of r.m.s. voltage irrespective of the waveform.

A.C. voltmeters may be average-responding, peak-responding, or r.m.s.-responding, but in each case it is generally the r.m.s. value that is of interest and these instruments are therefore usually calibrated in r.m.s.

The most common type of a.c. electronic voltmeter is average-responding. The waveform to be measured is rectified and amplified and fed to a conventional moving-coil meter. This of course means that it is not a true r.m.s. voltmeter type.

Average-responding electronic voltmeters take two basic forms:

a) a.c. amplifier/rectifier types,
b) rectifier/d.c. amplifier types.

a) A.C. amplifier/rectifier type
The arrangement is shown in fig. 10.2. The input is applied via a high-impedance attenuator. The voltage is then amplified using a wideband

Fig. 10.2   Electronic voltmeter – a.c. amplifier/rectifier type

amplifier and rectified. The instrument is usually calibrated in r.m.s., although there will be some waveform error if the waveform is non-sinusoidal. The frequency response is limited by the bandwidth of the a.c. amplifier (see section 2.12). Typical performance figures are:

Input resistance   10 MΩ
Voltage range   100 μV to 300 V
Frequency range   10 Hz to 10 MHz
Accuracy   1% to 5%, depending on frequency

b) Rectifier/d.c. amplifier type
This type has the advantage that it may be used for measurement of a.c. and d.c. voltages. It is shown in fig. 10.3. When used for measuring a.c. voltages, the waveform is first rectified and then amplified by a d.c. amplifier. The

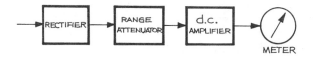

Fig. 10.3 Electronic voltmeter –rectifier/d.c. amplifier type

frequency response is thus limited only by the capacitance of the rectifier. The sensitivity of this type is, however, less than that of the a.c. amplifier/ rectifier type. When used for measurement of d.c. voltages the rectifier is excluded.

Typical performance figures are

for a.c. measurement·

Input resistance   5 MΩ at 1 kHz
Voltage range   25 mV to 300 V
Frequency range   20 Hz to 1500 MHz
Accuracy   2% to 3%

for d.c. measurement:

Input resistance   100 MΩ
Voltage range   10 mV to 1000 V
Accuracy   2%

A typical example is shown in fig. 10.4.

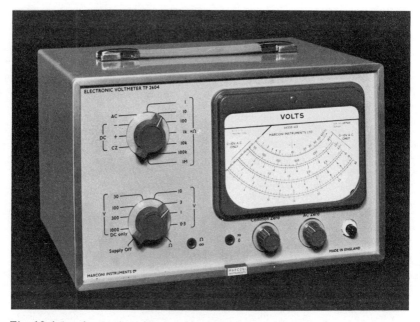

Fig. 10.4 An electronic voltmeter for precision measurement of a.c. voltages within the range 20 Hz to 1500 MHz with further facilities included for measurement of a wide range of d.c. voltages and resistance

10.4 True r.m.s. voltmeter
One method of obtaining a true measurement of the r.m.s. value of a wave- form is to use a thermocouple instrument. The instrument measures the heating

effect of the waveform and gives a correct measurement irrespective of the waveform. However, these instruments have a sensitivity which is limited by the thermocouple. Maximum frequency response is about 20 MHz, while the minimum frequency response is about 50 Hz because the thermocouple output will follow a low-frequency wave rather than provide the r.m.s. value.

An alternative non-thermal true r.m.s. voltmeter uses an analogue circuit which has a square-law transfer function similar to that of a thermocouple.

10.5 Harmonic content of waveforms

The inherent error of an average-responding instrument is a function of the magnitude of the distortion of the waveform being measured from a pure sine wave, and of the harmonic content and phase of the distortion. The most commonly occurring harmonic distortions of sinusoidal waveforms are second- and third-harmonic (i.e. sine waves of two or three times the fundamental superimposed on the fundamental frequency).

Harmonic distortion is most readily seen by displaying the waveform on a cathode-ray oscilloscope. Examples of second-harmonic distortion are shown in fig. 10.5 and third-harmonic distortion in fig. 10.6.

For measurements of a.c. voltages with about 10% of second-harmonic distortion, the measurement error ranges from about 0.1% to 0.5% depending on the phase relationship. (The degree of harmonic distortion is usually given as 'percentage harmonic distortion'. This is the ratio of the r.m.s. value of the harmonic to the r.m.s. value of the fundamental and is measured by using a harmonic-distortion meter.)

With 10% of third-harmonic distortion the measurement error ranges from about +3% to −4%, depending on the phase.

It is evident that second-harmonic distortion introduces only a small error into the measurement of an r.m.s. value using an average-responding instrument. The error introduced by third-harmonic content is slightly higher.

Whether the required accuracy of measurement justifies the cost of the purchase of a true r.m.s. voltmeter depends on the requirements of the user.

10.6 Use of the CRO

In order to inspect the shape of a waveform, a cathode-ray oscilloscope (normally abbreviated to 'CRO' or 'scope') is an essential instrument. It may be used to make reasonably accurate measurement of voltage amplitude and frequency; to compare the phase relationship of two waveforms; to determine whether the waveform is sinusoidal, square, triangular, etc.; or to give an indication of the degree of distortion.

The CRO has a good frequency response, typically of the order of 30 MHz, and a high impedance of the order of 10 MΩ.

Use of the CRO to measure waveforms

The oscilloscope provides an accurate method of measuring the peak value and frequency of a waveform. For waveforms which are well defined – such as sine, square, triangular, sawtooth, etc. – the ratio of the peak value to the r.m.s. value is defined as the *crest factor* and is readily calculated. Since the CRO can

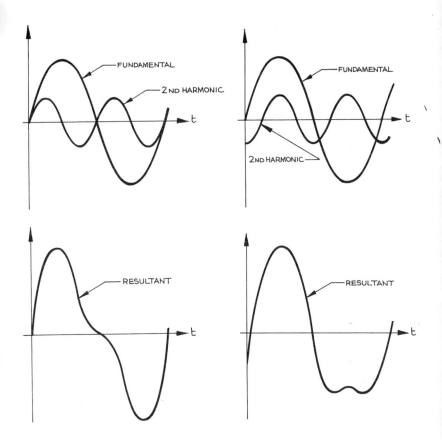

Fig. 10.5 Second-harmonic distortion

only be used to measure the peak value, it is necessary to know the crest factor to be able to calculate the r.m.s. value. The crest factors of some commonly encountered waveforms are given in Table 10.2.

Table 10.2 Crest factors of common waveforms

Waveform	Crest factor
Sine wave	1.41
Square wave	1.00
Triangular wave	1.74
Sawtooth	1.74
Full-wave rectified sine wave	1.41
Half-wave rectified sine wave	2.0
Pulse waveform (16 : 1 duty cycle)	4.0

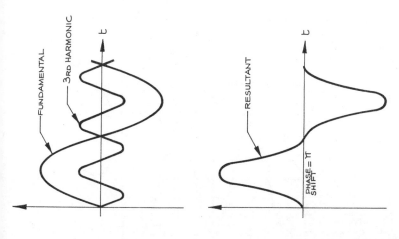
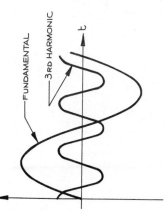
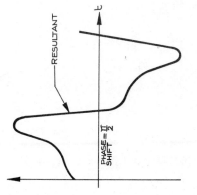
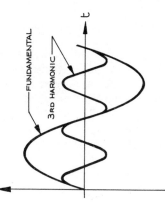
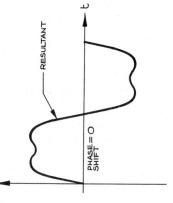

Fig. 10.6 Third-harmonic distortion

Example   For the waveform displayed in fig. 10.7, calculate (a) V_{p-p}, (b) V_p, (c) $V_{r.m.s.}$, (d) $V_{av.(half\text{-}wave)}$, and (e) the frequency. Assume that the amplitude scaling is 10 V/cm and the time base 100 ms/cm.

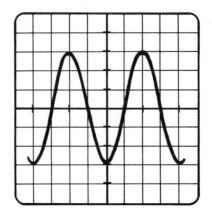

Fig. 10.7

a) V_{p-p} = 60 V

b) V_p = 30 V

c) $V_{r.m.s.} = \dfrac{V_p}{\sqrt{2}} = \dfrac{30\,V}{\sqrt{2}} = 21.21\,V$

d) $V_{av.(half\text{-}wave)}$ = 0.637 × 30 V = 19.11 V

e)   Waveform period T = 400 ms

$\therefore \quad f = \dfrac{1}{T} = \dfrac{1}{400 \times 10^{-3}}$ Hz = 2.5 Hz

To measure current waveforms, the current may be passed through an accurately known resistor as shown in fig. 10.8(a) and the CRO be used to measure the voltage across the resistor. A more commonly used alternative is a current probe as shown in fig. 10.8(b). This is a type of current transformer in which the core may be opened to allow for the insertion of the current-carrying conductor. This is of course suitable only for a.c. waveforms and gives sensitivities of 1 mA/V over a bandwidth of 1 kHz to 200 MHz. A similar probe incorporating a Hall-effect device is available for d.c. currents. (The Hall effect is a magnetic effect in which a probe of semiconductor material carrying a current and situated in a magnetic field at right angles to the plane of the probe will have a voltage produced across the probe proportional to the magnitude of the magnetic flux.)

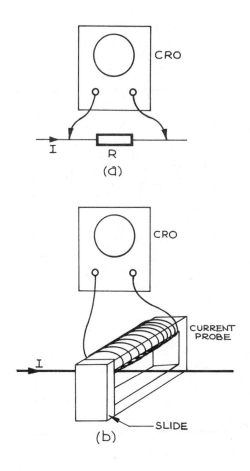

Fig. 10.8 Use of CRO to measure current

10.7 Use of the CRO to measure phase and frequency

Phase measurement
A CRO may be used to measure the phase relationship between two wave-forms. There are two methods.

a) The dual-trace method The horizontal axes of the two waveforms are lined up as shown in fig. 10.9 and then measurement is made of t and T. The phase angle is then found from

$$\frac{\phi}{360°} = \frac{t}{T}$$

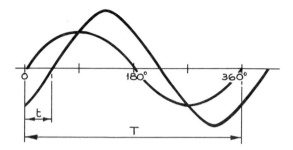

Fig. 10.9 Two waveforms out of phase

b) Lissajou's figures By connecting one waveform to the Y-plate and the other to the X-plate (and therefore disconnecting the time base), a figure is displayed on the CRO screen which depends on the phase relationship between the two waveforms. Several examples are shown in fig. 10.10 for sinusoidal waveforms of the same frequency.

The phase relationships in these figures are

a) in-phase
b) $90°$ out-of-phase,
c) $180°$ out-of-phase,
d) between 0 and $90°$ out-of-phase.

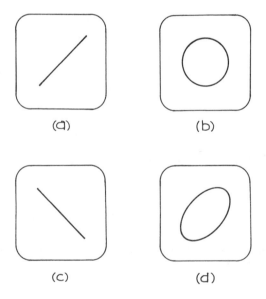

Fig. 10.10 Use of Lissajou's figures for phase measurement: (a) in-phase, (b) $90°$ out-of-phase, (c) $180°$ out-of-phase, (d) 0–$90°$ out-of-phase

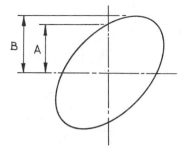

Fig. 10.11

The method of calculating the phase relationship is shown in fig. 10.11, where the phase difference ϕ is given by

$$\sin \phi = \frac{A}{B}$$

Frequency measurement
The method of Lissajou's figures may also be used to compare the frequencies of two waveforms. In the examples shown in fig. 10.12, the frequency relationships are

a) 2 : 1
b) 3 : 2

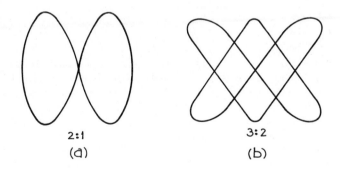

2:1
(a)

3:2
(b)

Fig. 10.12 Use of Lissajou's figures for frequency measurement

An alternative method of measuring phase and frequency is to use a phase meter or a frequency meter.

10.8 A.C. bridges
The measurement of values of passive components such as inductance L, capacitance C, and resistance R is carried out using a 'universal a.c. bridge'.

This is a standard piece of laboratory equipment sometimes called an 'L-C-R bridge'.

The a.c. bridge is similar to a Wheatstone bridge, except that the supply is an alternating one and the detector must therefore be sensitive to alternating currents.

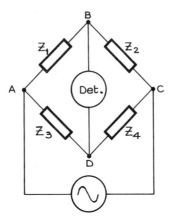

Fig. 10.13 Basic a.c. bridge

The basis of the a.c. bridge is shown in fig. 10.13. The bridge is said to be balanced when the current through the detector is zero. At balance,

$$\frac{Z_1}{Z_2} = \frac{Z_3}{Z_4}$$

One of the bridge arms contains the unknown impedance to be measured, and the other arms contain fixed or variable comparison standards. Balance is more difficult to achieve than with the Wheatstone bridge, since both the magnitude and phase of the voltages at B and D must be equal to obtain a balance. This means that balance is achieved by successive adjustment of *two* variable standard components. When balance is achieved, the unknown impedance may be expressed in terms of the comparison standards.

There is a wide variety of a.c. bridges used for measurement of inductance and capacitance.

Example 1   As an example of the method of derivation of the balance conditions for an a.c. bridge, fig. 10.14 shows the Owen bridge which is used to measure the inductance L and resistance r of a coil by using fixed and variable standard resistors and capacitors. By suitable choice of bridge components, a wide range of inductance values can be measured.

From the original equation,

$$Z_1 Z_4 = Z_2 Z_3$$

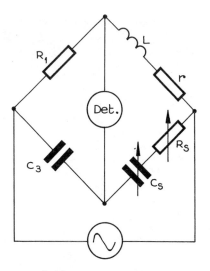

Fig. 10.14 The Owen a.c. bridge

$$\therefore \quad R_1 \left(R_s + \frac{1}{j\omega C_s} \right) = (r + j\omega L) \times \frac{1}{j\omega C_3}$$

Equating the imaginary (quadrature) terms,

$$r = R_1 \frac{C_3}{C_s}$$

Equating the real (in-phase) terms,

$$L = C_3 R_1 R_s$$

Notice that two variable standards are required: C_s and R_s.

A typical commercially available 'universal bridge' is shown in fig. 10.15. It is a self-contained instrument with an internal 1 kHz oscillator for a.c. measurements of L, C, and R; or a 9 V battery for d.c. measurements of R. Facilities are provided for the application of external a.c. or d.c. supplies for measurements over an alternative range of frequencies.

The component to be measured is connected across the two large terminals and the selector switch is turned to select L, C, or R measurement. Balancing the bridge entails adjusting the main BALANCE controls, in conjunction with the LOSS BALANCE control for reactive components, in order to bring the meter to as near zero deflection as possible. The SENSITIVITY control allows the detector sensitivity to be reduced for a clearer meter indication of approaching balance with components of unknown value. The main BALANCE controls consist of a RANGE MULTIPLIER switch linked to a variable control.

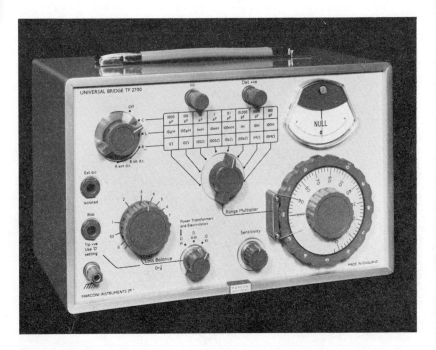

Fig. 10.15 A universal bridge for measurement of inductance, capacitance, and resistance

The LOSS BALANCE control is used to balance out the resistive loss of the inductor or capacitor under test, so that the true reactance of the component may be measured more accurately. In addition to measuring the value of a component, this LOSS BALANCE provides a measure of the dissipation factor D or of the Q factor of the component.

When measuring capacitors on this bridge the LOSS BALANCE controls are normally set to D, which gives the result in terms of a series capacitance C_s and a series resistance R_s.

The dissipation factor is given by

$$D = 2\pi f C_s R_s$$

Measurements on inductors are more dependent on their core loss for LOSS BALANCE setting. Normal air-cored coils are measured in terms of series inductance L_s and series resistance R_s, with the LOSS BALANCE at the Q setting.

Here $$Q = \frac{2\pi f L_s}{R_s}$$

High-Q coils, such as ferrite-cored filter coils and laminated iron-cored inductors, are measured in terms of parallel values L_p and R_p on the D range. In this case the Q factor may be easily obtained from the relationship

214

$$Q = \frac{1}{D}$$

Also, at values of Q greater than 10, $L_p \simeq L_s$ (within 1%).

The minimum deflection on the meter is obtained by alternate adjustment of the BALANCE and the LOSS BALANCE controls.

For further details, the manufacturer's operating instructions should be consulted.

Example 2   A coil is measured on a universal bridge and a minimum deflection is obtained with the balance control set at 12.7 mH and the loss-balance control set at a dissipation factor of 0.02. Calculate the Q factor of the coil and the effective series loss resistance of the coil. Assume the measurements are taken using the internal oscillator of frequency 1 kHz.

$$Q = 1/D$$

where $D = 0.02$

$\therefore$ $Q = 1/0.02 = 50$

Now $Q = \dfrac{2\pi f L_s}{R_s}$

$\therefore$ $R_s = \dfrac{2\pi f L_s}{Q}$

For values of $Q > 10$, $L_p \simeq L_s$

$\therefore$ $L_s = L_p = 12.7 \, \text{mH} = 12.7 \times 10^{-3} \, \text{H}$

and $f = 1 \, \text{kHz} = 10^3 \, \text{Hz}$

$\therefore$ $R_s = \dfrac{2\pi \times 10^3 \, \text{Hz} \times 12.7 \times 10^{-3} \, \text{H}}{50} = 1.6 \, \Omega$

i.e. the coil Q factor is 50 and the effective series resistance is 1.6 Ω.

10.9 The decibel

It is sometimes convenient to express the ratio of two powers P_1 and P_2 in logarithmic form. If a logarithm to base 10 is used, the ratio is measured in *bels*. Since this is a rather large unit, the decibel (abbreviation dB) is used:

$$\text{power ratio in decibels} = 10 \log_{10} \frac{P_2}{P_1}$$

It was originally intended that 1 dB would approximate to the smallest power-level difference detectable to the human ear. In fact about 2.5 dB is the smallest audible change.

One advantage of the use of a logarithmic scale is that, if it is required to calculate the overall power gain of a number of amplifiers in cascade (i.e.

connected serially), then the overall dB gain is simply found by *adding* the individual dB gains.

If a reference power is adopted for P_1, then the decibel can be used to state absolute power. The usual reference level is 1 mW, and the symbol dBm is used to indicate that 1 mW is used as the reference. Thus a power level of say 5 W corresponds to

$$10 \log_{10} \frac{5\,\text{W}}{1\,\text{mW}} = 37\,\text{dBm}$$

whereas a power level of 0.5 mW corresponds to

$$10 \log_{10} \frac{0.5\,\text{mW}}{1\,\text{mW}} = -3\,\text{dBm}$$

Notice that the minus sign indicates a power level below the reference, while a positive sign indicates a larger power than the reference.

The decibel in terms of voltage and current ratios

Power ratio may be expressed in decibels as

$$\text{power ratio in dB} = 10 \log_{10} \frac{P_2}{P_1}$$

If power P_1 is dissipated in resistance R_1 and P_2 in resistance R_2, then

$$\text{power ratio in dB} = 10 \log_{10} \frac{V_2{}^2/R_2}{V_1{}^2/R_1}$$

Now, if we arrange that $R_1 = R_2$, then

$$\text{power ratio in dB} = 10 \log_{10} \left(\frac{V_2}{V_1} \right)^2$$

$$= 20 \log_{10} \frac{V_2}{V_1}$$

Voltage gains of amplifiers are often stated in dB using this equation. Strictly speaking, the equation should not be used if the resistances are not the same, but in practice it is used extensively.

In many communication systems, source and load resistances are arranged to have a standard value of 600 Ω for impedance matching (see section 2.13). In this case the equations may be used correctly.

Example An amplifier has an input voltage of 100 mV and an output voltage of 14.5 V. Calculate the dB gain, assuming that the input and load resistances are equal. What attenuation would need to be inserted in series with the amplifier to reduce the overall gain to 100?

Now   dB gain $= 20 \log_{10} \dfrac{V_2}{V_1}$

$$= 20 \log_{10} \dfrac{14.5\,\text{V}}{0.1\,\text{V}}$$

$$= 43.2\,\text{dB}$$

An overall gain of 100 is an overall dB gain of

$$20 \log_{10} 100 = 40\,\text{dB}$$

$\therefore$ required attennuation $= 43.2\,\text{dB} - 40\,\text{dB}$

$$= 3.2\,\text{dB}$$

i.e. the amplifier gain is 43.2 dB, and to reduce the overall gain to 100 requires the insertion of a network with -3.2 dB gain.

The dB ratio may be expressed in terms of the current instead of the voltage, since

power ratio in dB $= 10 \log_{10} \dfrac{P_2}{P_1}$

$$= 10 \log_{10} \dfrac{I_2{}^2 R}{I_1{}^2 R}$$

$$= 20 \log_{10} \dfrac{I_2}{I_1}$$

Exercises on chapter 10
1   Five common types of electrical indicating instrument are classified as moving-coil, moving-iron, dynamometer, rectifier, and thermocouple. State which types are suitable for measurement of (a) alternating and direct current or voltage, (b) direct current or voltage only, (c) alternating current or voltage only.

An a.c. voltmeter is required to measure a sinusoidal voltage in the range 0 to 10 V (r.m.s.) within a frequency range of 50 Hz to 10 kHz. State which of the above types of instrument would be suitable, giving reasons for the choice.
2   State, giving brief reasons, the type of voltmeter which would be selected for each of the following specifications: (a) d.c./a.c., 25 Hz to 100 Hz, r.m.s.-responding; (b) d.c./a.c., 25 Hz to 1 MHz, peak-responding; (c) a.c., 25 Hz to 20 kHz, average-responding; (d) square wave, 25 Hz to 10 kHz with minimum waveform error.
3   State, giving brief reasons, the type of instrument that would be most suitable for performing each of the following measurements: (a) high-tension

voltage from a d.c. power-supply unit (250 V, 500 mA, 50 Hz); (b) base current of a transistor (20 μA, 0.6 V d.c.); (c) cathode-ray tube, cathode-to-earth voltage (20 kV d.c.); (d) voltage across a tuned i.f. circuit (4 V, 470 kHz); (e) the voltage across a semiconductor diode when obtaining the reverse leakage characteristic (30 V).

4   State the type and approximate range of instrument required for use in each of the following circuits: (a) to measure the current in the shunt field circuit of a d.c. generator having a maximum output of 5 kW at 200 V; (b) to measure the p.d. across a capacitor rated at 3.3 μF, 350 V d.c. max.; (c) to measure the collector current of a single-stage audio transistor amplifier in common-emitter configuration; (d) to measure the output voltage of a tuned radio-frequency amplifier; (e) to measure the true r.m.s. voltage of a square wave of frequency 10 kHz.

5   Show how an alternating voltage may be measured using a diode, a d.c. amplifier, and a moving-coil milliammeter. Give a typical frequency response that you would expect of this instrument and explain what is meant by 'waveform error' with reference to this type of voltmeter.

6   A d.c. milliammeter with a full-scale deflection of 1 mA is converted into an a.c. voltmeter by connecting it in series with a suitable resistor and a single rectifier diode. Neglecting the effects of the resistances of the milliammeter and the rectifier element, calculate the value of the series resistor in order that the full-scale reading as an a.c. voltmeter may be 200 V, assuming a sinusoidal waveform. State whether the instrument would be suitable for measurement of 200 V d.c., giving reasons for your answer. [90 kΩ]

7   a) With the aid of a circuit diagram, describe a method of obtaining a calibration curve for an a.c. voltmeter (range 0 to 250 V).

   b) A sinusoidal a.c. supply of peak value 155 V is applied to a circuit with the following components in series: (i) a half-wave rectifier with forward resistance 1 Ω and infinite reverse resistance, (ii) a moving-coil ammeter of resistance 0.1 Ω, (iii) a resistor of 23.9 Ω. Calculate the readings obtained on the instrument.   [1.97 A]

8   With the aid of a diagram, explain the operation of an electronic volt-meter. With the aid of a simple circuit, explain how an electronic voltmeter may be used to measure resistance, and compare this with the way in which a multimeter measures resistance.

9   With the aid of diagrams, describe the operation of (a) an a.c. amplifier/ rectifier type of voltmeter and (b) a rectifier/d.c. amplifier type of voltmeter and compare their usefulness in terms of voltage and frequency ranges. Give typical performance figures in each case.

10   Obtain a copy of the manufacturer's instruction manual for one type of electronic a.c. voltmeter and write a brief essay on the instrument, including specification, operating procedure, and any precautions to be taken when using the instrument.

11   A batch of coils all marked as 0.3 H 40 Ω is to be checked to confirm that the inductances are within a tolerance of ± 10%. The test is made using an a.c. bridge, and the following components are available: (a) a standard

fixed capacitor, (b) a standard variable capacitor, (c) two decade resistance boxes, (d) an a.c. voltmeter for use as a detector. Using a circuit diagram, explain how a simple a.c. bridge may be constructed using these components and choose a suitable range for the standard components.

12   Explain why a Wheatstone d.c. bridge requires only one standard variable component while an a.c. bridge requires two. Relate this to the balance controls available on a universal a.c. bridge.

A capacitor is measured on a universal a.c. bridge and balance is obtained with the balance setting at $0.15 \mu F$ and the loss-balance setting at a dissipation factor D of 0.05. Calculate the capacitor series loss resistance and loss angle δ, given that $D = \tan \delta$. (Assume that the bridge internal oscillator frequency is 1 kHz.)   [$53 \Omega; 2.9°$]

13   A $0.2 \mu F \pm 20\%$ capacitor is to be tested on a universal bridge by an unskilled operator. Write brief operating instructions which will allow a pass/ fail test to be carried out.

14   a) With the aid of test-circuit diagrams, describe how a CRO may be used to obtain the following characteristics for an electronic amplifier: (i) the frequency response, (ii) the phase shift.

b) Sketch the front-panel layout of a typical dual-beam CRO and clearly label each main control.

15   A cathode-ray tube is used to measure the phase difference between two sinusoidally alternating voltages of the same frequency by applying one voltage across the X-plates and the other across the Y-plates of the tube. The Y-plate voltage has a peak value of 100 V, and the X-plate voltage has a peak value of 50 V. The deflectional sensitivities of the tube in the X and Y directions are the same at 0.50 mm/V. Draw dimensional sketches showing the pattern of the trace on the screen when the phase difference between the two voltages is (a) $0°$, (b) $60°$, (c) $90°$. Derive an expression which may be used to determine the phase difference from measurements taken from the trace.

16   a) List four measurements that may be carried out using a cathode-ray oscilloscope.

b) Describe two of these in detail showing any necessary connection circuits.

c) State the reasons for using a low-capacitance probe when making high-frequency measurements from a high-impedance source.

d) Explain one method of measuring the phase relationship between two sinusoidal waveforms, using a cathode-ray oscilloscope.

17   A sinusoidal alternating voltage is measured on a CRO using an atten-uation probe with an attenuation factor of 10. The peak-to-peak deflection is 5 cm on the CRO graticule, and the voltage-amplification setting is 2 V/cm. Calculate the r.m.s. value of the voltage.   [35.4 V]

18   a) Explain the advantage of using decibels as a measure of power gain.

b) Calculate the magnitude of the output quantity for each of the following gains: (i) +10 dBm, (ii) −4 dBm, (iii) +5 dB with respect to 1 mV.

c) Two amplifiers, A and B, are connected via an 8 dB voltage attenuator. The voltage gains of A and B are 25 dB and 43 dB respectively. Calculate the overall dB voltage gain and the output voltage of amplifier B if the input to amplifier A is 3 mV. (Assume the attenuator is correctly matched to both amplifiers.)   [60 dB; 3 V]

19   The following table gives the voltage gain of an audio amplifier. The table also shows the reduction of gain in decibels due to the introduction of a negative-feedback circuit. Using log–linear graph paper, plot the graph of voltage gain in dB against log frequency for the amplifier without feedback and with feedback. Calculate the amplifier bandwidth in each case.

Frequency (kHz)	0.04	0.1	0.25	0.5	1.0	2.5	5.0	10	20
Voltage gain	7.92	19.8	34.6	43.5	50	45.5	30	12	3.46
Gain reduction (dB)	4.4	5.5	6.0	6.5	6.6	7.0	6.6	3.8	1.4

11   Thyristors

11.1 Introduction

The term 'thyristor' refers to a group of semiconductor devices which have a very rapid switch-on characteristic. They are all basically four-layer devices, being made up as a p–n–p–n sandwich, and their 'snap-on' switching action is referred to as 'pnpn regenerative feedback'. They can have two, three, or four terminals, depending on the device. Some devices pass current only one way (undirectional), while others pass current both ways (bidirectional).

The most senior and influential member of the family is the silicon controlled rectifier (SCR), which may be referred to as a 'reverse-blocking triode thyristor' or just simply as a 'thyristor'. We shall refer to the SCR as the 'thyristor'.

The thyristor is essentially a power diode which can be switched into the conducting state by a low-power switching signal applied to a control input terminal called the 'gate'. It may be considered as a static latching switch; that is, a device which has no moving parts and which can be switched on or 'latched' by the brief application of a gate control current (for about 1 μs).

The thyristor is not like a transistor and does not require the control current to be maintained once it has latched. As a latching switch it is basically 'on' or 'off' and can therefore handle much more power than a transistor (since power is only dissipated during the switching period). With only a few microwatts of control power, a thyristor can switch hundreds of watts, giving it a power gain of the order of ten million.

Since it has no moving parts, its life is virtually unlimited. It can be hermetically sealed (in a metal can against moisture) and works well under harsh conditions of atmosphere, vibration, and shock.

The range of thyristors available makes it possible to handle currents from tens of milliamperes to more than 1000 amperes at voltages up to several thousand volts.

The main advantages of thyristors are:

a) low 'on' resistance,
b) high 'off' resistance,
c) rapid switching,
d) low control power,
e) long life.

They find particular application in speed control of rotating electrical machines and in heating control, but are also used in a very wide range of other applications such as car ignition circuits, lamp dimmers, and many more.

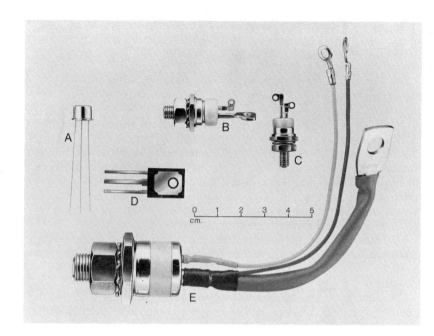

Fig. 11.1 A selection of thyristors, including low-power types (A, B, C) a plastics-encapsulated device primarily for domestic (washing machine) applications (D), and a large 70 A industrial device (E)

A selection of thyristors is shown in fig. 11.1.

11.2 Action of the thyristor
The thyristor (SCR) is a three-terminal device with an anode (A), a cathode (K), and a gate (G). The symbol for a thyristor is shown in fig. 11.2.

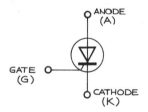

Fig. 11.2 Thyristor symbol (p-gate)

The thyristor is basically a power diode which can be switched into conduction by a signal applied to the control terminal, called the gate. Current will then flow between anode and cathode (but not in the reverse direction).

222

Once in the forward-conducting state, the device conducts like a normal diode and the gate current can be removed without switching the device off. The gate now loses control over the switching of the device and cannot be used to switch it off.

The thyristor is switched off by reducing the anode current below its holding level. (This is normally done by reducing the anode voltage to zero.)

A useful analogy is with a flush toilet – once the handle has been pulled, the handle loses control over the water flow, and flow ceases only when the cistern is empty. (The engineer makes use of analogies to clarify explanations – this rather bizarre analogy was suggested to me by a colleague.)

Example 1 The anode-to-cathode and gate-to-cathode voltages across a thyristor are as shown in fig. 11.3. Sketch the current waveform.

The current waveforms are shown in the figure.

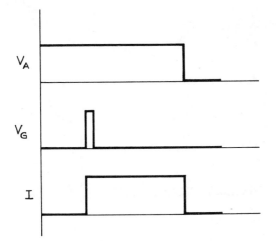

Fig. 11.3

Example 2 Repeat example 1 using fig. 11.4(a) and (b).

The current waveforms are shown in the figures.

11.3 Thyristor operation
The thyristor is a four-layer device as shown in fig. 11.5(a). Its operation may best be understood by considering it as being made up of two transistors as shown in fig. 11.5(b). This two-transistor model is shown in transistor-symbol form in fig. 11.5(c).

One of the transistors is a pnp and the other an npn type. They are interconnected to form a regenerative-feedback pair. This means that the collector current of one provides the base-current drive for the other and vice-versa. We are considering here a p-gate thyristor (referred to as a 'conventional' thyristor).

223

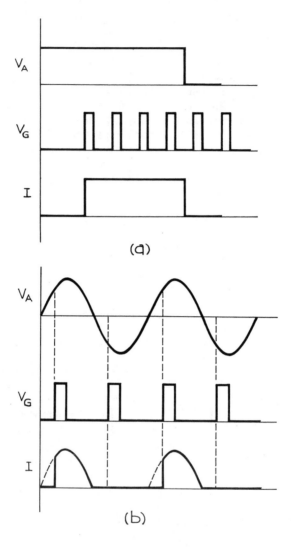

V_A

V_G

I

(a)

V_A

V_G

I

(b)

Fig. 11.4

When normal bias is applied to the thyristor (i.e. with the anode positive and the cathode negative) and there is no gate signal applied, then only leakage current flows through the device. This is called the high-impedance 'off' state or the forward-blocking state. In this condition, the common-base current gain (α) of the transistors is low and the positive feedback around the loop is therefore less than unity.

To switch to the low-impedance 'on' state requires the loop gain to be raised to unity. When this condition occurs, the regenerative feedback action

224

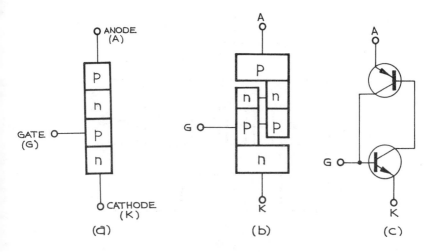

Fig. 11.5 The two-transistor model of a thyristor

takes place and each transistor drives its mate into saturation. All three junctions become forward-biased and the thyristor assumes the characteristic of a single pn diode junction. In this condition the anode current is limited only by the external circuit.

One way of increasing the loop gain to unit is by injecting a pulse of current into the gate (i.e. the base of the npn transistor). This causes an increase in the emitter current of that transistor with a consequent increase in its current gain (α). This provides base-current drive to the pnp which in turn drives the npn further into conduction and triggers off the regenerative action. The gate current can now be removed without the device switching off.

In practice, a pulse of a few volts applied to the gate is sufficient to trigger the thyristor into conduction.

The device just considered is a 'conventional' p-gate thyristor which requires a positive pulse applied to the gate with respect to the cathode. An alternative device is the 'complementary' n-gate thyristor which requires a negative voltage pulse for switch-on.

11.4 Thyristor characteristic

The thyristor (SCR) characteristic is shown in fig. 11.6. It is similar in certain respects to that for a semiconductor diode. In the reverse direction, only a very small leakage current flows until avalanche breakdown occurs. The device must not be allowed to move into this region.

In the forward direction with no applied gate current ($I_G = 0$), the characteristic is similar to that in the reverse direction, and only a small leakage current flows until, at the forward breakover voltage (V_{BO}), avalanche breakdown occurs and the voltage across the thyristor suddenly falls to the on-state voltage (V_T). The thyristor is rarely if ever used in this manner and is more

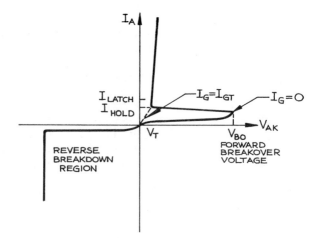

Fig. 11.6 Thyristor characteristic

commonly used at anode voltages below the forward breakover voltage, the
switching being controlled by the gate current.

When a gate current ($I_G = I_{GT}$) is fed to the gate, the characteristic is
similar to that of a forward-biased diode. Provided the anode current exceeds
the latching current, the gate current can now be removed without switching
the thyristor off. The device will remain on as long as the anode current
exceeds the holding-current level.

The thyristor is normally used at voltages below the forward breakover
voltage and it is the characteristic effect of triggering the device into conduction by applying a gate current which is important. Alternative methods of
switching into conduction (such as by exceeding the forward breakover voltage) should be avoided.

11.5 Control methods
Since the thyristor is basically a rapid-action switch, one of its broad areas of
application is in signal and power control.

There are two basic methods of thyristor control:

a) *static switching*, in which thyristors are used to perform simple switching
   where they open or close a circuit *completely*, rather like a non-static switch
b) *a.c. phase control*, in which they thyristor is used to connect an a.c. supply
   to the load for a *controlled fraction of each cycle*. By this means, the
   average power delivered to a load may be accurately controlled.

A further technique which is rapidly becoming popular is *zero-voltage
switching*, which is considered at the end of this section.

Static switching

Static-switching circuits may be either a.c. or d.c. Static a.c. switching uses an a.c. supply, and the reversal of the voltage waveform is used as the means of turning the thyristor off. In d.c. static-switching circuits, some alternative circuit arrangement must be made for switching the thyristor off. We shall consider only static a.c. switching.

A simple arrangement is shown in fig. 11.7(a). An electromechanical switch such a relay may be used to switch the supply on to the gate. The thyristor then conducts during the period that the switch is closed. A typical gate-control voltage waveform is shown in fig. 11.7(b), and the corresponding load current may be seen to flow for this period during positive half cycles

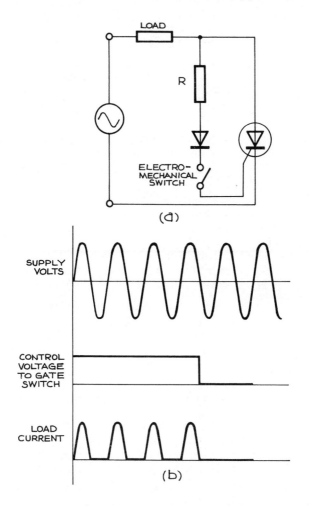

Fig. 11.7 A simple static switching circuit for a thyristor and its waveforms

227

of the supply voltage. The thyristor acts as a half-wave rectifier while switched on. The diode in the gate circuit is to prevent reverse current flowing through the thyristor gate.

The use of a reed switch operated by a small d.c. coil allows complete electrical isolation between the control circuit and the switched power output.

If full-wave operation is required, then the thyristor may be replaced by a triac (discussed in section 11.8). This device allows conduction on both halves of the a.c. waveform and therefore makes the arrangement suitable for switching on and off loads such as induction motors.

An alternative arrangement for full-wave operation is to use a diode-bridge circuit as shown in fig. 11.8(a), giving a current waveform as in fig. 11.8(b).

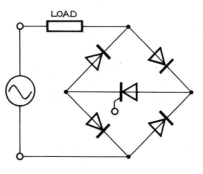

(a)

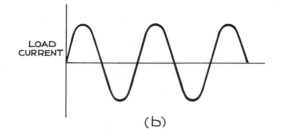

(b)

Fig. 11.8 A thyristor full-wave bridge circuit with a.c. load

This circuit can be used for a d.c. load by placing the load in series with the thyristor as shown in fig. 11.9(a). An unsmoothed full-wave-rectified current can thus be made to flow through the load as shown in fig. 11.9(b).

As well as the switching of a.c. and d.c. loads, static switching is used in applications such as lamp flashers, protection circuits against overload transients and short-circuit currents, logic counters, and time-delay circuits.

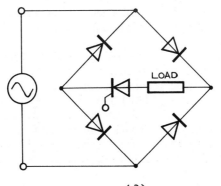

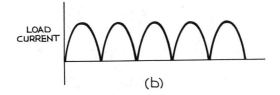

Fig. 11.9 A thyristor full-wave bridge circuit with d.c. load

A.C. phase control

A.C. phase control is the switching on of the a.c. supply to a load for a con-trolled fraction of each cycle. It is an effective method of controlling the average power to loads such as motors, heaters, lamps, etc.

The point on the waveform at which the thyristor fires is arranged by a control circuit which is usually some sort of phase-shifting circuit. Once fired, the thyristor will conduct for the remainder of that half cycle.

This method of control is ideally suited to applications where a smooth supply of controllable power is required. One disadvantage of phase control is that, unless precautions are taken, interference occurs of both mains and radio-frequency types.

The simplest form of a.c. phase control is the half-wave circuit for fig. 11.10(a). The control provides the gate signal which turns the thyristor on, and the thyristor switches off when the supply voltage falls to zero, as shown by the current waveform of fig. 11.10(b).

Various forms of phase control are possible. Figure 11.11 shows a method of phase control providing full-wave control. This allows control from zero to full power with the waveform shown.

An alternative form is shown in fig. 11.12. This allows the use of the same control circuit to fire each thyristor.

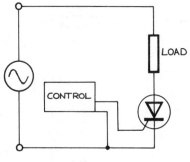

(a)

GATE
VOLTAGE

LOAD
CURRENT

(b)

Fig. 11.10 A.C. phase control of a thyristor

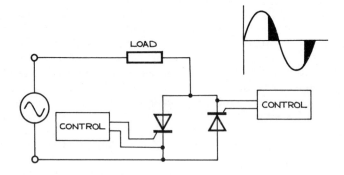

Fig. 11.11 Full-wave phase control

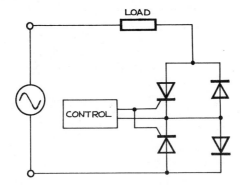

Fig. 11.12 Alternative circuit for full-wave phase control

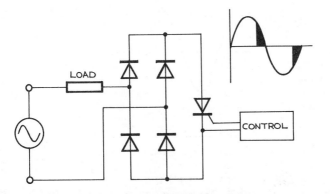

Fig. 11.13 Full-wave phase control using one thyristor

To achieve full control with only one thyristor, the circuit of fig. 11.13 may be used. This circuit incorporates the thyristor within a full-wave bridge circuit and provides the waveform shown.

By placing the load in series with the thyristor, the circuit may be used to provide full-wave rectified control of unsmoothed d.c. current.

By far the most simple, reliable, and efficient method of controlling a.c. power is to use a triac as shown in fig. 11.14. The triac (considered in section 11.8) allows control in both directions, as shown, using only a single gate input.

Many of the phase-control trigger circuits use either diacs or unijunction transistors. The description of the control circuits is therefore considered in section 11.10.

Zero-voltage switching
When a power circuit is turned 'on' or 'off', high-frequency electromagnetic radiation is generated which can cause interference problems. If the switching

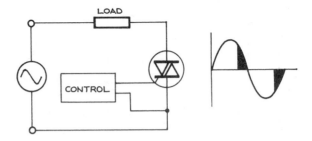

Fig. 11.14 Use of a triac in a.c. power control

can be made to take place as the current through the switch approaches zero, then these interference problems can be virtually eliminated. The thyristor is an ideal device in this respect in its turn-off characteristic, since it turns off only when the anode current is below the holding-current level.

Interference-free turn-on can be arranged by using special trigger circuits which trigger the thyristor as the voltage waveform passes through zero. The method is known as *zero-voltage switching*, and various circuits are available using both discrete-component and integrated-circuit assemblies.

This method is used particularly in heating control where radio and TV interference would be a problem.

11.6 The diac, triac, and unijunction transistor
There is a whole family of pnpn regenerative switching devices, of which we have only considered the thyristor (SCR).

Other devices are the triac, the silicon unilateral switch (SUS), the silicon bilateral switch (SBS), the silicon controlled switch (SCS), the bidirectional diode switch (diac), and light-activated devices.

We shall consider the diac and the triac, as well as a device often used for triggering thyristors called the unijunction transistor (UJT).

11.7 The diac
The diac is a two-terminal device which may be referred to as a bidirectional trigger diode. It has the symbol shown in fig. 11.15(a) and has basically a transistor structure. When the voltage across the terminals exceeds a certain voltage (the breakdown voltage V_{BR}), then the characteristic moves into a negative-resistance region as shown in fig. 11.15(b). A typical diac has a breakdown voltage V_{BR} of about 30 V.

The diac is used to provide a simple trigger circuit as shown in fig. 11.16. The capacitor C_1 charges via R_1 until its voltage reaches V_{BR}, at which voltage the diac conducts and discharges C_1 through R_2, thus producing a voltage pulse across R_2. Once the capacitor is discharged, the process is repeated. The charging time of C_1 is controlled by variation of R_1.

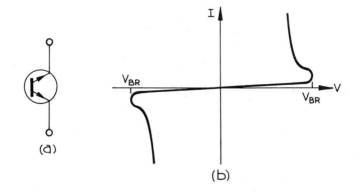

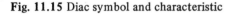

(a)

(b)

Fig. 11.15 Diac symbol and characteristic

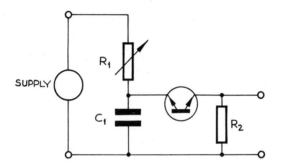

Fig. 11.16 Use of a diac in a trigger circuit

11.8 The triac

The triac is defined as a bidirectional triode thyristor. The name stems from *triode a.c.* switch.

It is a device which can pass or block current in either direction and can therefore be used in place of two thyristors in inverse-parallel (back-to-back) configuration. It requires only a single gate electrode and – unlike the thyristor – can be triggered by either a positive or a negative pulse.

The triac is used to give full-wave control of a.c. power, and simplifies heat-sink design since there is only one device to consider.

Being a full-wave bidirectional device, it cannot be used in controllers for d.c. power control. It also has the limitation that, to guarantee switch-off, the supply voltage must be reduced to zero and held there for a sufficient length of time for recombination of any stored change (i.e. for the charge to dissipate). In most power-frequency (50 Hz) applications, switch-off does not present a problem.

233

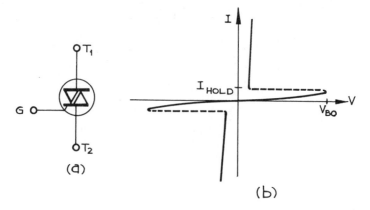

Fig. 11.17 Triac symbol and characteristic

The symbol for the triac is shown in fig. 11.17(a), where the terminals are referred to as main terminals T_1 and T_2 and a single gate G.

The triac characteristic is shown in fig. 11.17(b) and may be seen to be formed from positive parts of two thyristor characteristics.

The triac may be switched on by either a positive or a negative gate voltage. The theory of operation is complex and will not be considered here.

11.9 The unijunction transistor

The unijunction transistor (UJT) is a three-terminal device with an emitter E and bases B_1 and B_2 as shown in the symbol of fig. 11.18(a).

Under the normal bias conditions shown, the characteristic between B_2 and B_1 is that of an ordinary resistance of the order of 5 kΩ to 10 kΩ. However, it is the emitter E to base B_1 characteristic which is most useful in trigger-circuit applications. This characteristic is shown in fig. 11.18(b) for a base–base voltage V_{BB} of 10 V.

With V_E less than the emitter peak-point voltage V_P (see fig. 11.18(b)), only a small emitter leakage current flows. When V_E is equal to V_P, the device turns on and the resistance between E and B_1 becomes very small, the current being limited only by the external circuit resistance. The emitter peak-point voltage V_P can be controlled by variation of the voltage across B_1 and B_2, since V_P varies in proportion to V_{BB}.

A typical unijunction pulse trigger circuit is shown in fig. 11.19 and may be used to fire a thyristor in a similar manner to the diac. The capacitor C_1 charges through R_1 until the emitter voltage reaches V_P. At this point, the unijunction turns on, discharging C_1 through R_{B1}. The emitter voltage continues to fall until it reaches approximately 2 V, when the device ceases to conduct and the cycle is repeated. A trigger pulse is generated across R_{B1} with a period approximately equal to $C_1 R_1$.

234

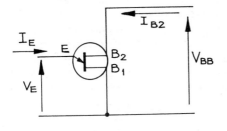

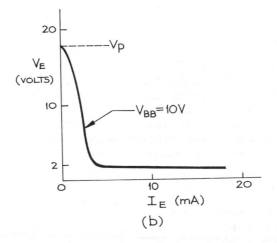

Fig. 11.18 Unijunction transistor symbol and characteristic

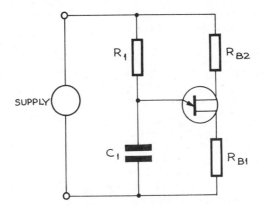

Fig. 11.19 Use of a unijunction transistor in a trigger circuit

235

11.10 Phase-control trigger circuits

The trigger circuits for phase control of thyristors make use of trigger devices such as the diac and the unijunction transistor. Some examples are shown in fig. 11.20(a), (b), and (c).

Figure 11.20(a) shows a phase-control circuit using a unijunction transistor in the manner described in section 11.9. Figure 11.20(b) shows a similar circuit using a diac.

Figure 11.20(c) shows the use of a diac to produce the trigger circuit for a triac, thus providing full-wave phase control.

Integrated circuits are now available for use in high-performance thyristor and triac control circuits specifically intended for use in the control of a.c. induction motors.

Controlled rectifiers may also be used in three-phase a.c. control. The basic requirements are the supply of a trigger turn-on signal and the provision of a turn-off circuit.

Fairly straightforward control circuits may be designed for speed control of universal a.c. motors and induction motors where the load is continually changing, such as in lathes, drilling machines, washing machines, etc.

Thyristor controllers are used in electric furnaces and for temperature control in domestic and industrial heating and air conditioning.

They are also used to convert from one voltage level to another in a variety of inverter circuits, this being previously performed by rotating electrical machines. These inverter applications may be classified as

a) rectifying from a.c. to d.c.,
b) inverting from d.c. to a.c.,
c) converting from a.c. to a.c. at different frequencies.

11.11 Thyristor ratings

The ratings of a device define limiting values for voltage, current, power dissipation, temperature, etc. Thyristors are generally rated on an absolute-maximum system, stating values which must not be exceeded. The symbols used are the usual ones of voltage and current (V and I), together with subscripts which specify the condition to which the rating applies.

Generally the first subscript defines whether the condition is the 'on' state (T) or the 'off' state (D), in the forward direction (F) or the reverse direction (R). The second subscript defines whether the value is the working value (W), the repetitive value (R), or the non-repetitive (surge) value (S).

There are numerous ratings used with regard to thyristors, and it is generally advisable to make full use of manufacturer's data sheets and applications advice when choosing a device for a particular application.

Some typical examples of more commonly used ratings are given below:

a) V_{RWM} – the working peak reverse voltage (the maximum instantaneous value of the reverse voltage across the thyristor);
b) V_T – the on-state voltage (the voltage across the thyristor in the 'on' state);

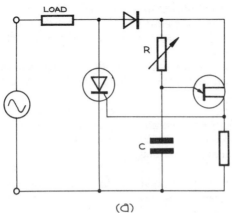

(a)

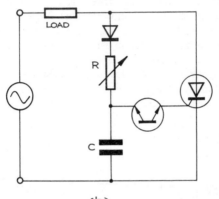

(b)

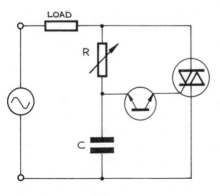

(c)

Fig. 11.20 Phase-control trigger circuits

c) $I_{T(r.m.s.)}$ – the r.m.s. value of on-state current (the total r.m.s. value of the current when in the 'on' state);

d) V_{GT} – the gate trigger voltage (the gate voltage required to produce the gate trigger current);

e) I_{GT} – the gate trigger current (the maximum gate current required to switch the thyristor from the 'off' state to the 'on' state).

Thermal ratings

With any power-control semiconductor device, it is very important to consider the choice and design of a suitable heat sink. This is to ensure that the junction temperature does not exceed its rated value at the operating power and current levels.

The heat developed at the junction is dissipated via the case and the heat sink. The junction temperature rises above the case temperature in proportion to the amount of heat developed at the junction. The thermal characteristics of the case and heat sink are therefore stated in terms of thermal resistance, with units °C/watt. A small heat sink thus has a high thermal resistance, whereas a large heat sink has a low thermal resistance.

Of course it is not possible to measure the junction temperature, and therefore the manufacturer provides a set of thermal design curves. From these curves, the user may determine the size of heat sink for his own particular application.

Exercises on chapter 11

1   Describe the action of a thyristor when switched on by the application of a short-duration voltage pulse to the gate. Why is it not possible to switch the thyristor off via the gate?

2   Draw the two-transistor model of a thyristor and explain the term 'regenerative'. Sketch the thyristor characteristic and identify the forward breakover voltage V_{BO} and the on-state voltage V_T. Why is the thyristor normally used well below the forward breakover voltage?

3   Explain the conditions necessary to switch an SCR 'on' and 'off'. A p-gate SCR is to be used to switch a 240 V a.c. supply on to a load for a certain period of time determined by the output of a NOR gate. Sketch the circuit diagram and draw suitable waveforms to explain your answer.

4   a) State two advantages that the thyristor has over a power transistor when used as a switch. Draw a p-gate thyristor showing the three junctions and indicate the positions of anode, cathode, and gate.

b) Sketch a full-wave bridge circuit using two thyristors to control a d.c. motor field circuit from an a.c. supply using a separate pulse-firing circuit. Draw waveforms of gate-voltage pulses and load current.

5   Explain the following terms: (a) radio-frequency interference, (b) zero-voltage switching.

Sketch a circuit diagram to show how a triac may be used to connect a single-phase induction motor to a 240 V a.c. 50 Hz supply for periods of time in excess of 1 s.

6 Distinguish between 'static switching' and 'a.c. phase control' as two possible methods of controlling the switching of a thyristor. Sketch a circuit diagram to show how a diac may be used to provide a simple phase-control trigger circuit for firing a thyristor. How is variation of the firing angle achieved?

7 Sketch circuit symbols for (a) a thyristor (SCR), (b) a diac, (c) a triac, (d) a unijunction transistor. Sketch the characteristic for each of these.

8 A triac is used together with a phase-control circuit to control the intensity of a 240 V 60 W filament lamp. Sketch the circuit diagram, assuming that a unijunction transistor is used in the control circuit. Sketch the waveform of the lamp current, and determine the average half-wave current if the firing angle is (a) 25°, (b) 35°. The triac on-state voltage may be ignored.   [0.21 A; 0.20 A]

9 A thyristor is connected in series with a 200 Ω load across a 240 V supply. If the trigger voltage is adjusted so that conduction starts 60° after the start of each cycle, calculate the readings on the following meters: (a) an average-reading ammeter connected in series with the load, (b) a true r.m.s. ammeter connected across the thyristor, (c) a wattmeter connected in the circuit so as to read the total power delivered by the a.c. supply.   [0.40 A; 0.61 A; 146 W]

12 Magnetic amplifiers

12.1 Introduction

A *transductor* is a control device consisting of a ferromagnetic core on which are situated two windings, rather like a transformer. One of the windings is connected in series with a load resistance, and an a.c. supply is connected across the combination as shown in fig. 12.1(a). The other winding is connected to a d.c. control voltage.

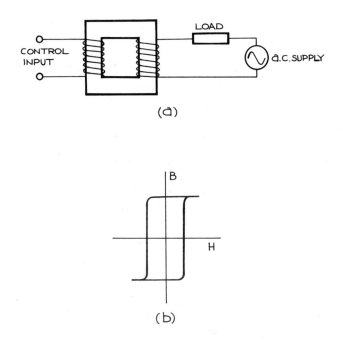

(a)

(b)

Fig. 12.1 A simple transductor and the *B–H* loop for the core material

The core material has a rectangular *B–H* loop, as shown in fig. 12.1(b), such that when the core is unsaturated the circuit impedance is high, but when the core becomes saturated with magnetic flux the circuit impedance suddenly becomes very low. The value of the d.c. current in the control winding sets the point in the load-current waveform at which the core suddenly becomes saturated with magnetic flux.

The d.c. voltage may thus be used to *control* the current flowing in the a.c. winding and hence in the load. The operation is decribed in more detail in section 12.2. The term 'transductor' (not to be confused with 'transducer') is a combination of the words *trans*former and in*ductor*. The transductor is sometimes referred to as a *saturable reactor.*

The *magnetic amplifier* uses transductors to provide amplification.

Transductors and magnetic amplifiers achieved popularity at a time when the thermionic valve was the only viable alternative as a means of control and amplification. They have the advantage of being rugged and reliable, with a long operating life and low failure rate. For this reason they were used in place of valve circuits in situations where reliability was of major importance, such as in autopilots and aircraft equipment. They also became widely used in theatre lighting control, electric-furnace heating control, and motor control.

They are now almost completely superseded by semiconductor control circuits and amplifiers.

12.2 Transductor operation

A simple transductor consists of two windings arranged on a magnetic core as shown in fig. 12.1(a).

The main winding is connected in series with the load resistance, and an alternating voltage is applied across the combination as shown. The control winding is connected to a controllable d.c. voltage.

The unique feature of the transductor is the material from which the core is made. This has a rectangular B–H loop as shown in fig. 12.1(b). When the core is unsaturated the permeability is very high, but when the core becomes saturated the permeability suddenly drops to a very low value.

Now we know that the reactance of an iron-cored coil is given by

$$X_L = \omega L$$

and that the inductance of the coil is given by

$$L = \frac{N^2}{S}$$

where N = number of turns

and S = reluctance of magnetic circuit

$$= \frac{l}{\mu A}$$

where l = length of magnetic circuit

         μ = permeability of the magnetic material

and A = cross-sectional area of the magnetic circuit

thus $X_L = \dfrac{\omega N^2 \mu A}{l}$

We may see from this equation that the reactance of an iron-cored coil is proportional to the permeability of the iron.

Referring back to the transductor, this means that the reactance of the main coil has two states – the reactance is very high when the core is unsaturated, and it is very low when the core becomes saturated. The transductor may thus be thought of as a switch which switches on and off once every cycle of the supply voltage. The point on the supply voltage waveform at which the transductor 'fires' is set by the control current. The control current *pre-sets* the flux to some value and thus controls the point at which the transductor suddenly saturates. The firing point is referred to as the *firing angle*.

The current waveform through the load is *not* sinusoidal, and the average load current (half-wave average) is proportional to the control current.

The transductor is used to control large a.c. power in a load by the application of a small amount of power to the control input.

The transductor has a high efficiency and a relatively fast response. It is used for controlling large power, but suffers from the disadvantages that it has only a low power gain. It also has the basic disadvantage that a.c. current flows in the control winding by transformer action from the main winding. This means that power is wasted and that the control winding must be insulated against large a.c. voltages which are induced in it. Also, if the transductor is being controlled from an instrument, then the a.c. voltage could cause instrument damage. This disadvantage may be overcome by using a 'balanced' circuit.

12.3 Balanced magnetic amplifier
The balanced magnetic amplifier overcomes the problem of a.c. coupling with the control winding.

In the shell-type construction shown in fig. 12.2, the load winding is made up of two coils wound on the outer limbs, and the control winding is situated on the centre limb.

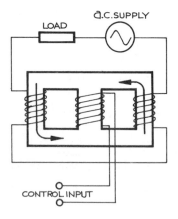

Fig. 12.2 Balanced magnetic amplifier – shell type

In this arrangement the load windings are connected in series opposition such that, when an a.c. current flows in the load windings, the alternating flux exists only in the outer limbs and there is no alternating flux in the centre limb. There is therefore no coupling from the load winding to the control winding, and there is no a.c. voltage induced in the control winding.

An alternative arrangement uses two separate cores as shown in fig. 12.3. In this case the induced e.m.f.'s in each half of the control winding exactly oppose each other, and the resultant e.m.f. is zero.

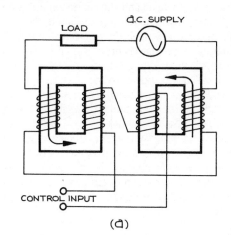

(a)

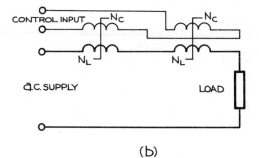

(b)

Fig. 12.3 Balanced magnetic amplifier – separate cores

In the idealised magnetic amplifier in which core losses and flux leakage are neglected, the control and average load currents are related by the turns ratio, just as is the case in the ideal transformer. We have

$$I_C N_C = I_L N_L$$

where $I_C N_C$ = control m.m.f.

and $I_L N_L$ = average load winding m.m.f.

243

$$\therefore \quad \frac{I_L}{I_C} = \frac{N_C}{N_L}$$

and $\quad I_L = I_C \dfrac{N_C}{N_L}$

Hence, for the idealised circuit conditions considered, the relationship between the control current and the load current depends only on the turns ratio.

The current characteristic for the magnetic amplifier is shown in fig. 12.4. Notice that the characteristic is symmetrical about the vertical axis. The relationship between the load current I_L and the control current I_C is approximately linear and has the slope N_C/N_L.

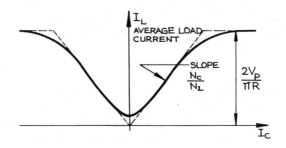

Fig. 12.4 Current characteristic for a magnetic amplifier

The magnitude of the supply voltage applied to the magnetic amplifier has no direct influence on the current relationship, except that full output is obtained when the whole of the supply voltage appears across the load. This gives a limiting average load current of $2V_p/\pi R$.

In the transductor, the ampere-turns balance given by the above equation is strictly valid only for cores of infinite permeability with the idealised B-H curve. For cores of finite permeability, small m.m.f.'s (analogous to the magnetising current of a transformer) are required for the core flux changes. These m.m.f.'s are the difference between the control and main circuit m.m.f.'s.

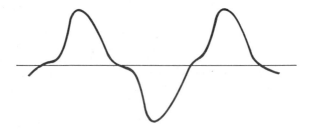

Fig. 12.5 Typical load-current waveform in a magnetic amplifier

It has been stated that the load current in the magnetic amplifier is *not* sinusoidal, and a typical waveform is shown in fig. 12.5. However, the shape of the waveform varies considerably with the choice of core material, with the control-circuit impedance, and with the type of load. In practice, the design of a magnetic amplifier is arrived at by experience and by building a prototype and carrying out tests to measure the voltage, current, and flux values, with subsequent modification until the desired characteristic is achieved.

12.4 Self-excited magnetic amplifier

One disadvantage of the balanced magnetic amplifier is the relatively low power gain. This may be improved by the application of positive feedback, but at the expense of increasing the time constant of the system. This is referred to as self-excitation.

One method of connection is shown in fig. 12.6, in which the feedback windings are fed with the rectified load current. The feedback coils are wound such that the rectified load current assists the control current, thus providing positive feedback.

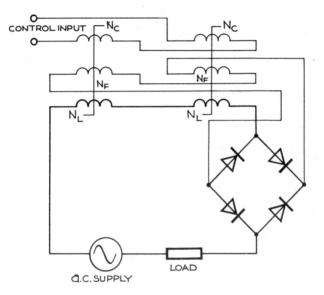

Fig. 12.6 Magnetic amplifier with feedback windings

The effect of this on the control characteristic is shown in fig. 12.7: the current gain is increased in one direction and reduced in the other. This is because in one direction (positive control current) the current in the feedback windings *aids* the control current, thus producing the required load current for a smaller value of control current. In the reverse direction (negative control current) the current in the feedback windings opposes the control current.

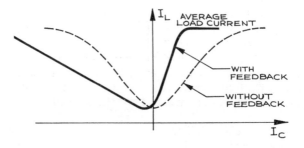

Fig. 12.7 Current characteristic for a magnetic amplifier with feedback

Notice also that the minimum point has been shifted to the left, due to the small load current (and hence feedback current) which flows even in the absence of any control current.

The new ampere-turns equation becomes

$$I_L N_L = I_C N_C + I_F N_F$$

Now, if $I_F = I_L$, then we may say

$$I_L N_L = I_C N_C + I_L N_F$$

$$\therefore \quad I_L(N_L - N_F) = I_C N_C$$

$$\therefore \qquad\qquad I_L = I_C \frac{N_C}{N_L - N_F}$$

$$= I_C \frac{N_C}{N_L(1 - N_F/N_L)}$$

Thus the current amplification has been increased as a result of feedback by the factor $1/(1 - N_F/N_L)$. The slope of the characteristic is thus dependent on the ratio N_F/N_L.

The self-excited magnetic amplifier has a high power gain but a large time constant.

12.5 Auto-self-excited magnetic amplifiers

In practice, the magnetic amplifier can be simplified by the use of a rectifier connected in series with the main winding. A single-element circuit is shown in fig. 12.8.

The diode allows current to flow in one direction only, with the result that an effect is achieved similar to that of the self-excited magnetic amplifier with full-excitation.

Consider the case with no control current. The core saturates on the positive half cycle of the supply voltage, and, since no current flows in the negative half cycle, the core flux does not reset. The core thus remains perman-

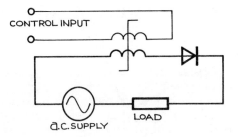

Fig. 12.8 Auto-self-excited magnetic amplifier

ently saturated and behaves as a low resistance. The circuit simply acts as a half-wave rectifier.

Now, by applying a control current, the flux may be reset by a controlled amount on the negative half cycle. The firing angle of the waveform on the positive half cycle may thus be controlled, and the control current may be used to control the average load current. The technique is referred to as 'auto-self-excitation', or simply 'self-saturation'.

The basic single-element circuit is not suitable for practical purposes, since transformer action occurs from the main winding to the control circuit and an e.m.f. of the same frequency as the load current is induced in the control winding. In practice this is overcome by using two elements to cancel out the fundamental-frequency current in the control circuit.

A two-element parallel auto-self-excited magnetic amplifier is shown in fig. 12.9. A controlled full-wave a.c. output is obtained with this circuit.

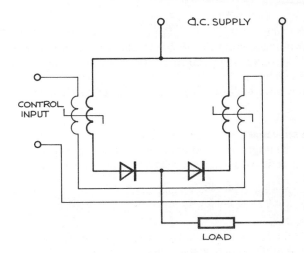

Fig. 12.9 Two-element parallel auto-self-excited magnetic amplifier

Magnetic amplifiers are generally designed for supply-voltage frequencies of 50 Hz or 400 Hz (for use in aircraft equipment). With increase of frequency, the core losses increase, but smaller physical size may be used.

12.6 Balanced amplifier arrangements

In many applications of magnetic amplifiers, the requirement is that the output voltage should reverse in direction with change of input control-signal direction, and also that the output voltage should be zero for zero control current. This is achieved by using two magnetic amplifiers in a push–pull arrangement such as that shown in fig. 12.10.

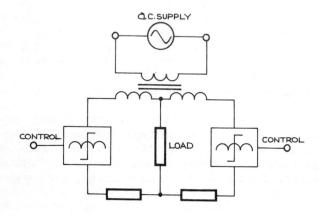

Fig. 12.10 Two magnetic amplifiers in push–pull

In this arrangement, the output of one magnetic amplifier is balanced against that of another with a similar characteristic. The control winding is arranged so that a positive control signal increases the output of one amplifier and decreases that of the other. Reversal of the direction of the control signal reverses the direction of the load current. The characteristic is shown in fig. 12.11.

12.7 Core material

The required properties of the core materials used in the construction of magnetic amplifiers are

a) high maximum permeability,
b) low coercive force and a narrow a.c. hysteresis loop,
c) a sharp knee at saturation and a low permeability after the knee,
d) a high saturation flux density.

The relative importance of these properties depends on the class of magnetic amplifier under consideration.

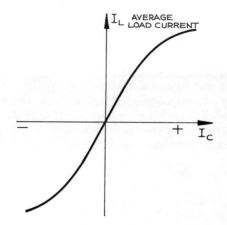

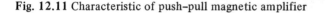

Fig. 12.11 Characteristic of push–pull magnetic amplifier

Low-power-input magnetic amplifiers up to 10 W use 70–80% nickel–iron with trade names such as Mumetal and Permalloy C. For medium-power devices up to 100 W, 50% nickel–iron is used such as HCR or Deltamax. These have a high saturation flux density and allow reduction of overall size. Large-power devices use silicon–iron cores for economic reasons.

12.8 Advantages and disadvantages of magnetic amplifiers
Magnetic amplifiers have the advantage of being robust and having a high reliability, which means that they have a long operating life. Their high efficiency (of the order of 75%) makes them particularly suitable for control of large power. These features can also be achieved with transistor circuits.

Magnetic amplifiers have the additional advantages that they are not temperature-sensitive and that the input is electrically isolated from the output.

Their disadvantages are that they are large and heavy and are in general limited to low-frequency applications, the signal frequency being limited to a fraction of the supply frequency. They have a relatively poor transient response (from several milliseconds to one second).

Exercises on chapter 12
1 a) Explain, using sketches, the principle of operation of a simple transductor (saturable reactor).
   b) Show how this principle is applied in a magnetic amplifier.
2 Sketch the circuit and explain the operation of a magnetic amplifier arranged so that the a.c. output is zero when the d.c. input is zero, and the phase of the a.c. output depends on the polarity of the d.c. input.
3 Explain how induced alternating voltages in the control winding of a saturable reactor may be avoided, and draw a circuit, using saturable-reactor

circuit symbols, to show how an additional set of feedback windings may be applied. Indicate on the diagram the control, feedback, and load windings and show where the control signal and a.c. supply are applied. Show the load circuit connected for d.c. output. Explain the purpose of the feedback windings and state one disadvantage of their use.

4 By means of a circuit diagram, explain how a saturable reactor may be used to control an a.c. load current with a variable d.c. control voltage.

5 Draw a suitable *B–H* curve for the core material of a saturable reactor and briefly explain how the current through a saturable reactor may be controlled by a separate d.c. control voltage. Show how the device may be likened to a switch.

Draw waveforms of supply voltage and load current to illustrate how the current drawn from an a.c. voltage source may be varied by the control voltage.

6 a) Explain the principle of operation of a simple saturable reactor.

b) Show how this principle is applied to a d.c. magnetic amplifier with external positive feedback.

c) How is a.c. kept out of the d.c. control windings?

d) Give a rough graph of output against input, showing the effect of positive and negative feedback.

7 A magnetic amplifier has a resistive load and gives the following load characteristic without feedback:

D.C. control current (mA)	0	4	8	12	16	18
Mean a.c. load current (mA)	8	44	80	118	152	162

With positive feedback applied the results are as follows:

D.C. control current (mA)	0	1	2	3	4	5	6
Mean a.c. load current (mA)	26	68	110	144	160	167	173

Draw a circuit diagram to show how positive feedback is applied. Plot both of the above characteristics to a base of control current and estimate the current gain for both conditions.   [9.4; 41]

Index